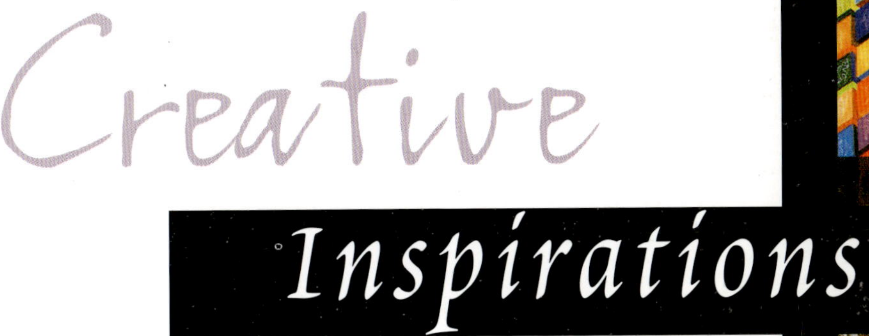

A Collection of Drawing and Painting Ideas for Artists

Includes work in:

- *Acrylic*
- *Colored Pencil*
- *Oil*
- *Pastel*
- *Watercolor*

First published in the United States of America by:
Quarry Books, an imprint of
Rockport Publishers, Inc.
33 Commercial Street
Gloucester, Massachusetts 01930-5089
Telephone: (508) 282-9590
Fax: (508) 283-2742

Distributed to the book trade and art trade in the United States by:
North Light, an imprint of
F & W Publications
1507 Dana Avenue
Cincinnati, Ohio 45207
Telephone: (800) 289-0963

Other Distribution by:
Rockport Publishers
Gloucester, Massachusetts 01966-1299

ISBN 1-56496-386-1

10 9 8 7 6 5 4 3 2 1

Designer: **Frederick Schneider / Grafis**
Cover Images: see pages 12, 26, 37, 40, 71, 79

Printed in Hong Kong.

Creative Inspirations

A Collection of Drawing and Painting Ideas for Artists

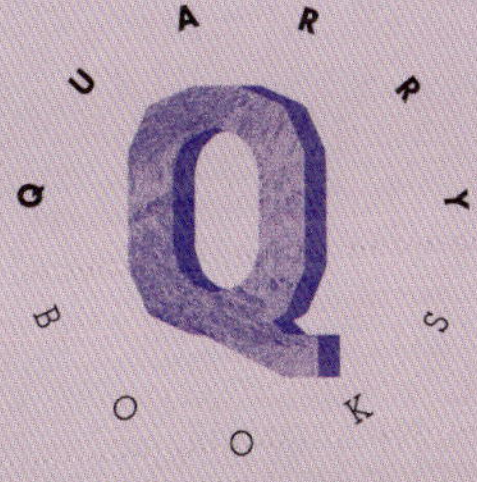

ROCKPORT PUBLISHERS, INC. • GLOUCESTER, MASSACHUSETTS
DISTRIBUTED BY NORTH LIGHT BOOKS • CINCINNATI, OHIO

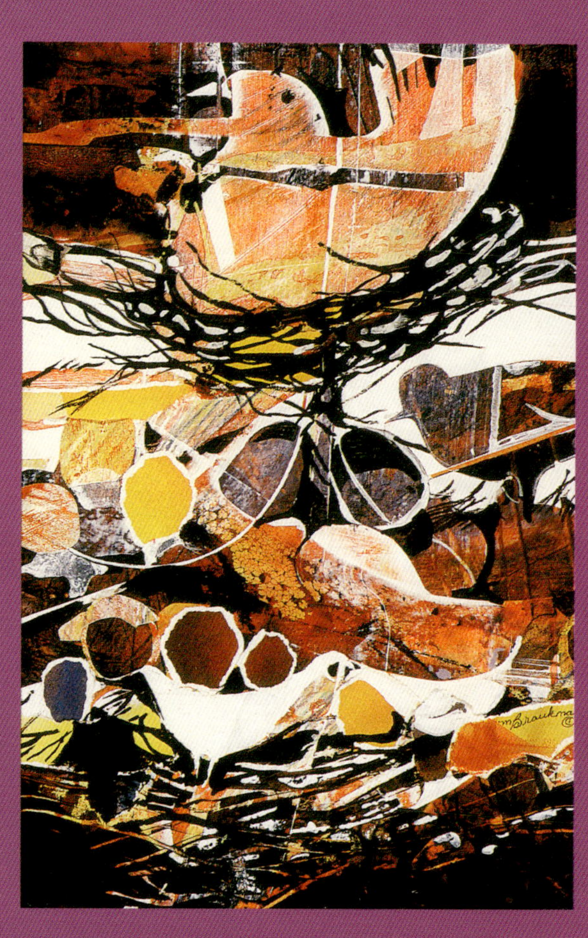

Introduction

It is self-evident that every person interprets everything they see in a different way. Mental factors, such a background and past experiences, as well as physical factors, right down to the amount of rods and cones in your eyes, will effect your perception of any outside object. It would seem to be virtually impossible to see something the way another person sees it. But this book allows you to do just that. By combining the many different ways these wonderful artists perceive their world, it affords all readers a tiny glimpse of someone else's perceptions.

Presenting paintings in a book has its limitations. The sizes of the paintings become somewhat standardized, and the topography of the paintings is lost in the flat, glossy sheets of paper. This does not mean that the book format is not useful. A book is able to present an enormous amount of work in a small space. This book in particular allows for the observation of many different things: styles, techniques, colors, applications. The number of beautiful images in this book is stunning.

Some of the included paintings almost appear to be studies of painting techniques. Every artist develops their own style and technique, many of them imaginative and innovative. Each painting works on two levels: investigation of theme and exploration of technique. Each media has a different consistency: think about the differences between watercolor and oil, and how they respond to the different surfaces. It is these explorations which make painting such a dynamic art.

Some of these paintings were inspired by actual places, people, objects, others are visual depiction of emotion. All were inspired by something, and can serve as inspirations themselves. We hope this book will provide hours of fascination.

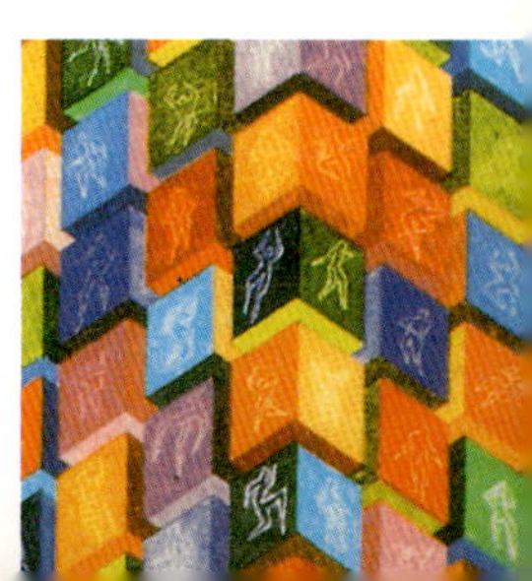

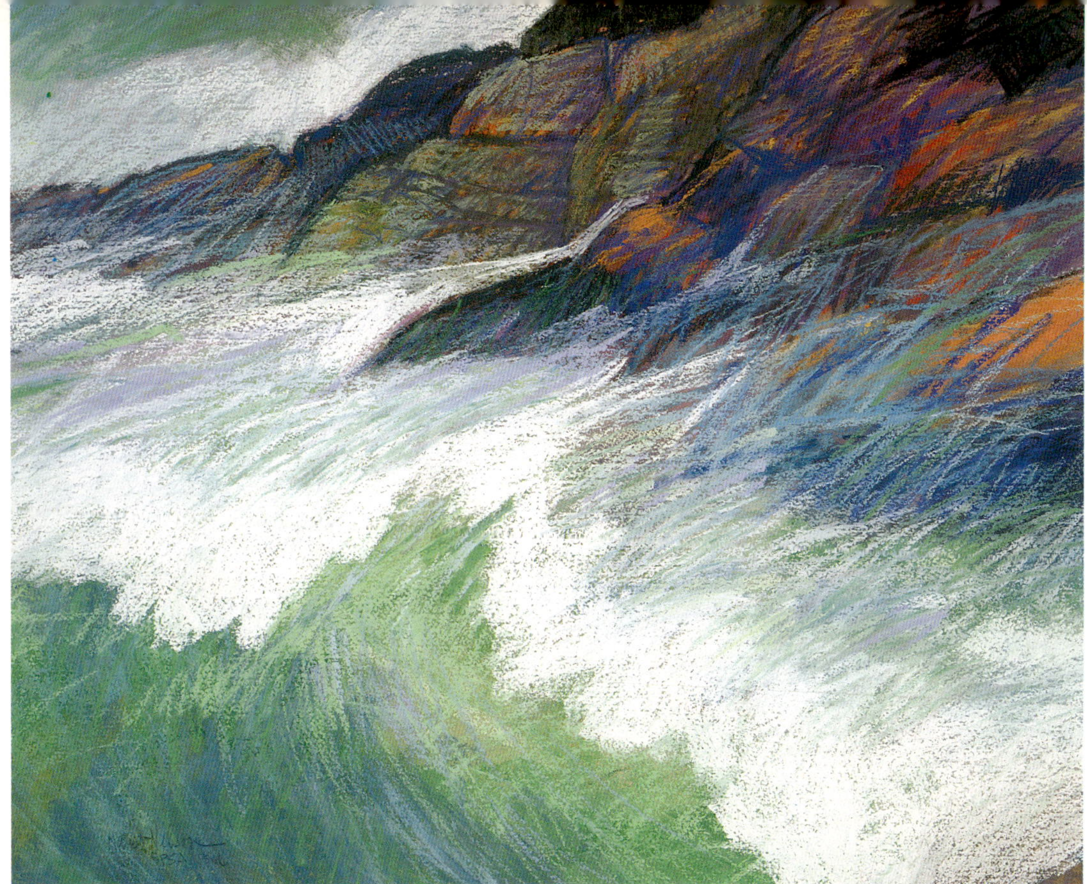

Marsh Nelson
Sea Rises
17.5" x 19.5" (44.5 cm x 49.5 cm)
Pastel with acrylic and extra fine pumice
Arches 140 lb. cold press paper

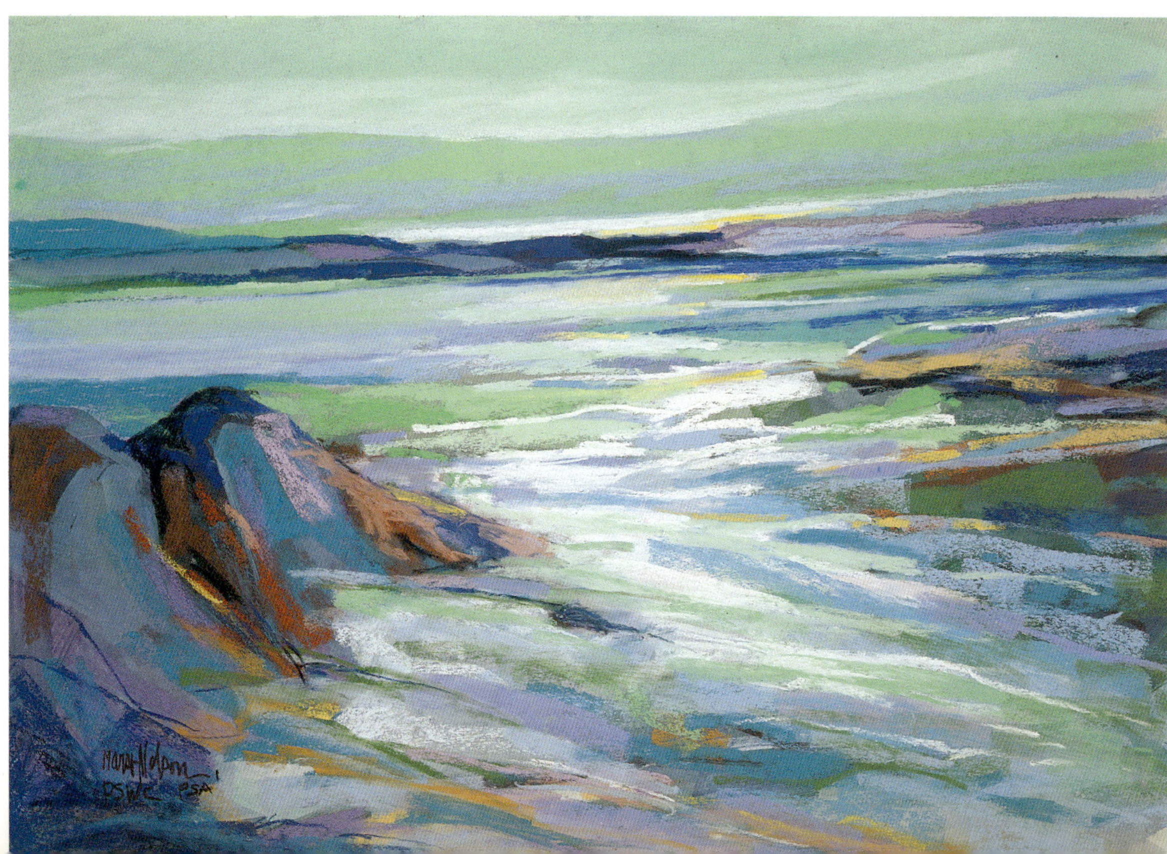

Marsh Nelson
Blue Surf
15" x 20" (38.1 cm x 50.8 cm)
Rising Stonehenge 100%
cotton acid-free paper

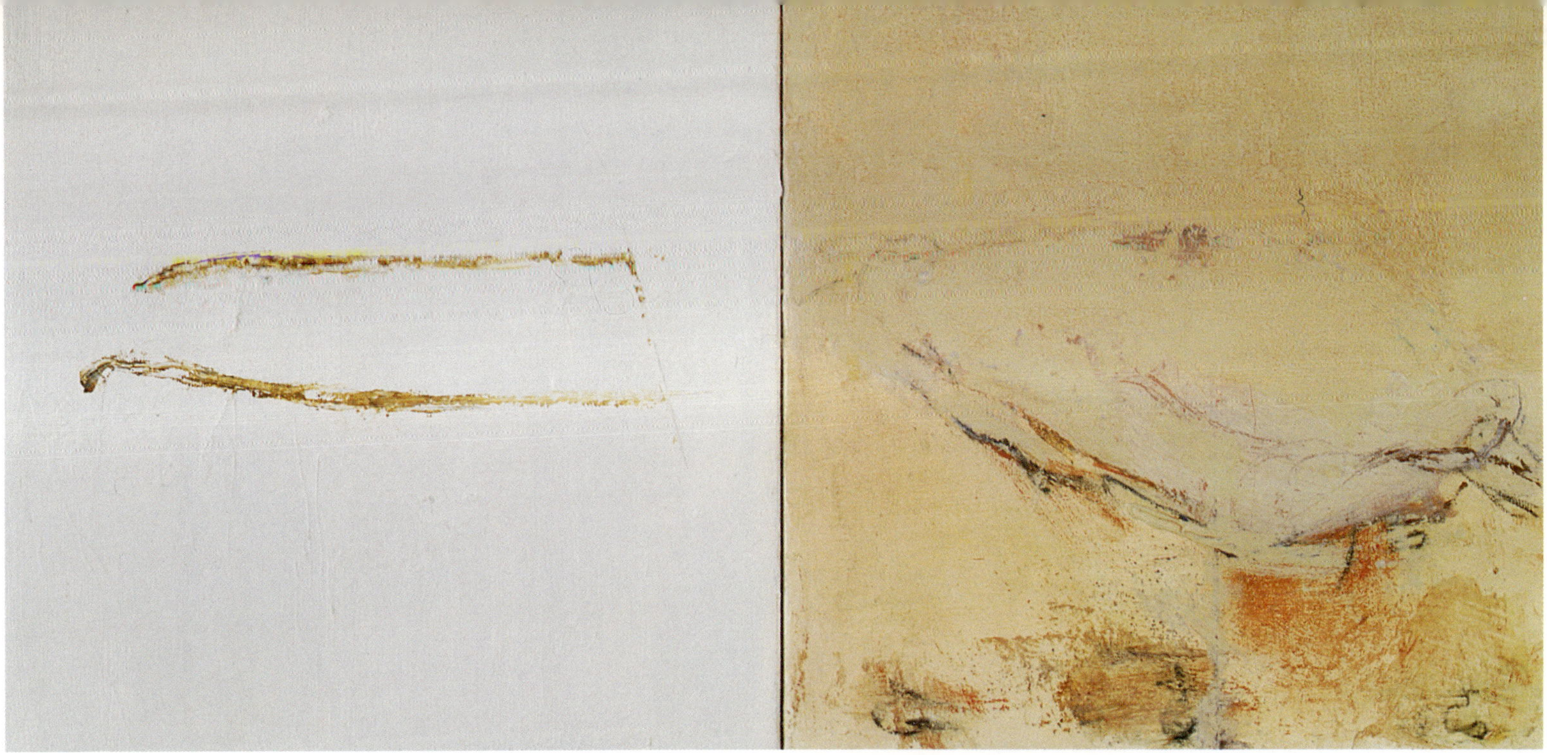

Kerri McLaughlin Smith
The Tissue of Hearts
12" x 24" (30.5 cm x 61 cm)
Canvas

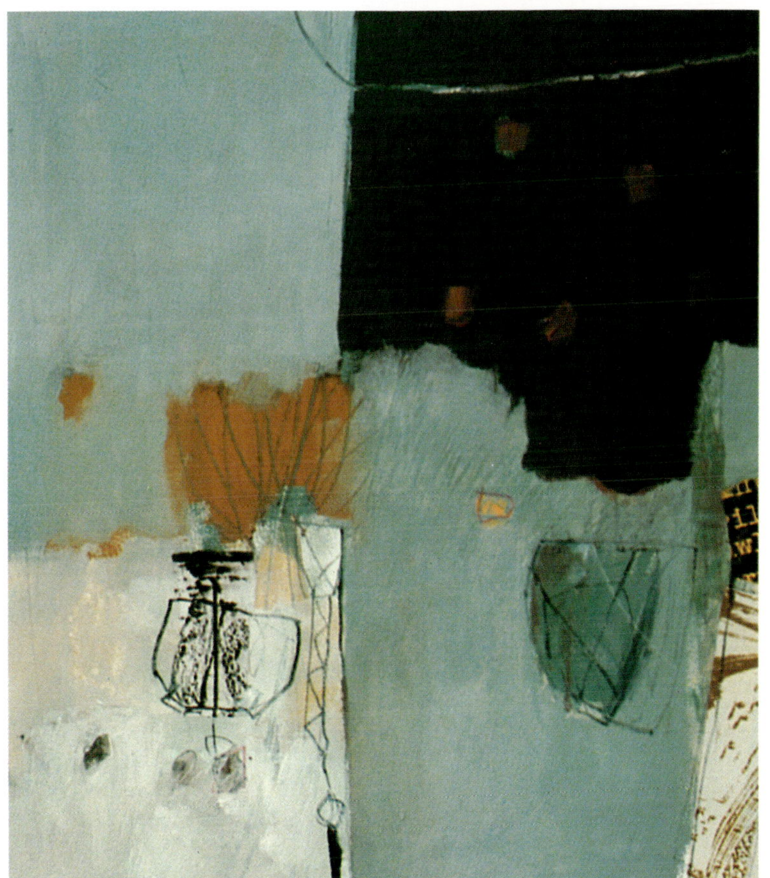

Katherine Chang Liu
Magic Carpet
17" x 17" (43.2 cm x 43.2 cm)
300 lb. Hot press paper
Oil with gesso

Mary Alice Braukman
Mythical Friends
22" x 30" (56 cm x 76 cm)
Acrylic with crayon and pastel
T.H. Saunders Waterford 300 lb. hot press paper

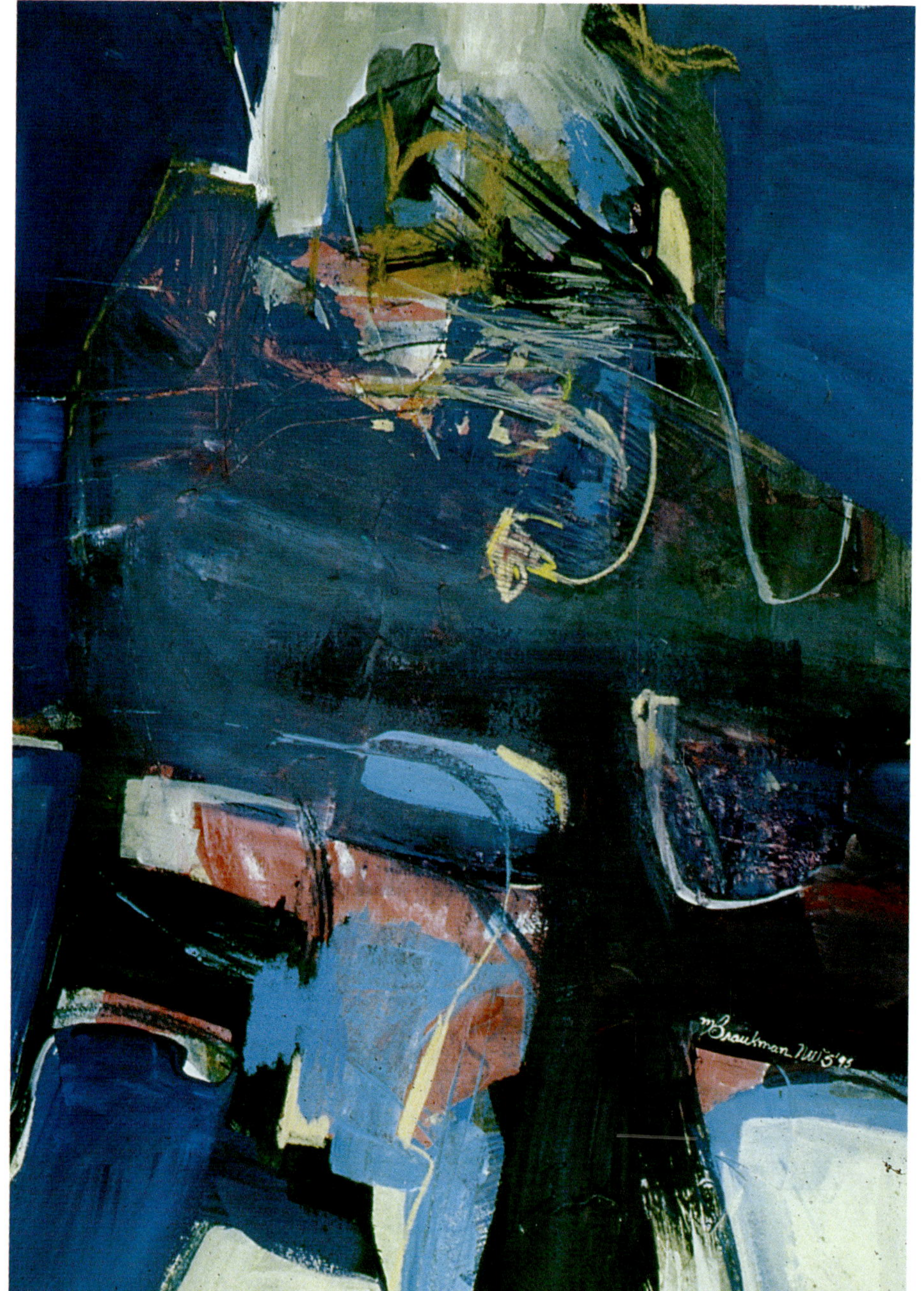

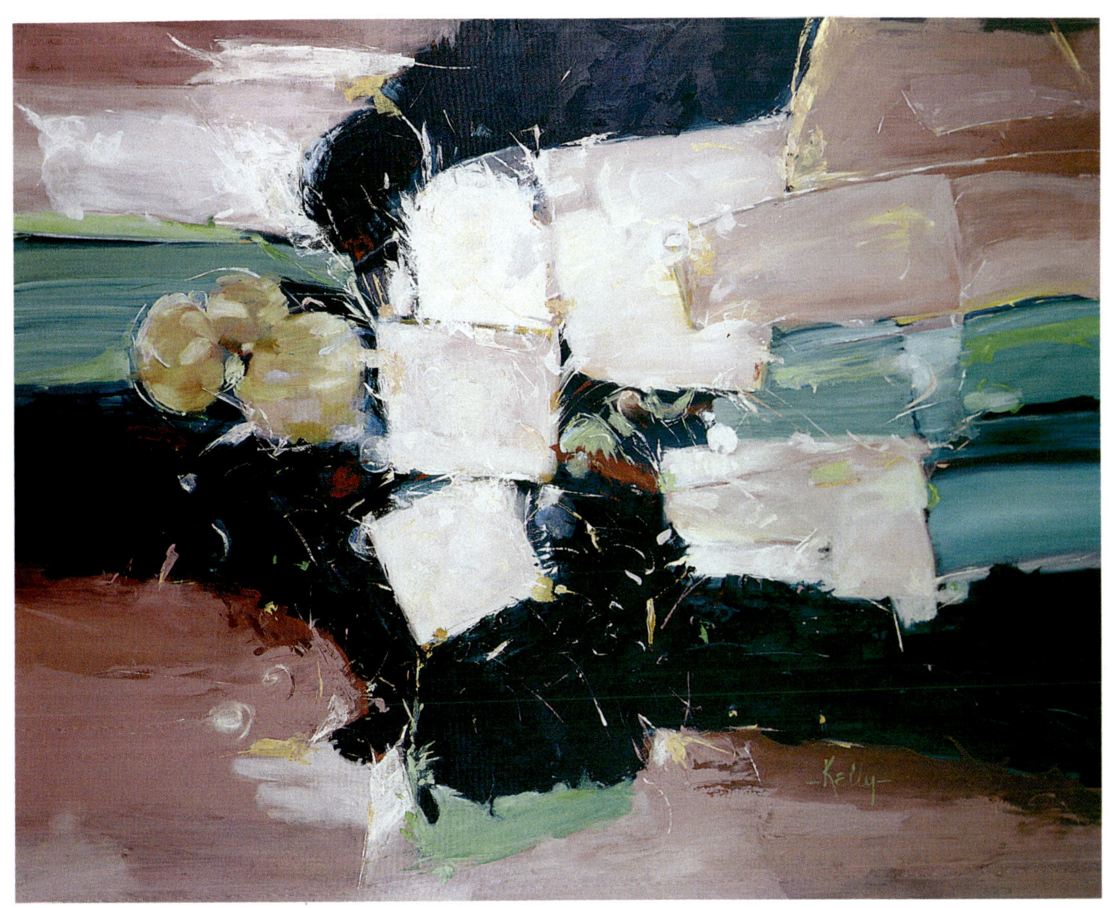

Joan D. Kelly
The Walls Come Tumbling Down
48" x 60" (121 cm x 151 cm)
Canvas

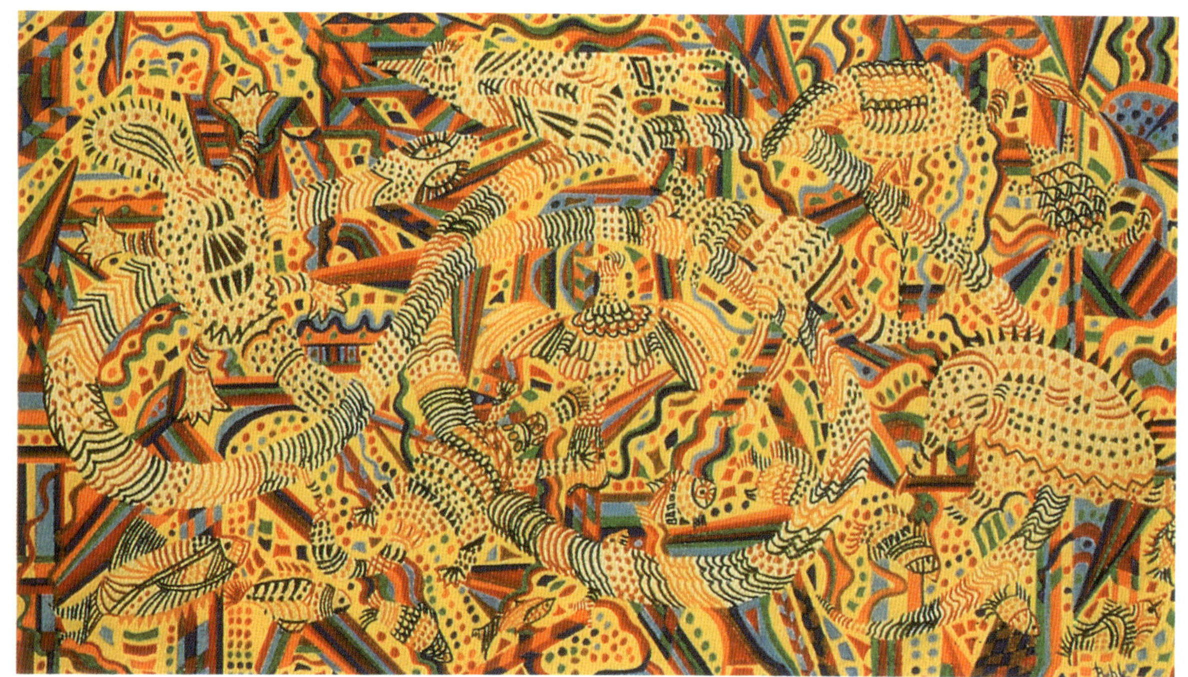

Meg Elliott-Behle
ABO Dream-Time
12" x 16" (30 cm x 40 cm)
Crane's stationery

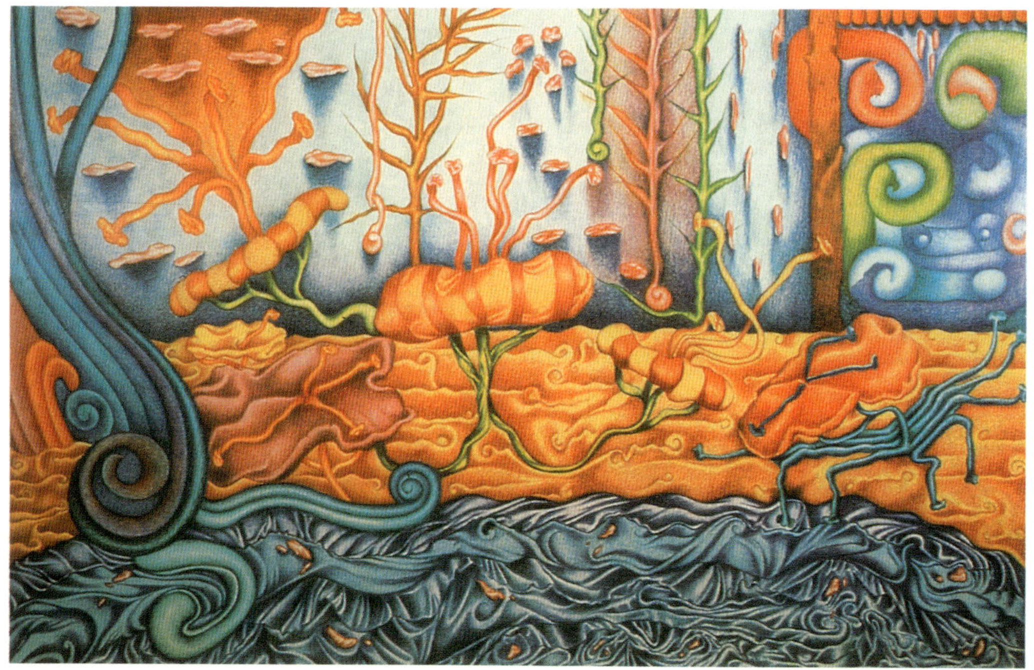

Deborah Friedman
A Happy Gulf Day
26" x 36" (66 cm x 91 cm)
Crescent cold press illustration board

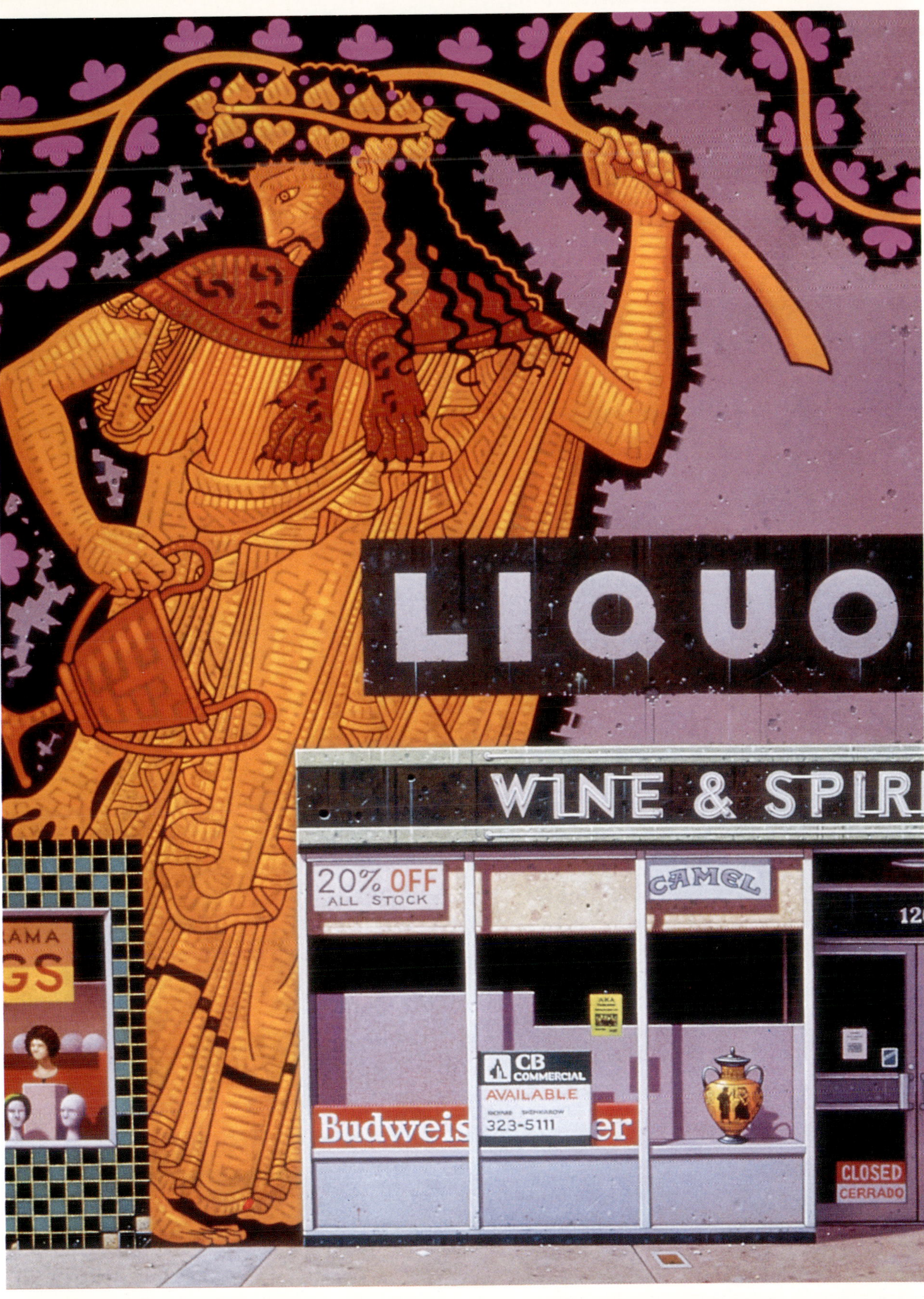

David VanDenBerg
Dionysos
40" x 30" (101.6 cm x 76.2 cm)
Canvas

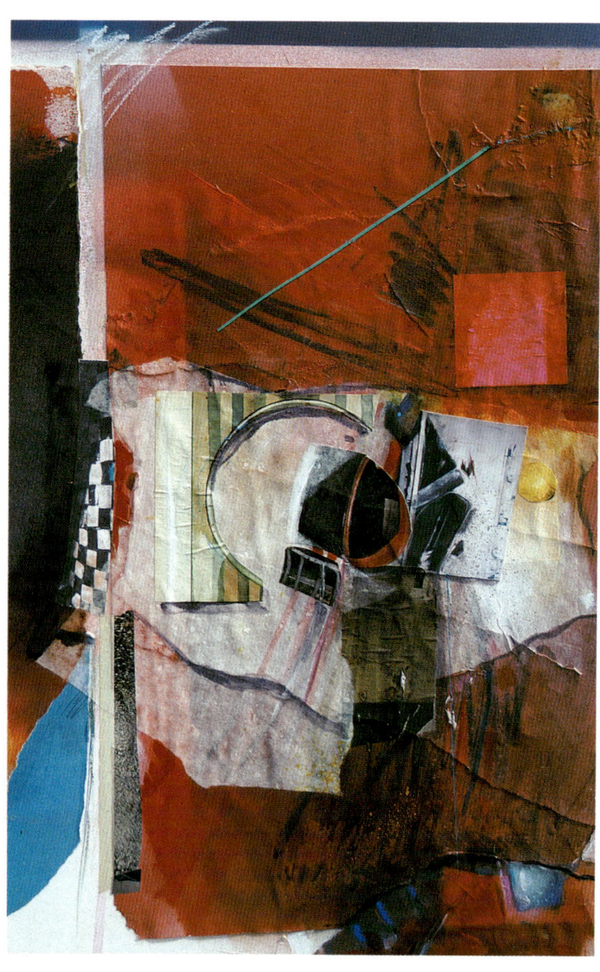

J. Luray Schaffner, N.W.S.
Color, Chain and Red
40" x 30" (101.6 cm x 76.2 cm)
4-ply museum board
Media: Watercolor collage

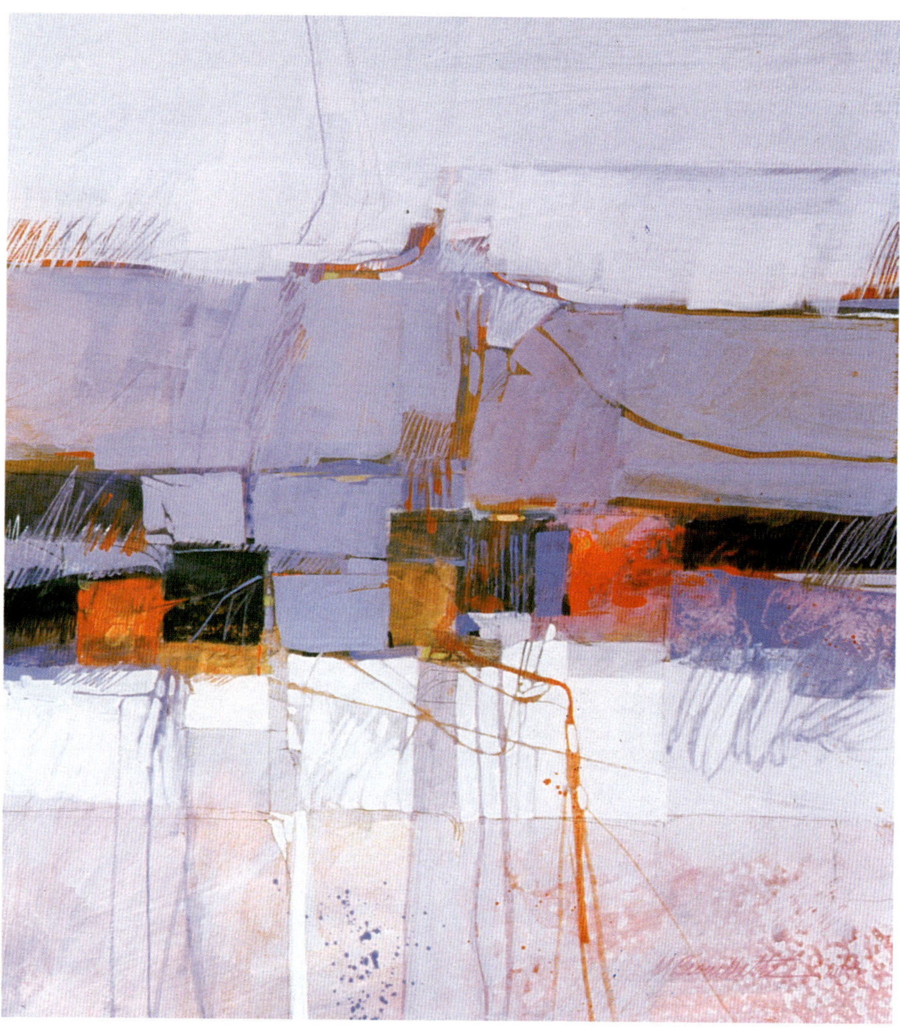

Al Brouillette
Horizons III
20" x 18" (50.8 cm x 45.7 cm)
Strathmore 500 board
Media: Transparent acrylic, semi-opaque and opaque watercolor

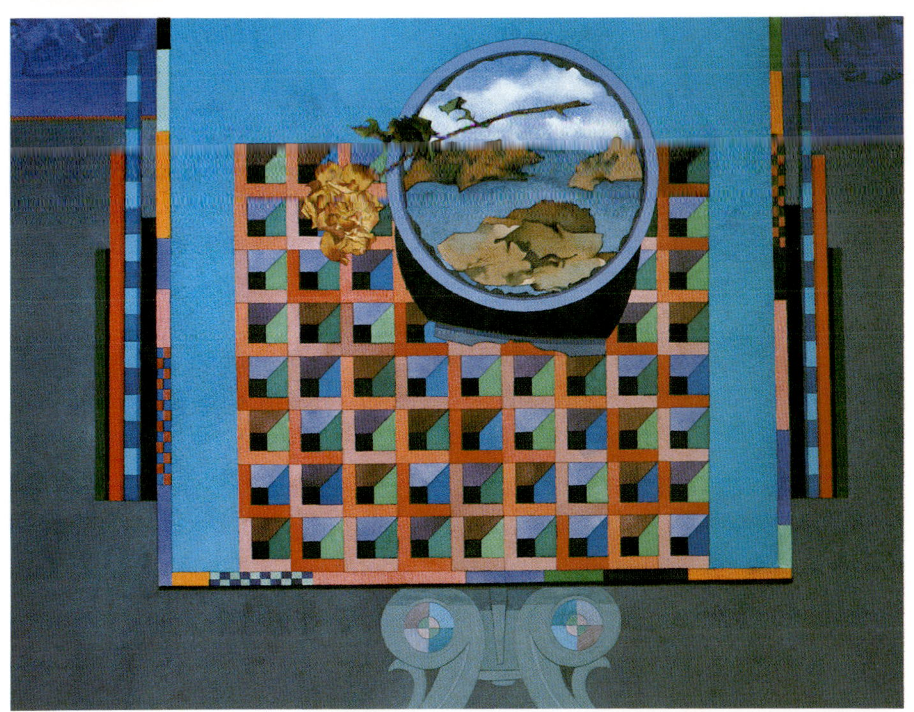

Edward Reep
How Did You Know
I Needed a Rose
28" x 38" (71.1 cm x 96.5 cm)
Arches 140 lb. rough

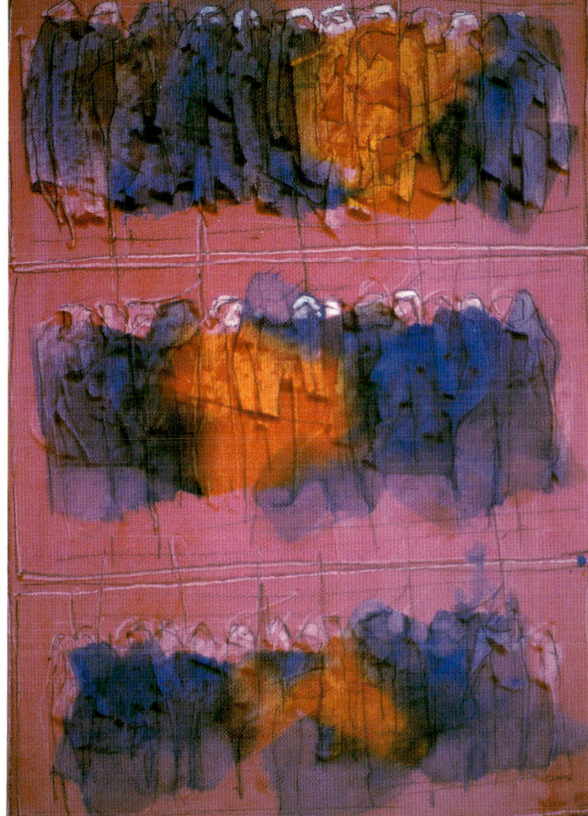
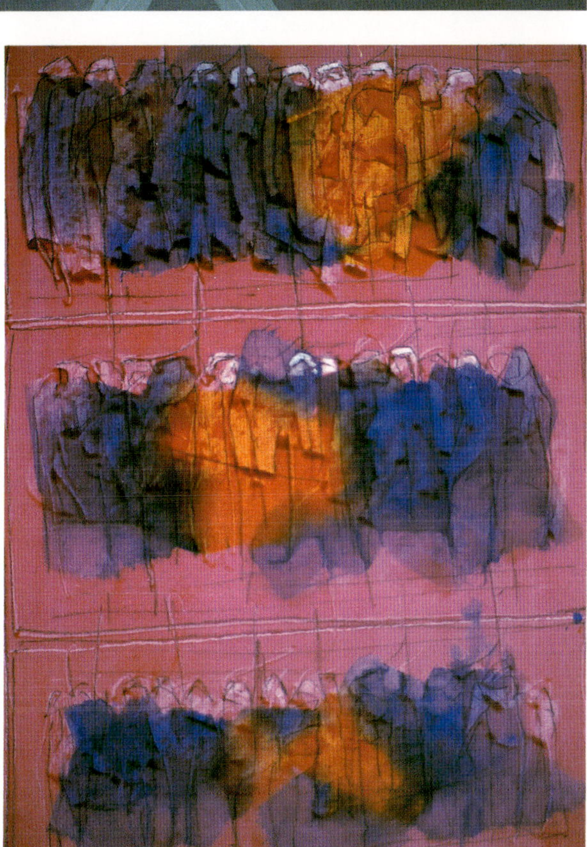

John McIver, A.W.S, N.W.S., W.H.S.
Parade IV
35" x 25" (89 cm x 63 cm)
Arches 260 lb. cold press, single elephant
Media: Acrylic wash, carbon line

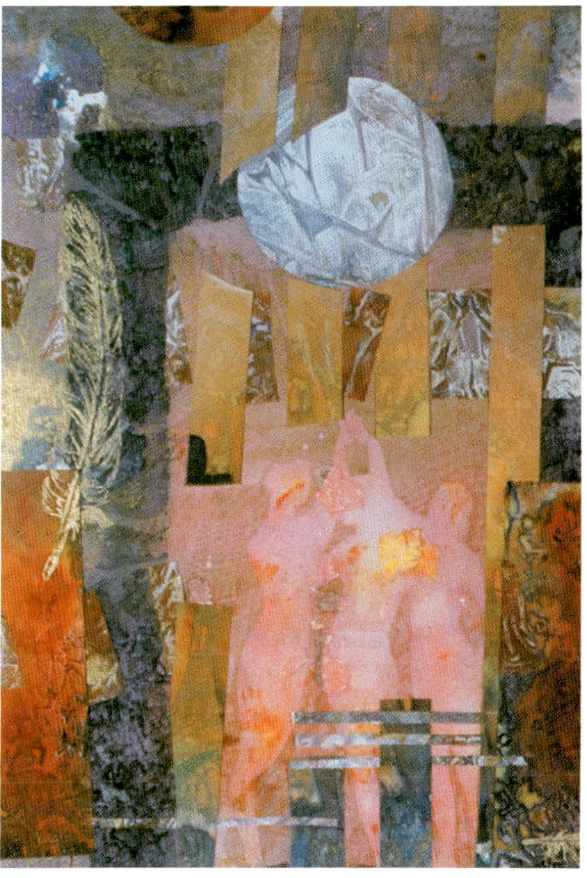

Kathleen Barnes
Moondance
15" x 20" (38.1 cm x 50.8 cm)
Strathmore Aquarius 90 lb.

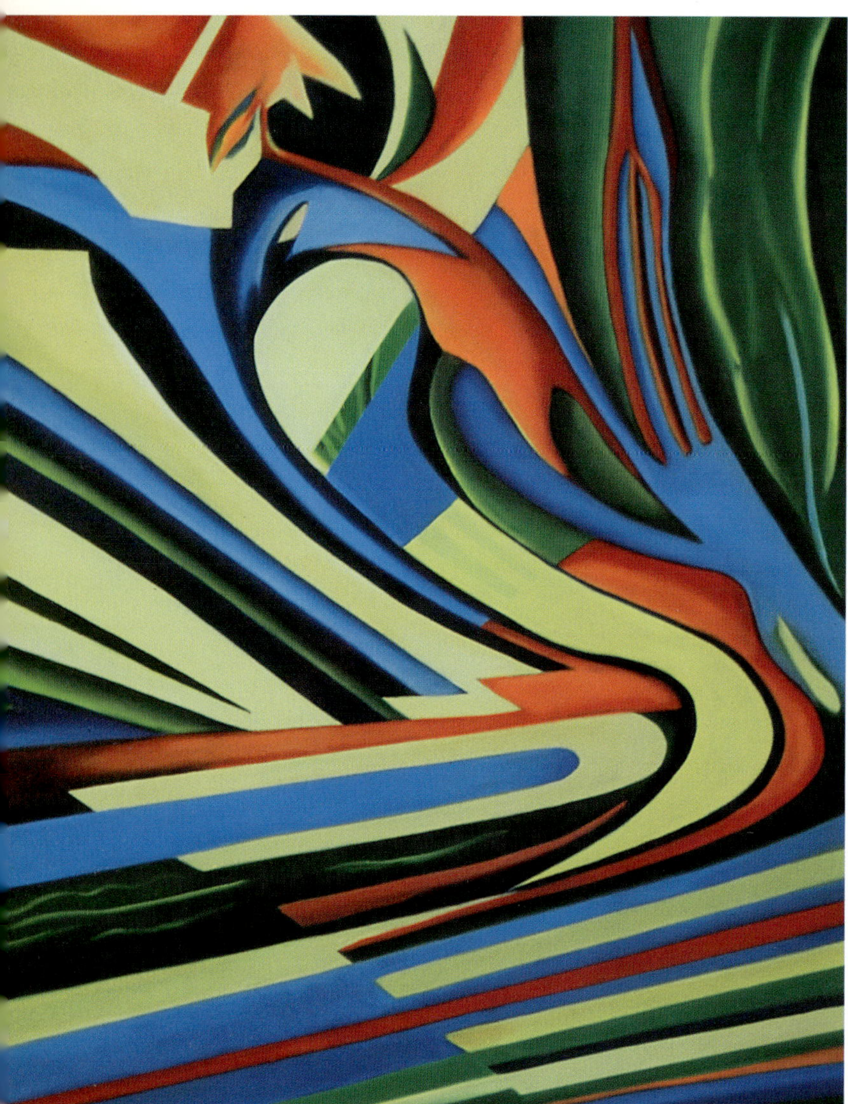

Patricia Brown
In the Beginning
36" x 30" (91.4 cm x 76.2 cm)
Linen canvas

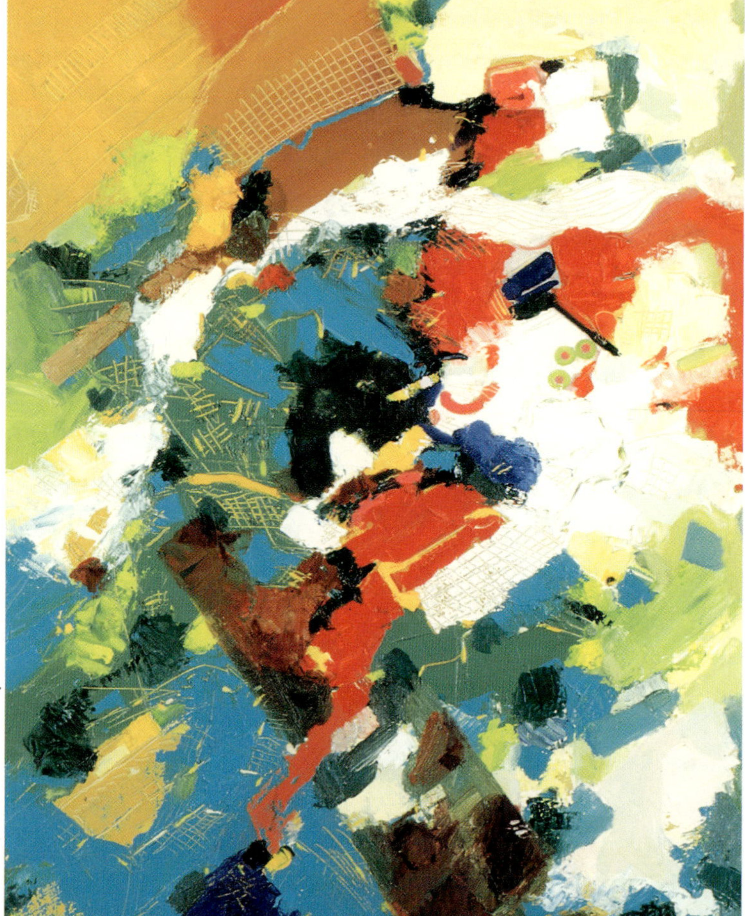

Atanas Karpeles
Crystal
48" x 36" (121.9 cm x 91.4 cm)
Linen canvas

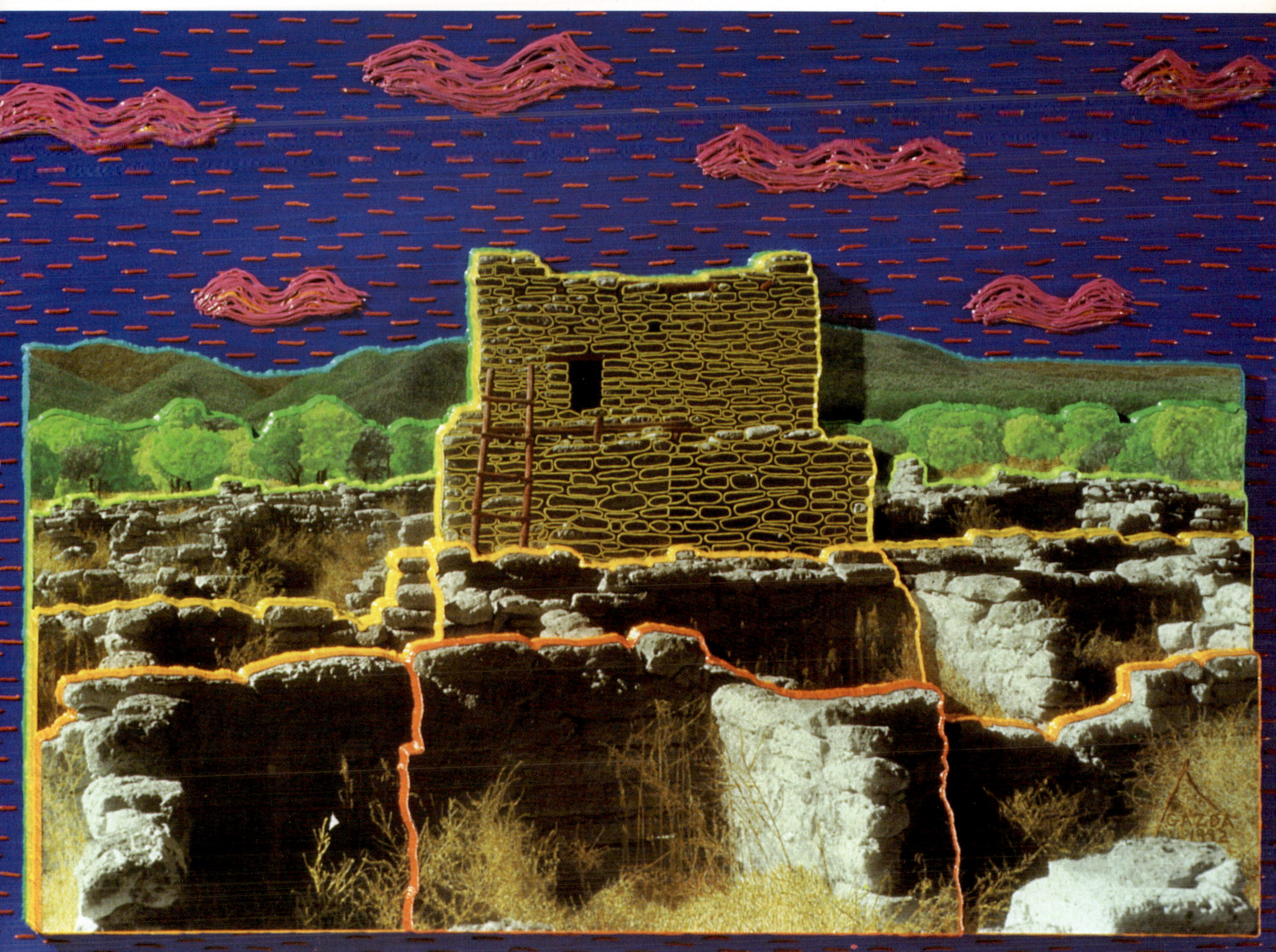

Paul Gazda
Second Pueblo
22" x 30" (55 cm x 75 cm)
Acrylic with black-and-white photographs
Foam board on canvas

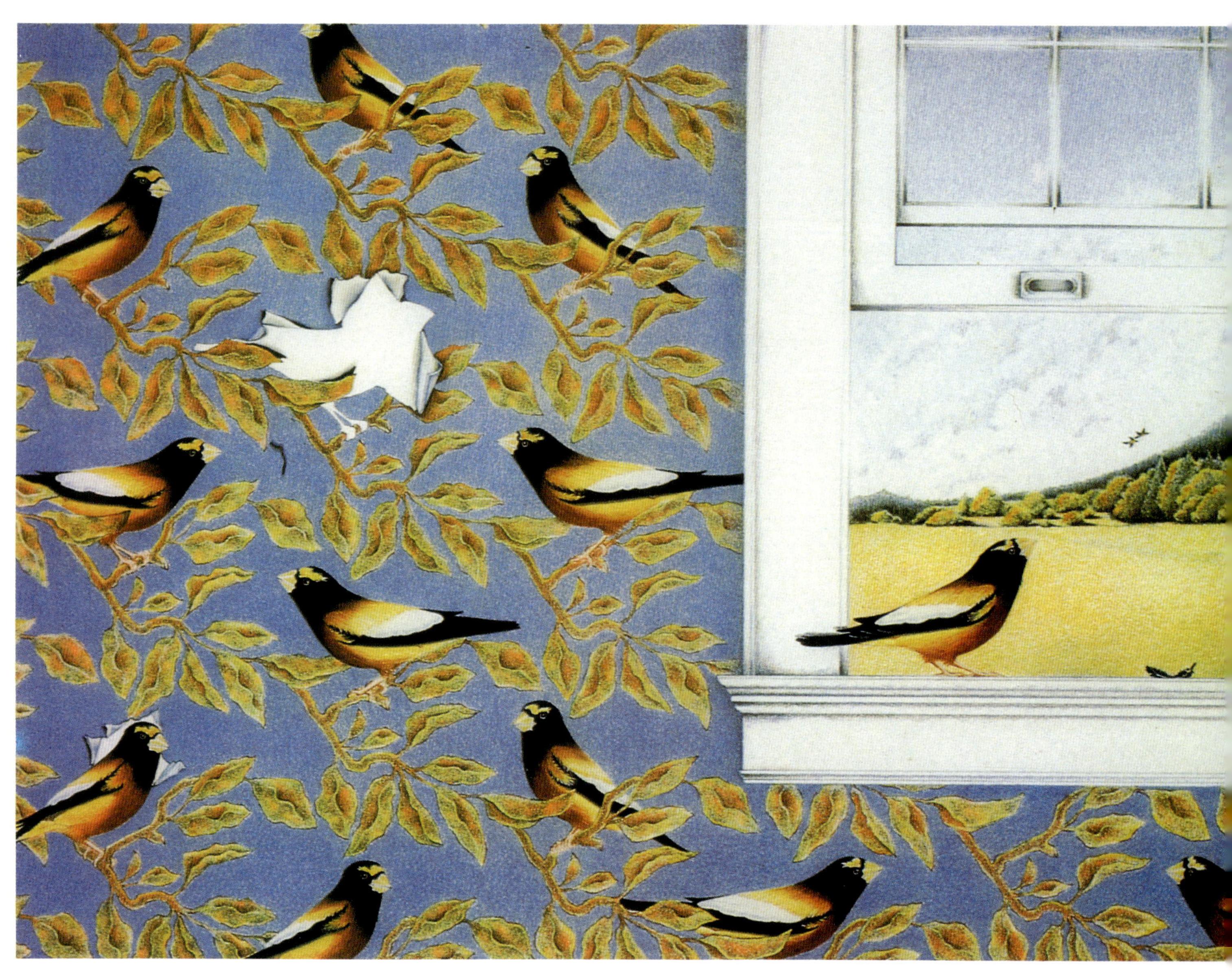

Linda M. Miller
Evening In September
21" x 26" (53 cm x 66 cm)
Rising museum board

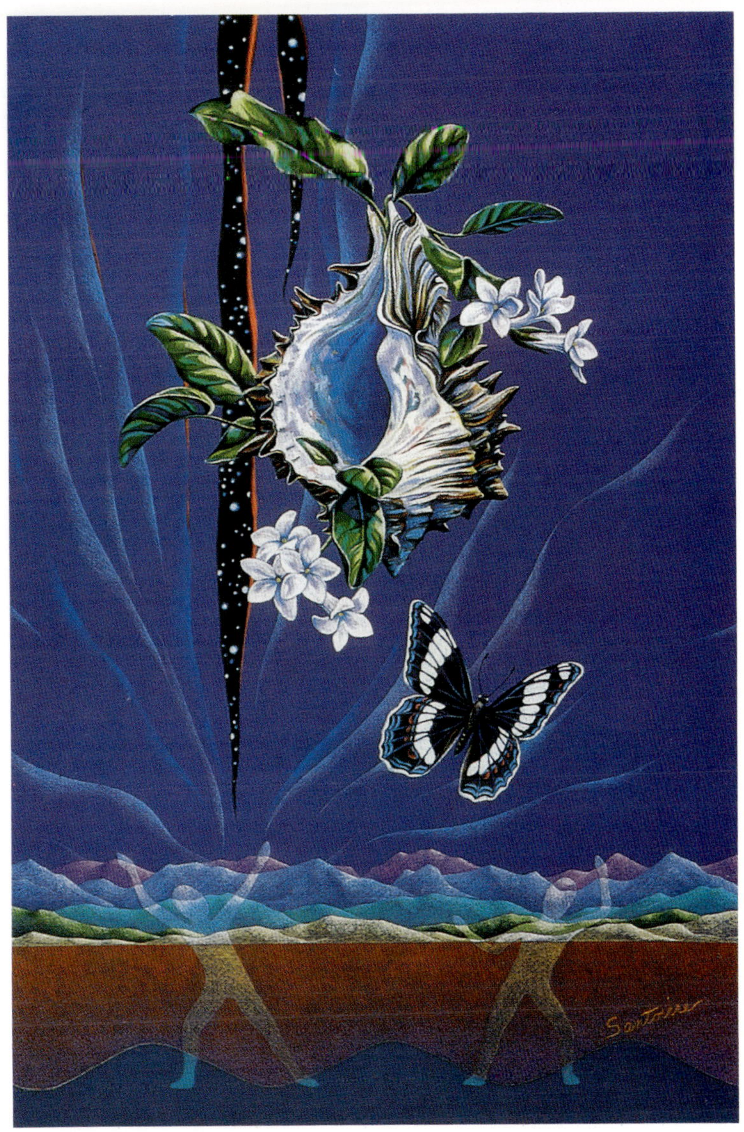

Timothy Santoirre
Fall from Grace
28" x 21" (71 cm x 53 cm)
Canson Mi-Tientes

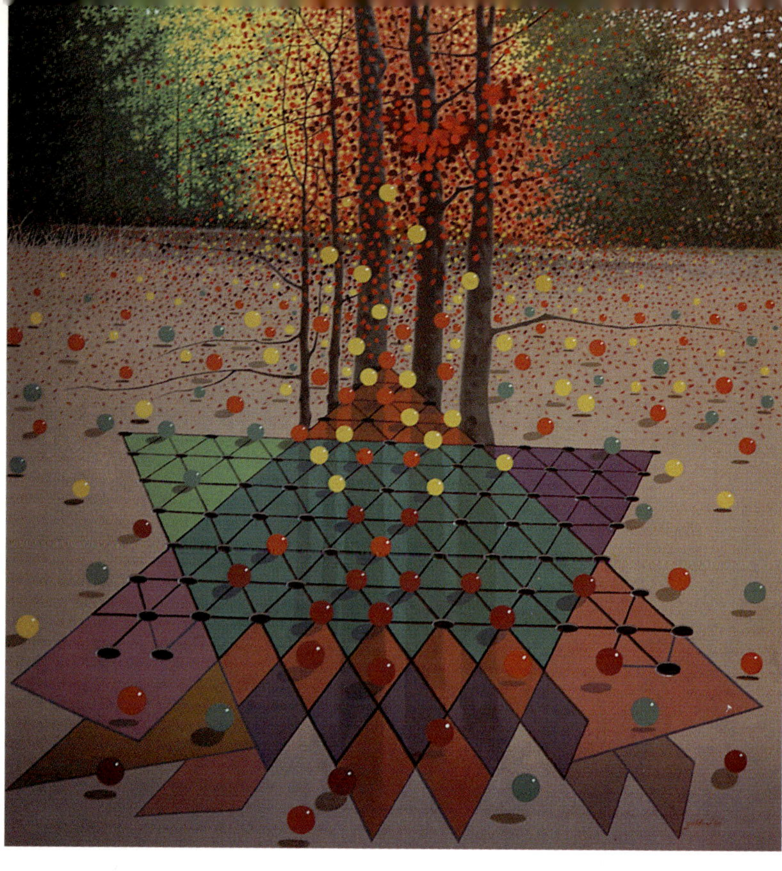

Rolland Golden
The Power of Relativity
48" x 36" (122 cm x 91 cm)
Canvas

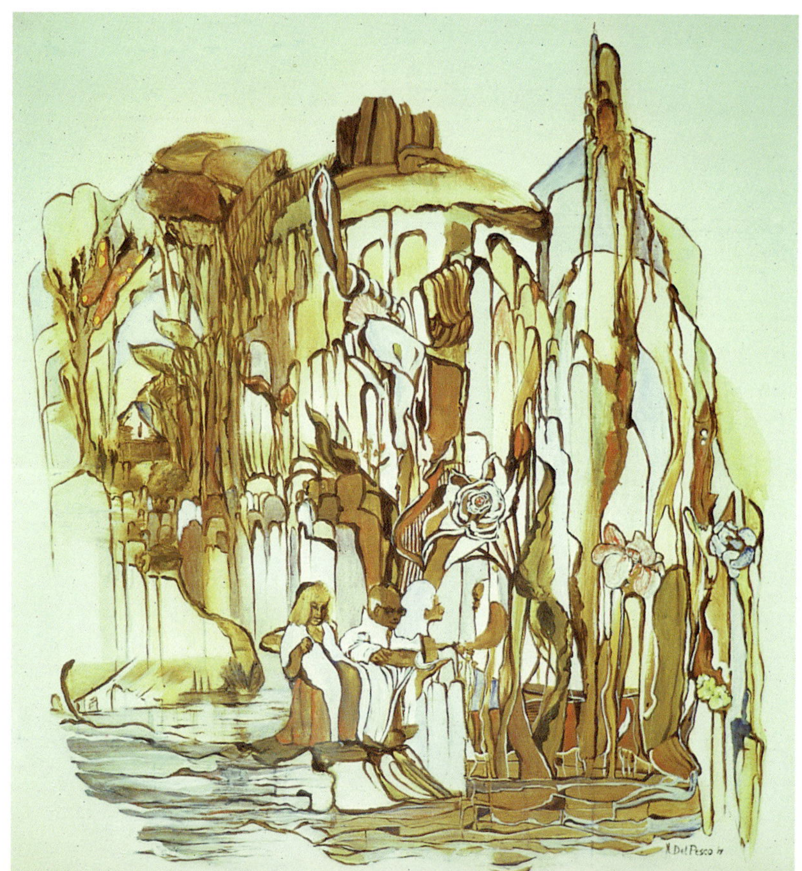

Nancy Del Pesco/Thornton
Waiting for Paradise
54" x 54" (137 cm x 137 cm)
Canvas

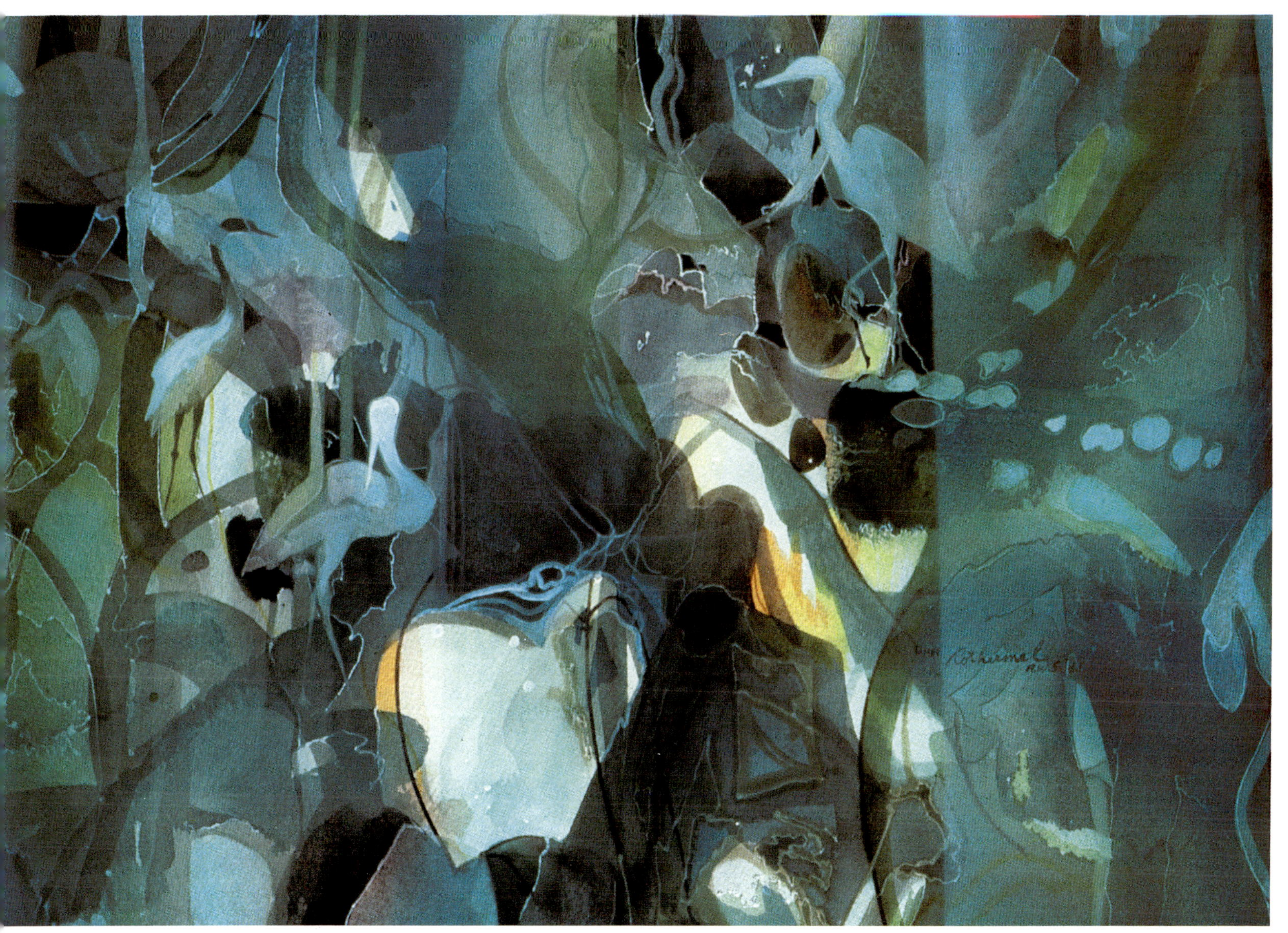

Joan Ashley Rothermel, A.W.S.
Heron Haven
12" x 18" (30.5 cm x 45.7 cm)
Arches 140 lb.

Pauline A. Braun
Under Clearwater
28" x 36" (71 cm x 91 cm)
Lana Aquarelle 140 lb. watercolor paper

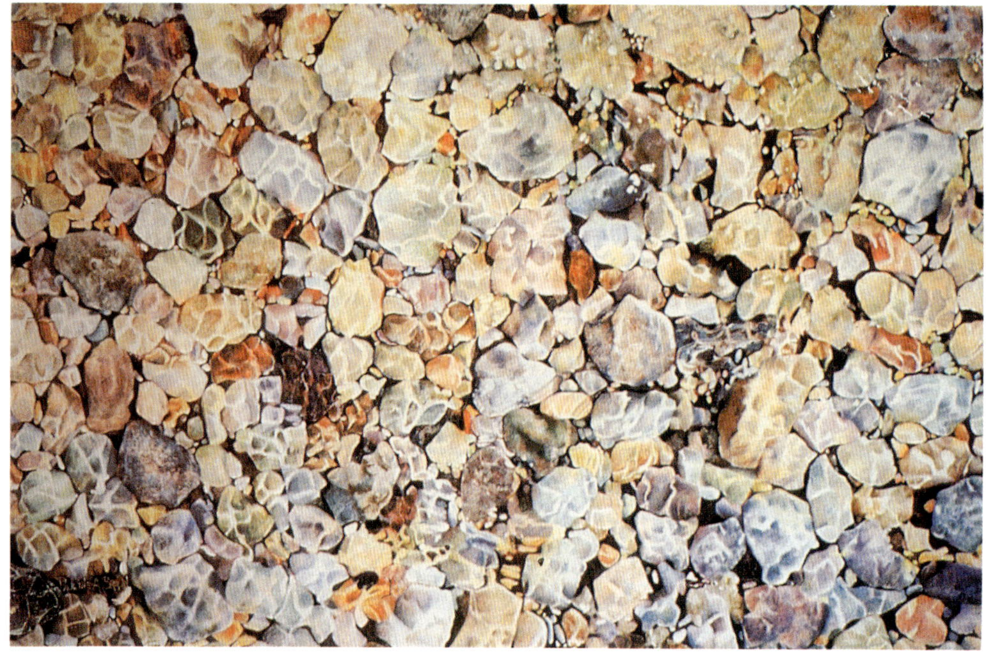

E. Michael Yefko
From Series Clear Cut V
20" x 23" (51 cm x 58 cm)
Meridian drawing paper

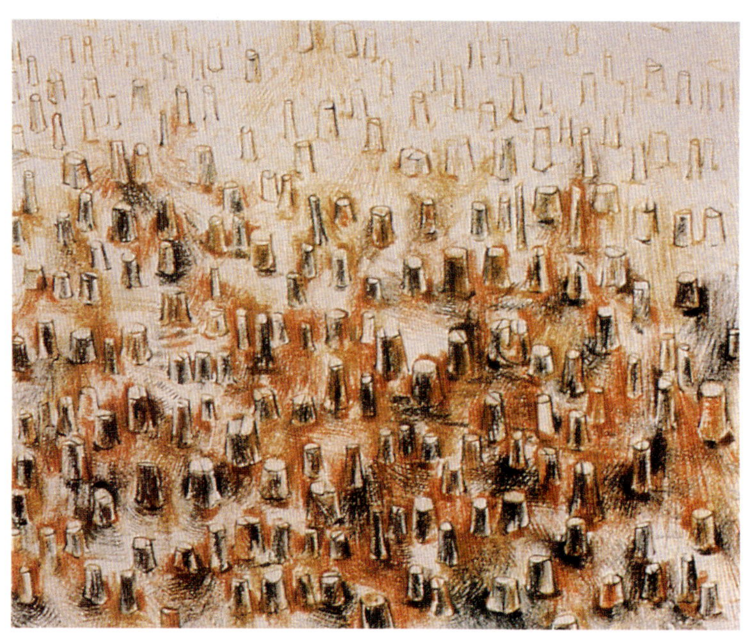

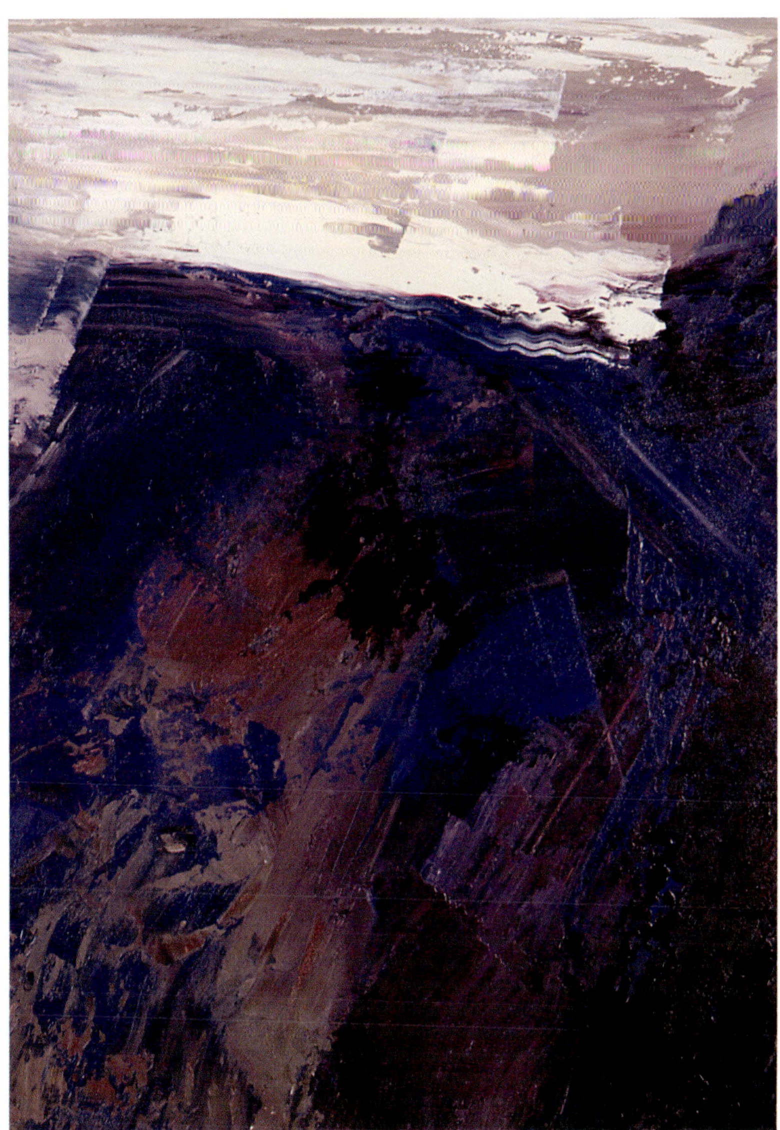

Patrick O'Kiersey
Blue Ridge
30" x 24" (76.2 cm x 61 cm)
Canvas

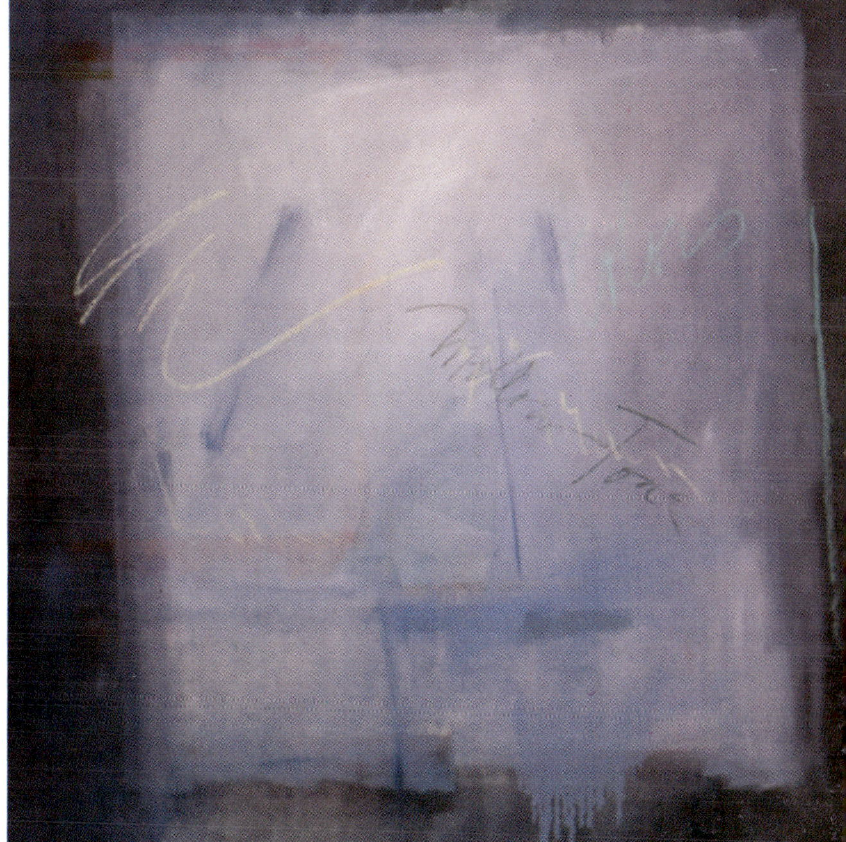

Esther Levy
Colors of the Duke No. 10
67" x 65" (170.2 cm x 165.1 cm)
Canvas

Alex Andra
Drifting
45" x 65" (114 cm x 165 cm)
Arches 300 lb. paper

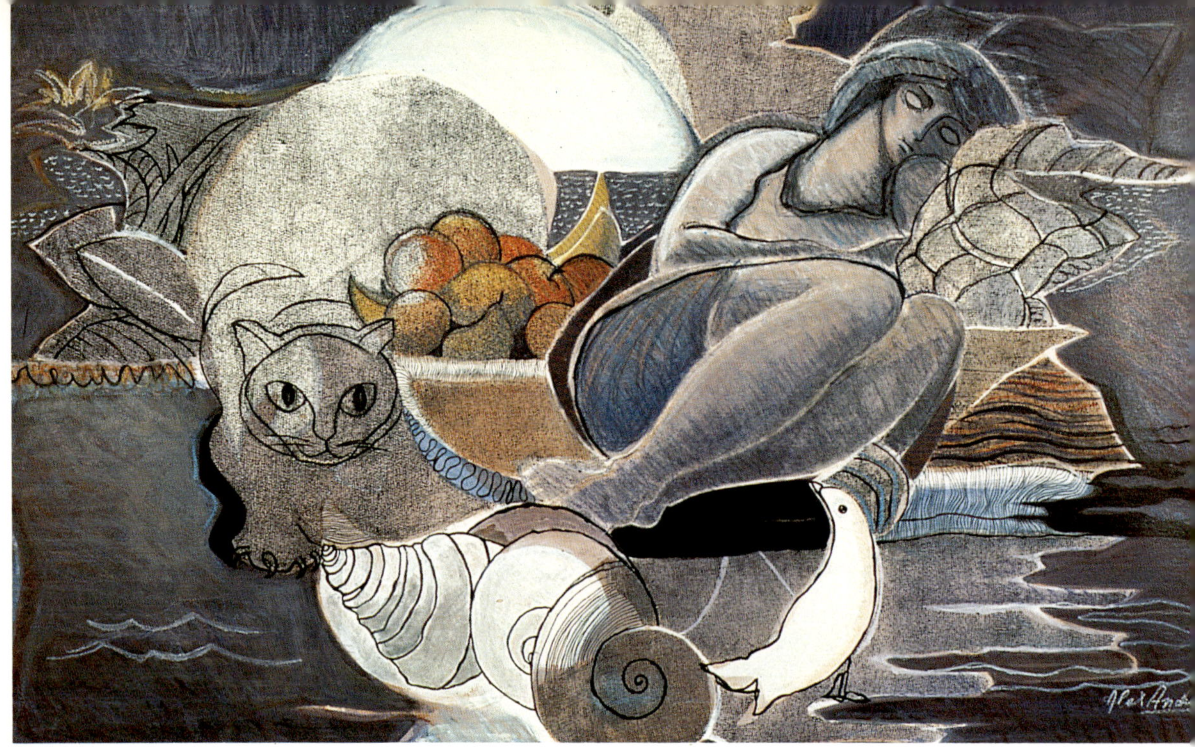

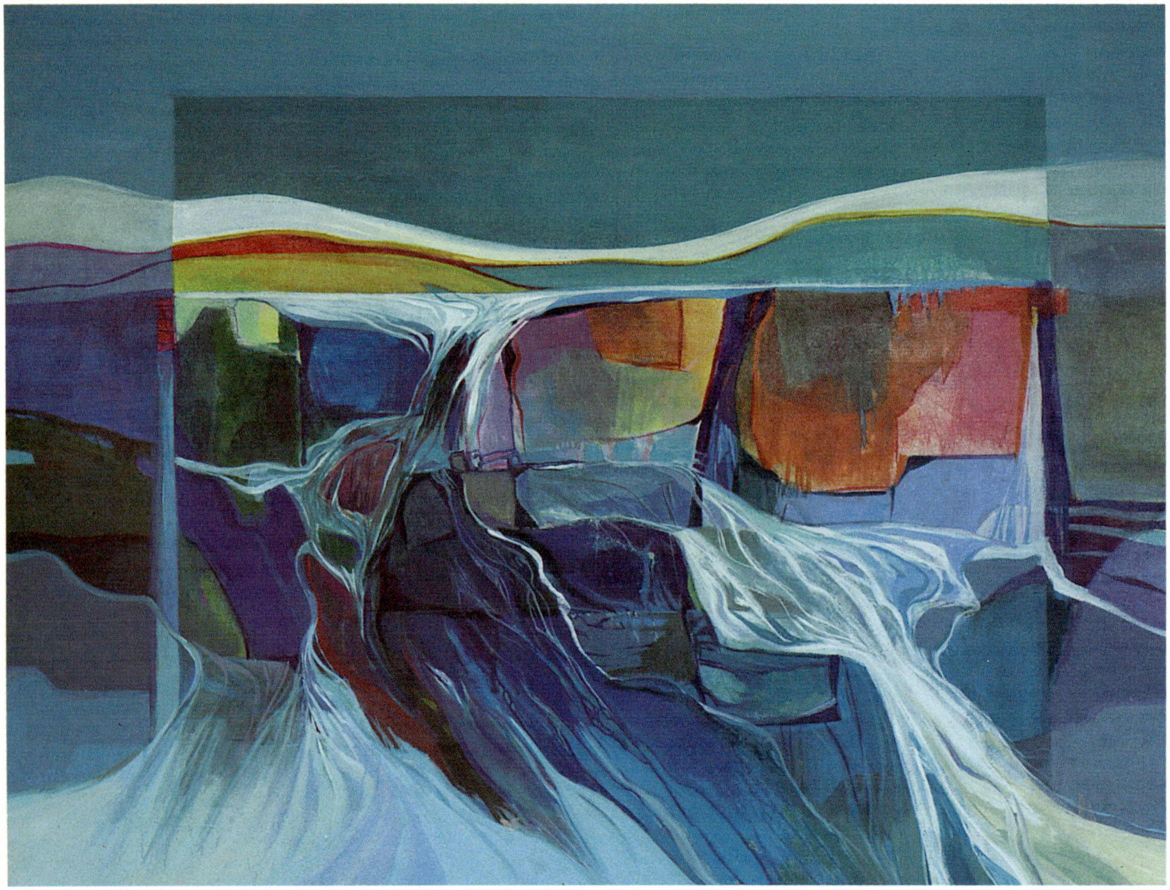

Edith Socolow
Window Series-Spring Thaw
38" x 49" (97 cm x 124 cm)
Canvas

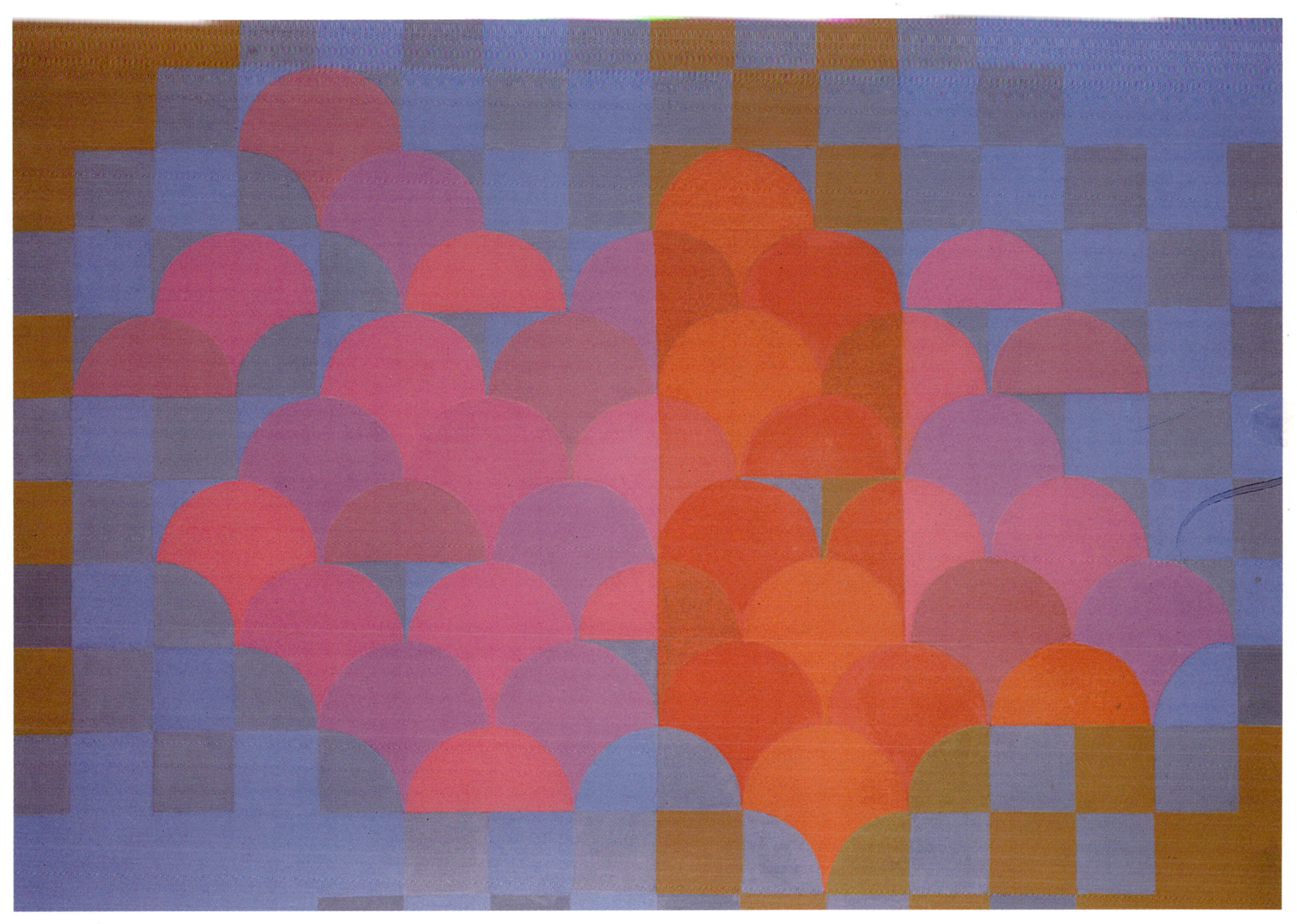

Marian Hettner Grunbaum
Light and Shade
36" x 48" (91 cm x 122 cm)
Canvas

Susan Lucas Updyke
Dune Grasses VI
22" x 30" (56 cm x 76 cm)
Strathmore Aquarius

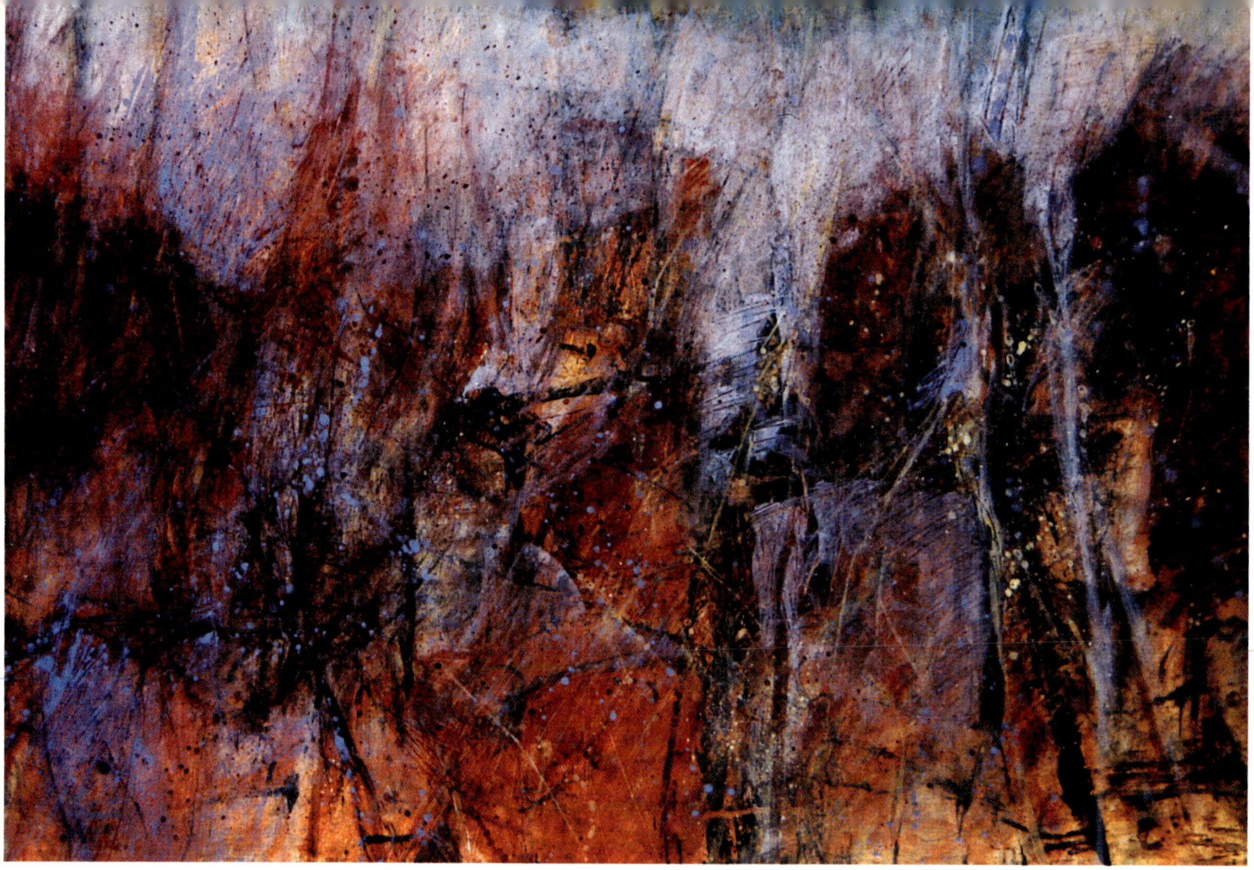

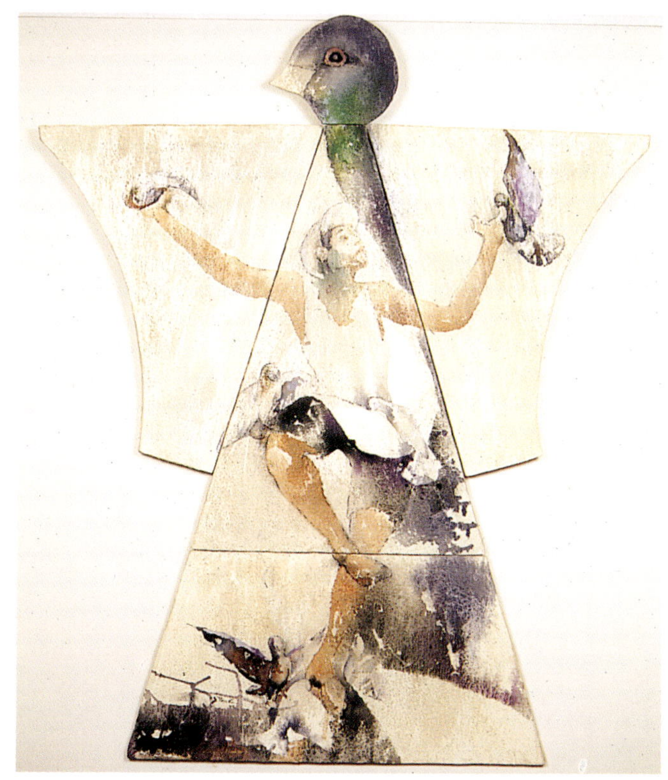

Doris Price
Birdflight
80" x 70" (203 cm x 178 cm)
Gatorboard sand- and gesso-coated foam core board

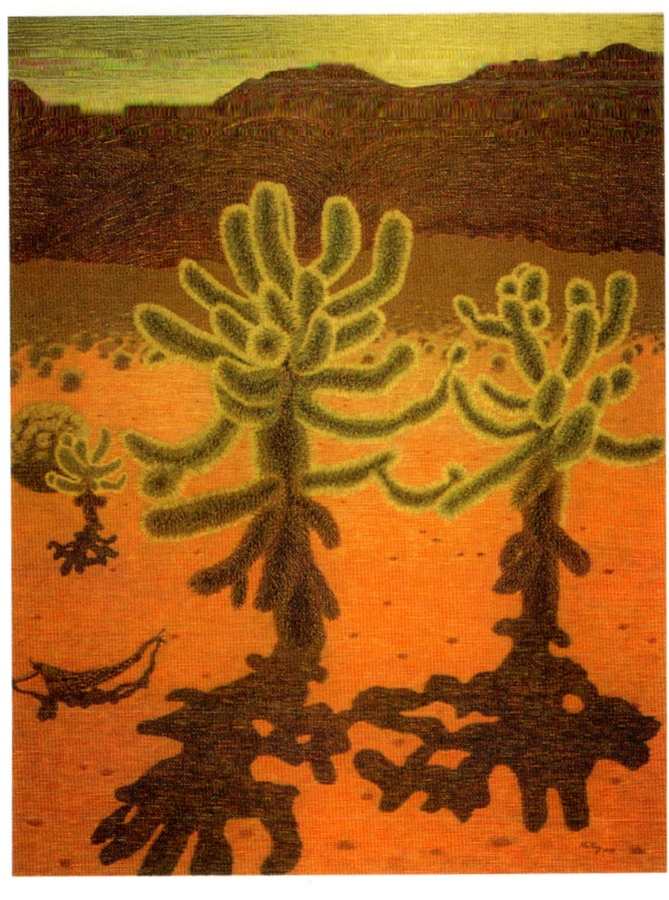

Katherine McKay
Anza-Borrego No 9: Cholla
31" x 25" (79 cm x 64 cm)
Canson Mi-Tientes

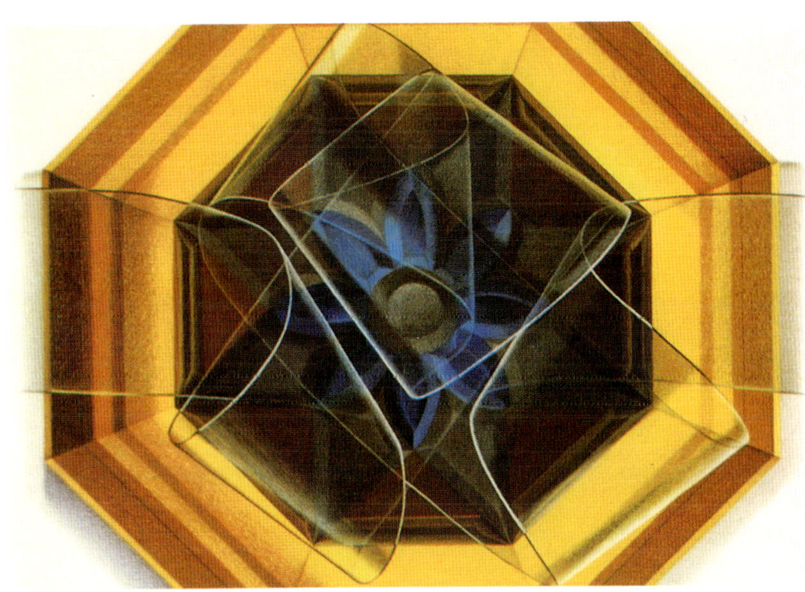

Lula Mae Blocton
Octagon Twist Clear Night
22" x 30" (56 cm x 76 cm)
Rives BFK rag paper

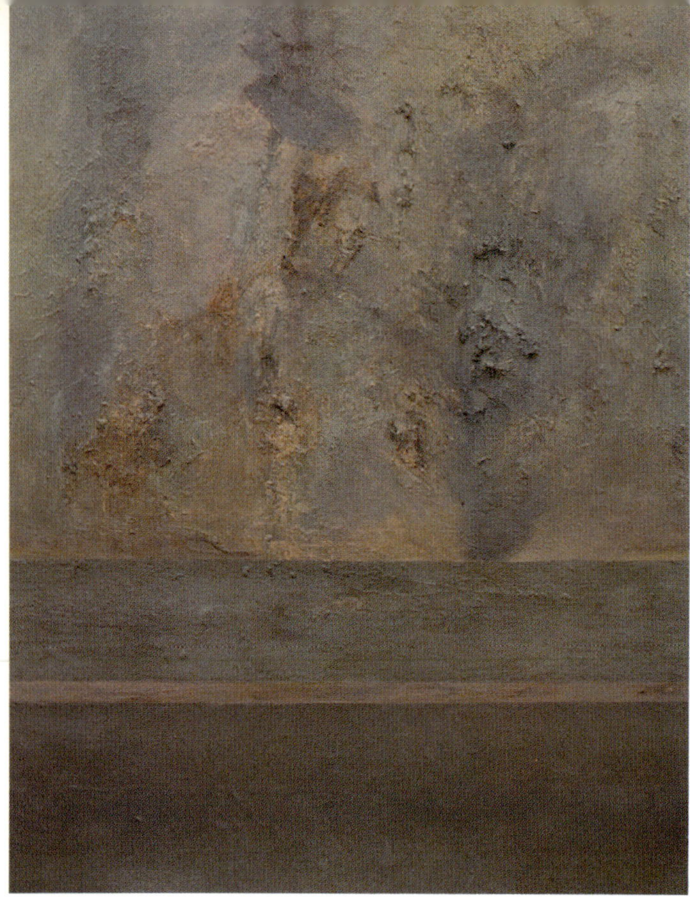

Lucille Dratler
Untitled
48" x 36" (121.9 cm x 91.4 cm)
Oil with wax
Canvas

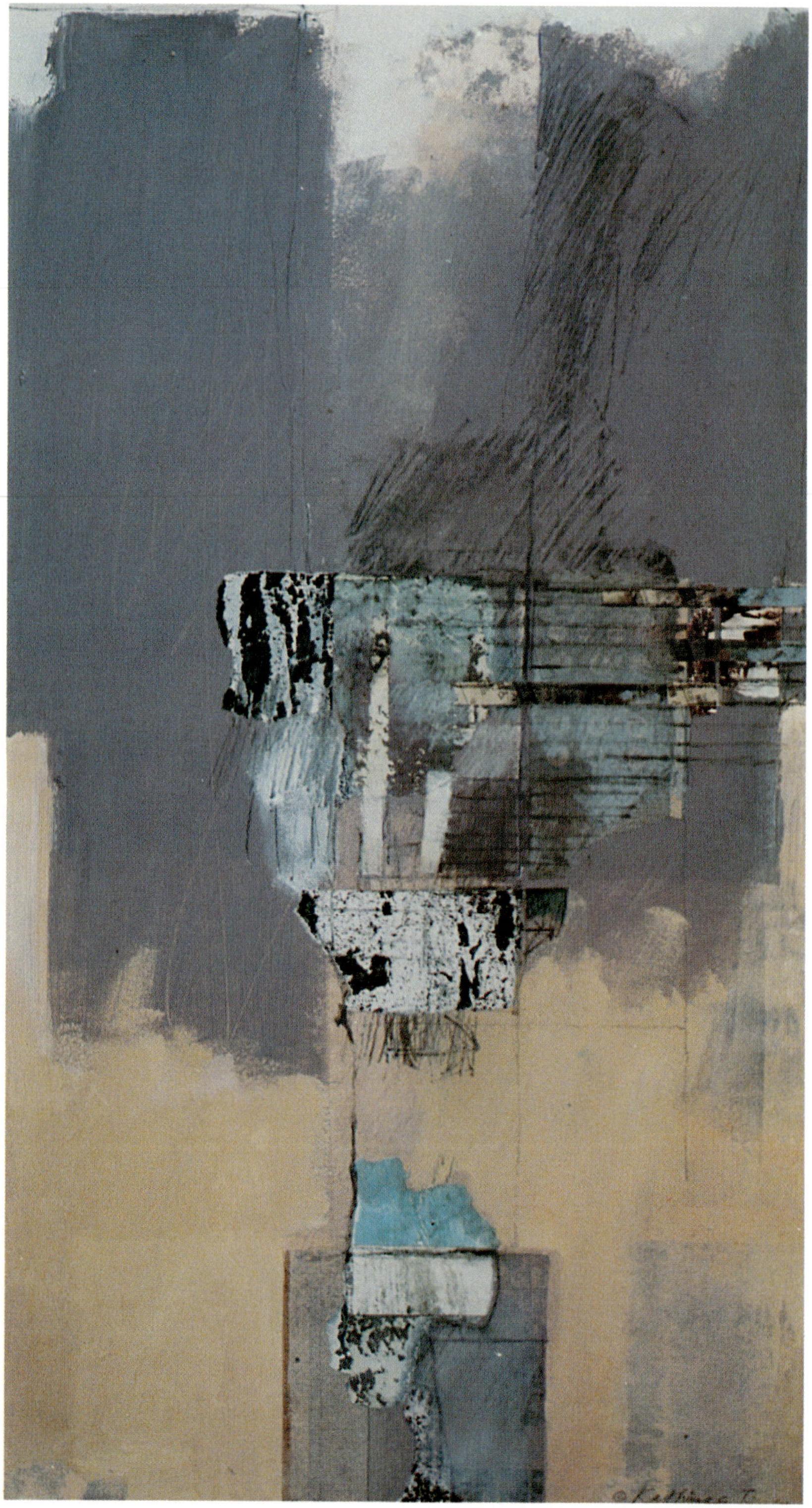

Katherine Chang Liu
I Knew a Flutist
23" x 12" (58.4 cm x 30.5 cm)
Oil with gesso
300 lb. Hot press paper

Leslie Masters

Mountain Rust

34" x 22" (88 cm x 57 cm)

Acrylic metal plate and barbed wire

Metal plate on stretched and

gesso-coated cotton canvas

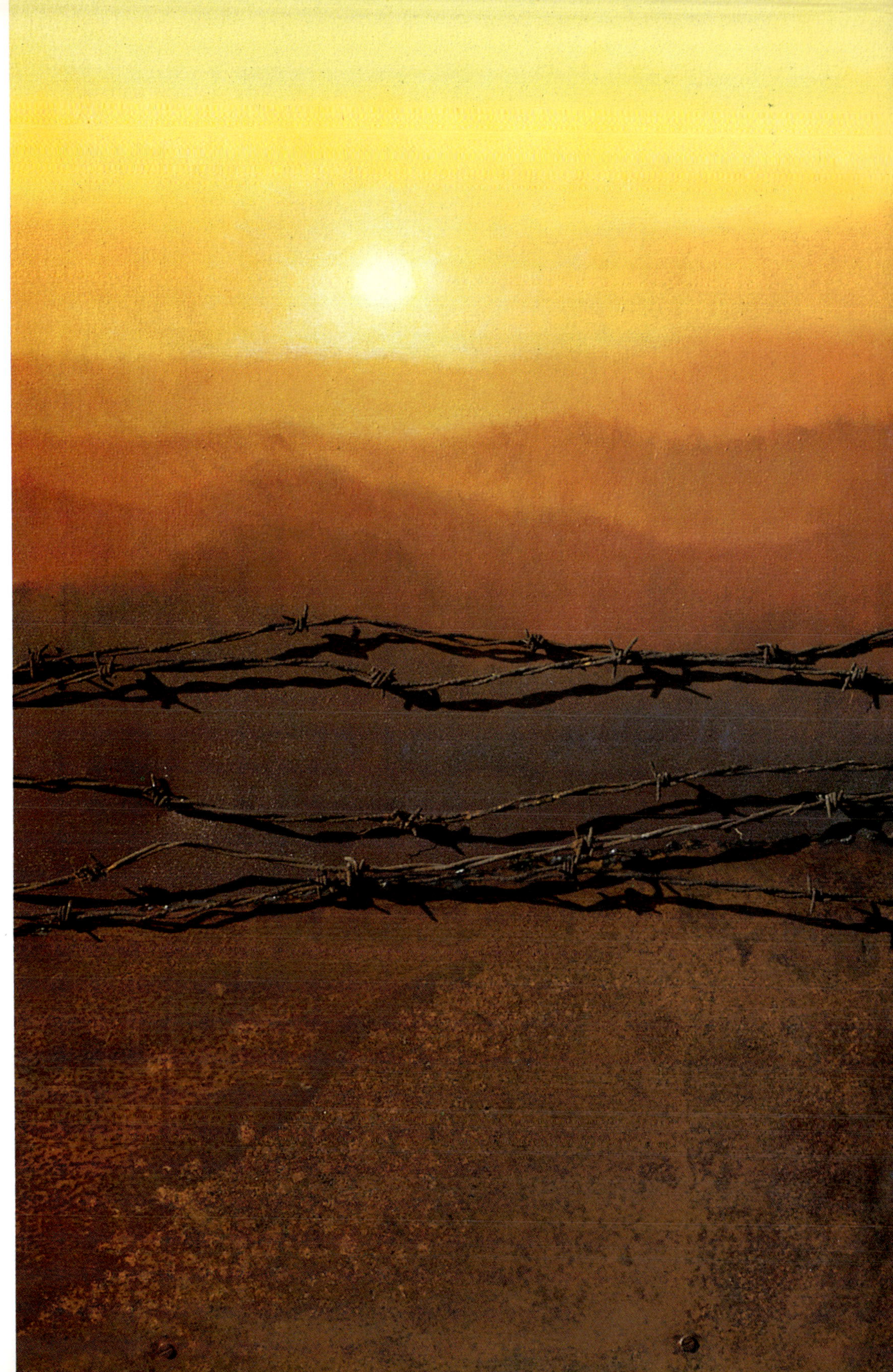

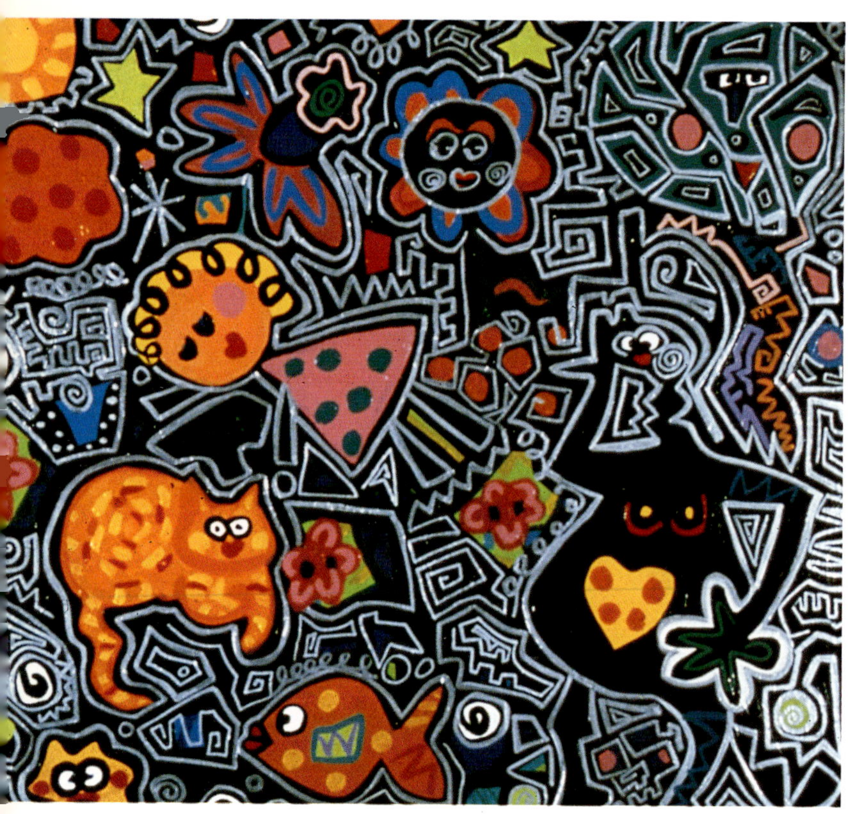

Jodi Cohen
Dreamland
52" x 52" (132 cm x 132 cm)
Canvas

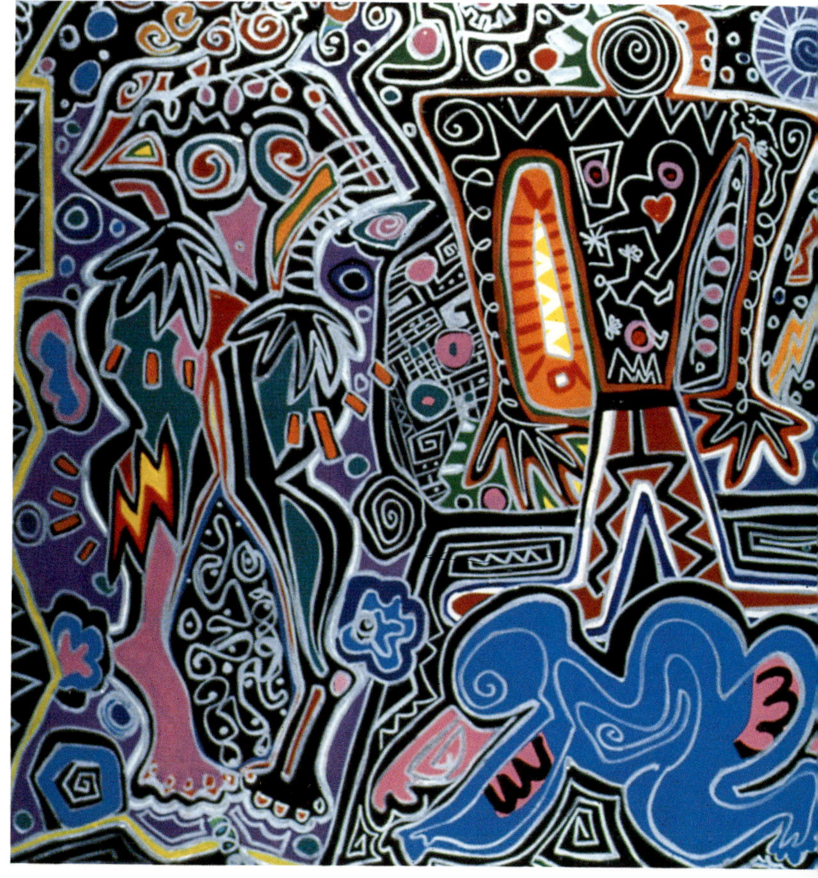

Jodi Cohen
The Nuclear Family
50" x 50" (127 cm x 127 cm)
Canvas

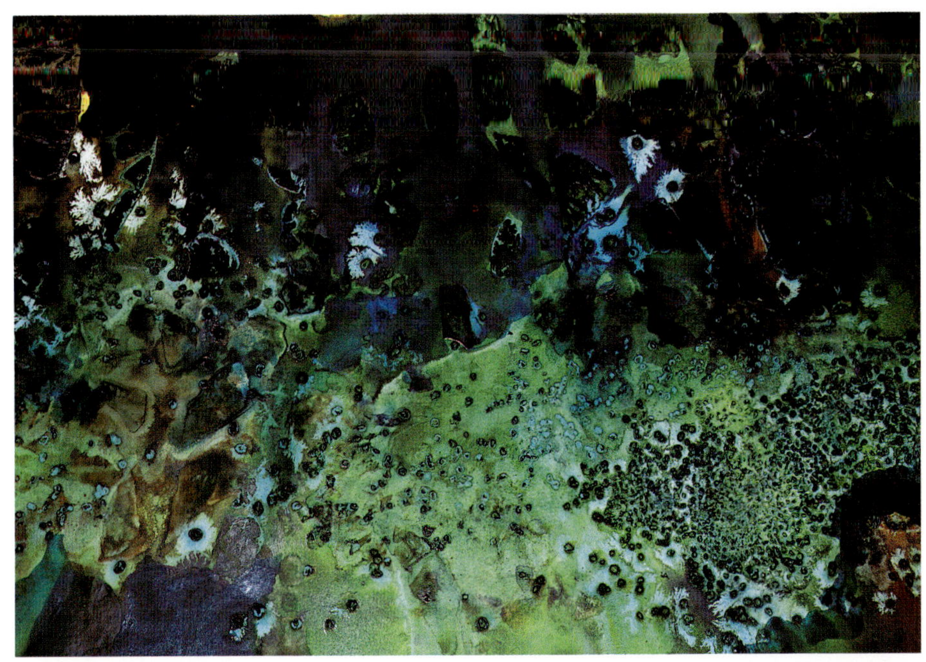

Jean Munro
Things That Go Bump in the Night
26" x 34" (66 cm x 86.4 cm)
Arches 140 lb. cold press
Media: Ink, shapes in plastic, rock salt

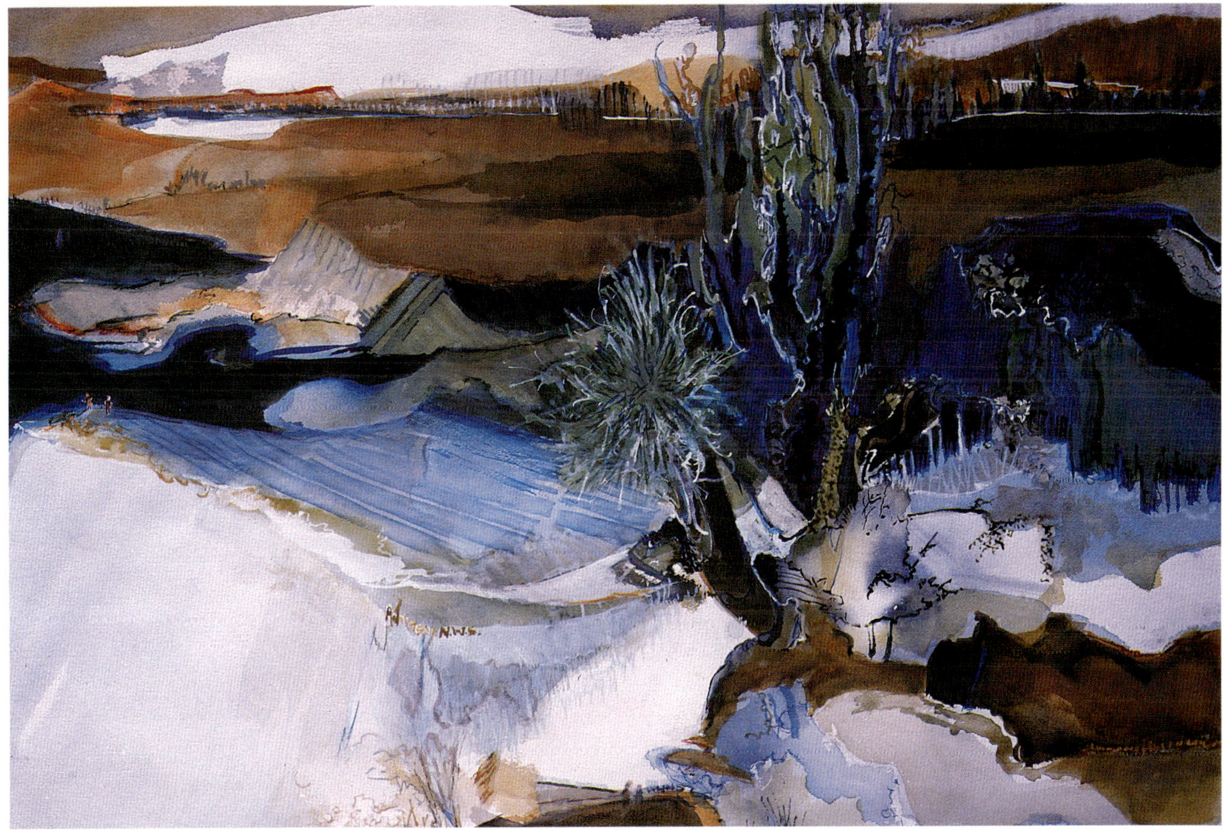

Astrid E. Johnson, N.W.S.
Colorado River
22" x 30" (55.9 cm x 76.2 cm)
Arches 140 lb.

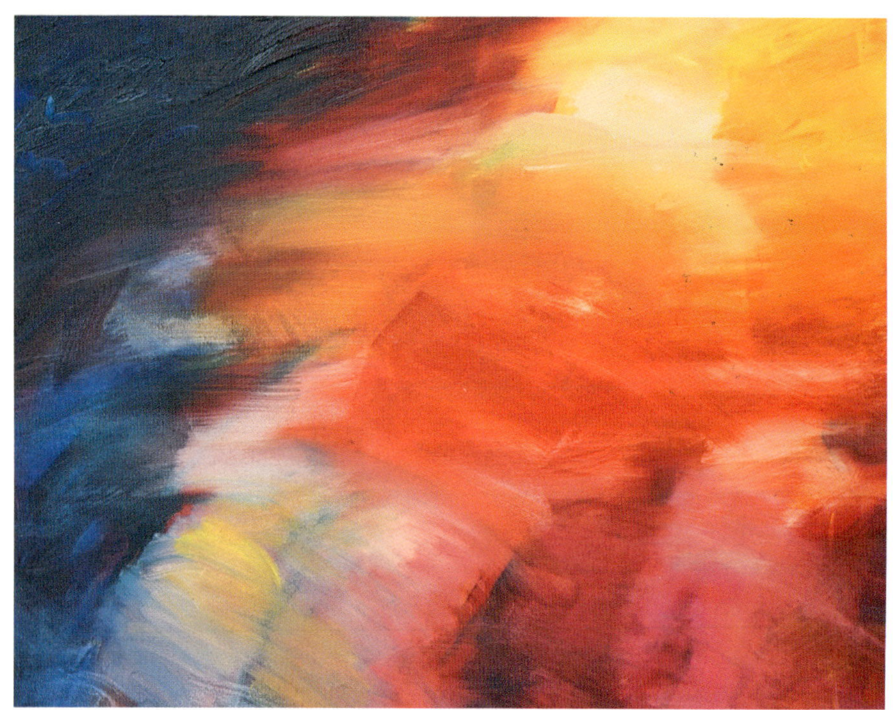

Maxine Warren
Shaman's Light Dance #4
24" x 30" (61 cm x 76.2 cm)
Stretched canvas

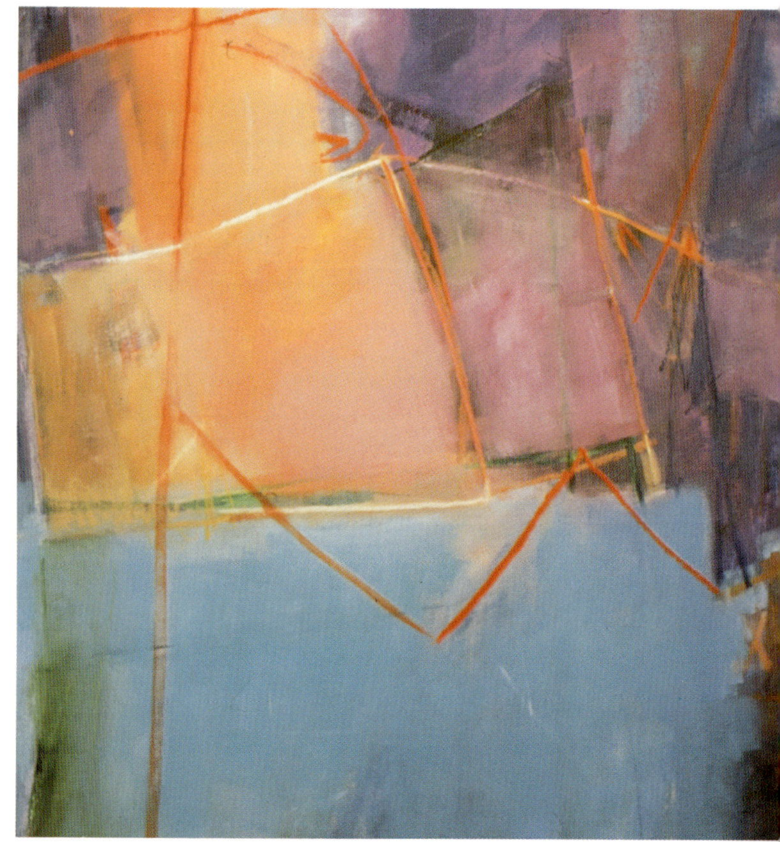

Esther Levy
Colors of the Duke No.1
67" x 66" (170.2 cm x 167.6 cm)
Canvas

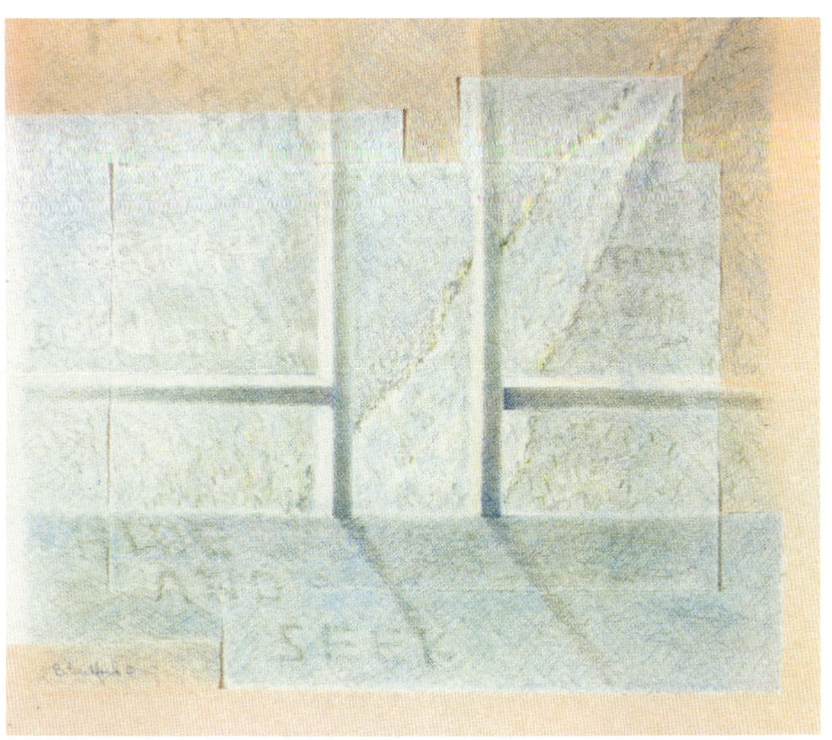

Bobbie Bradford
Nine Words
20" x 21" (51 cm x 53 cm)
Canson Mi-Tientes

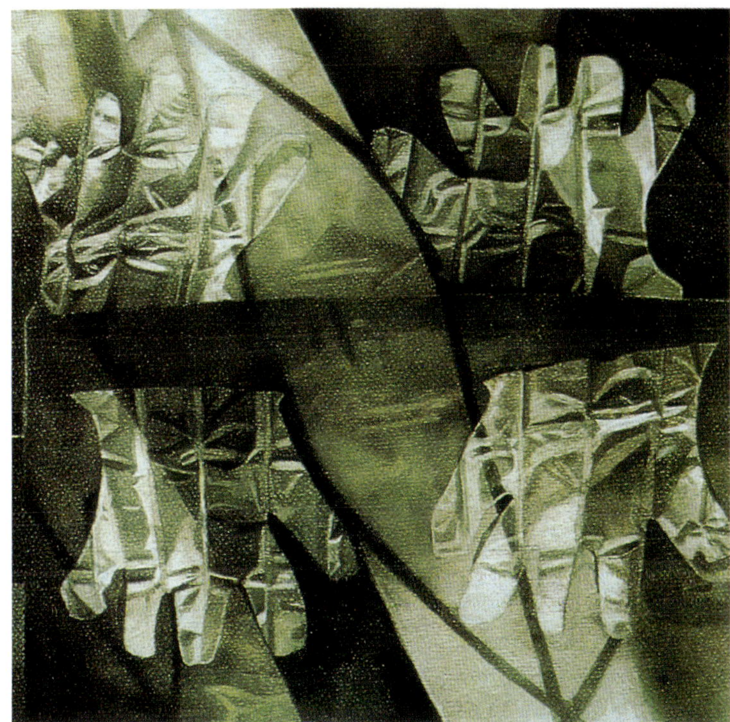

Lee Sims
Crisscross
18" x 18" (46 cm x 46 cm)
Canson Mi-Tientes

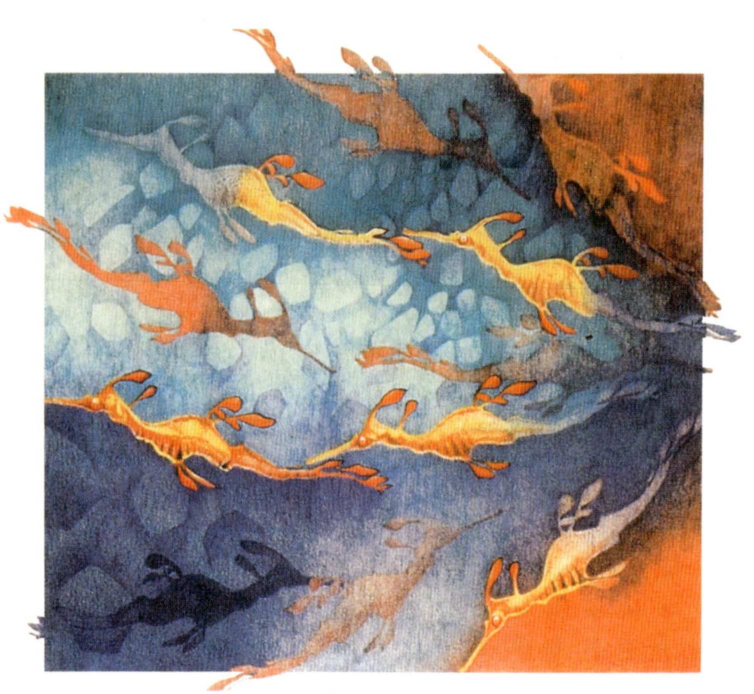

Jan Rimerman
Vanishing Dragons
33" x 32" (84 cm x 81 cm)
100% rag board, 8-ply vellum

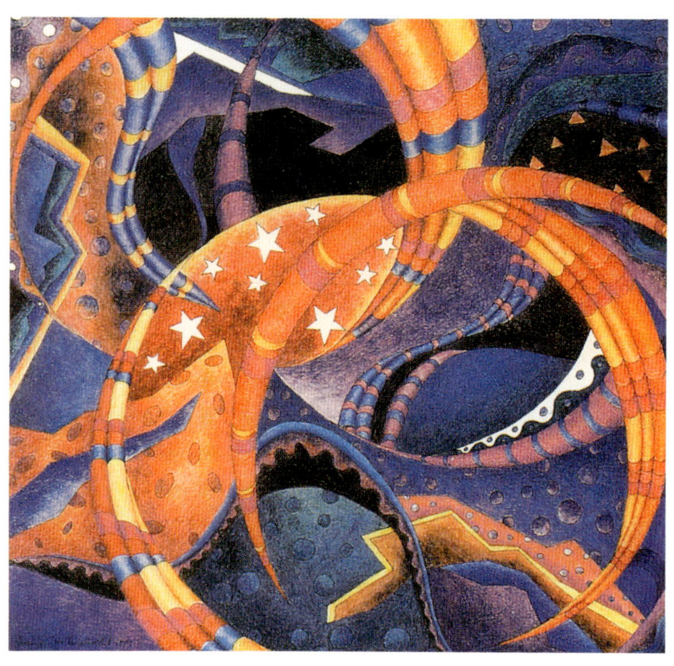

Joan C. Hollingsworth
Pursuit
14" x 14" (36 cm x 36 cm)
Crescent 5-ply

Anne Bagby
Queens Diamond
20" x 20" (50 cm x 50 cm)
Canvas

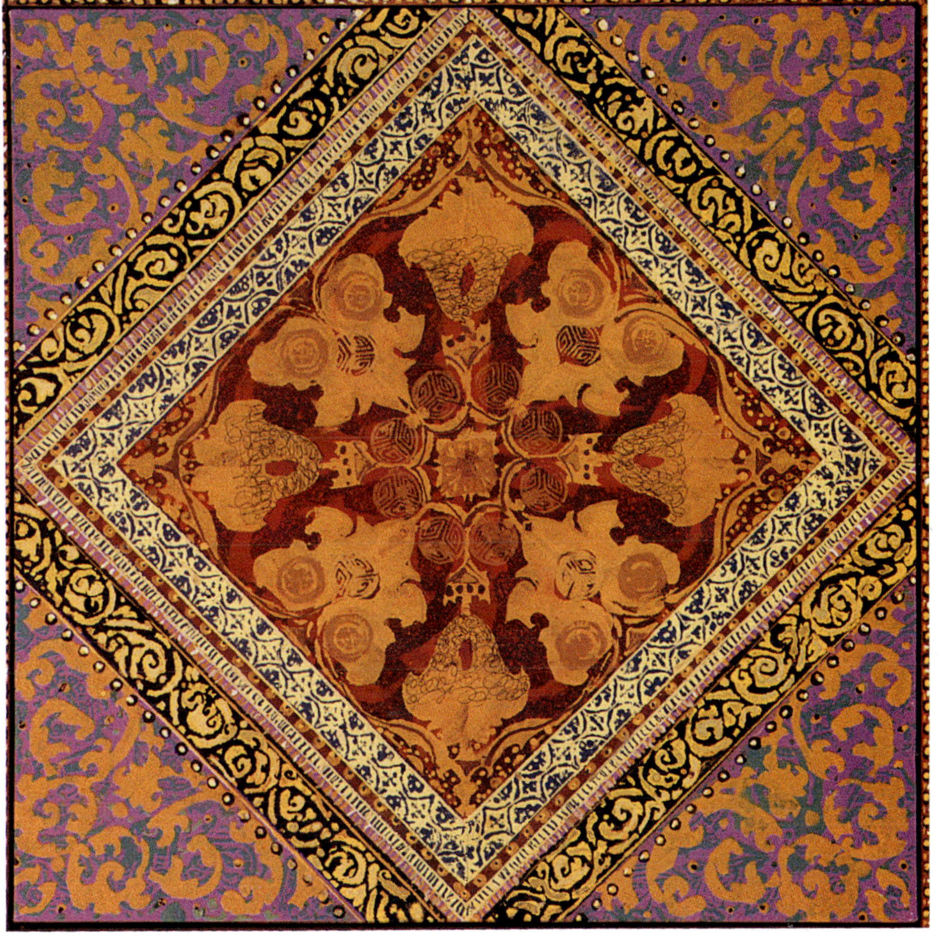

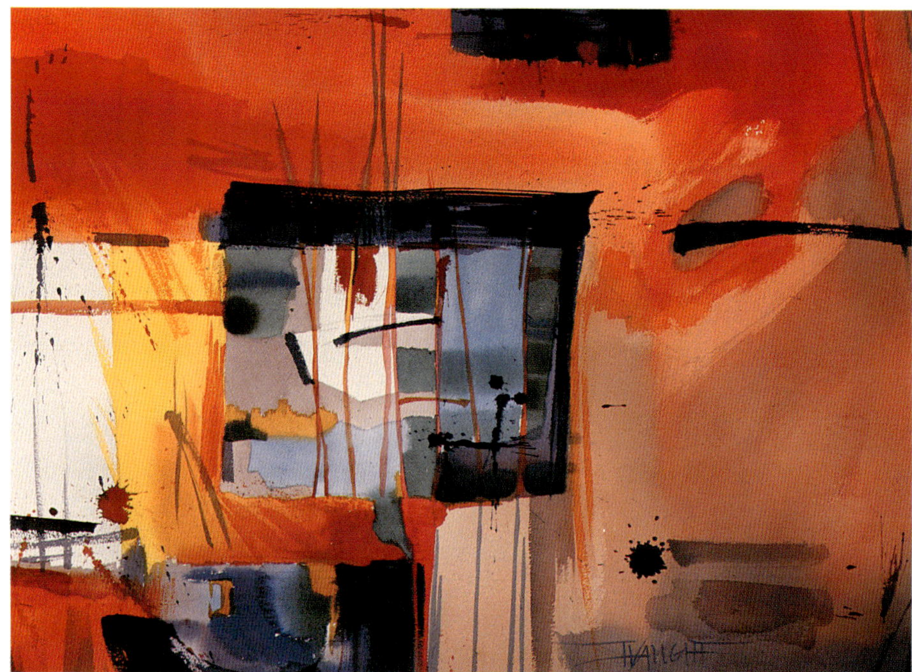

Ted Vaught
On the Warpath
21" x 29" (53.3 cm x 74.7 cm)
Arches 140 lb. rough

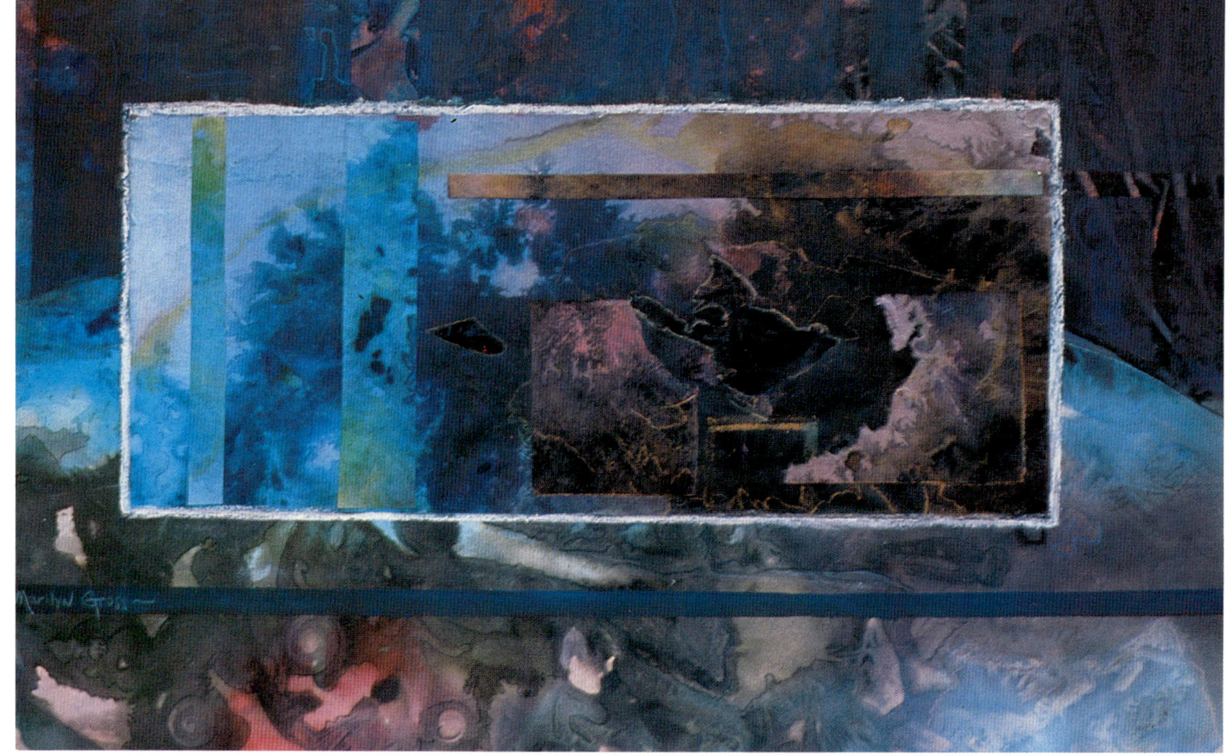

Marilyn Gross
Life Forms
15" x 21" (38.1 cm x 53.3 cm)
Arches 140 lb. cold press
Media: Watercolor, light fast inks, quilling paper

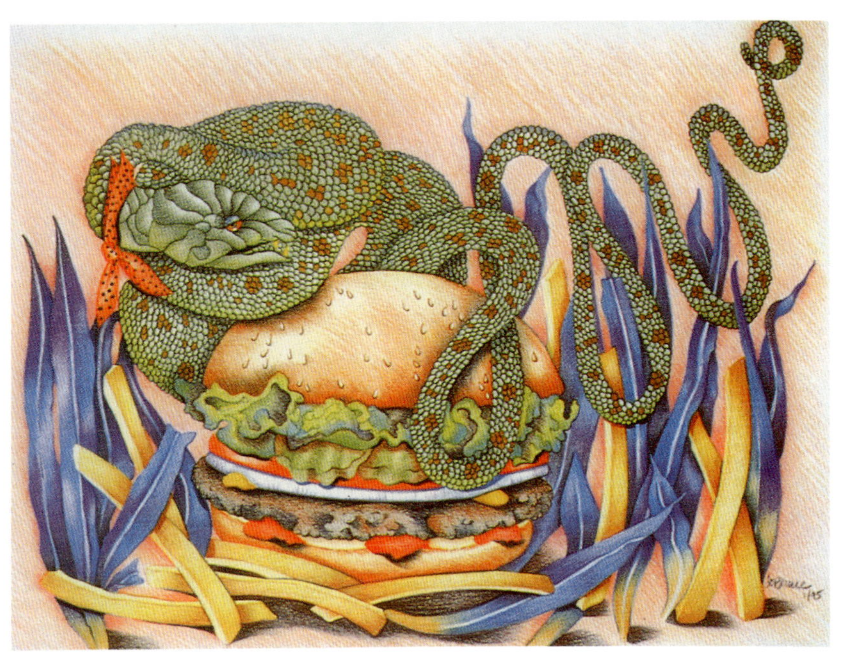

Judith Orner Bruce
Burger, Snake, and Fries
14" x 23" (36 cm x 58 cm)
2-Ply rising museum board

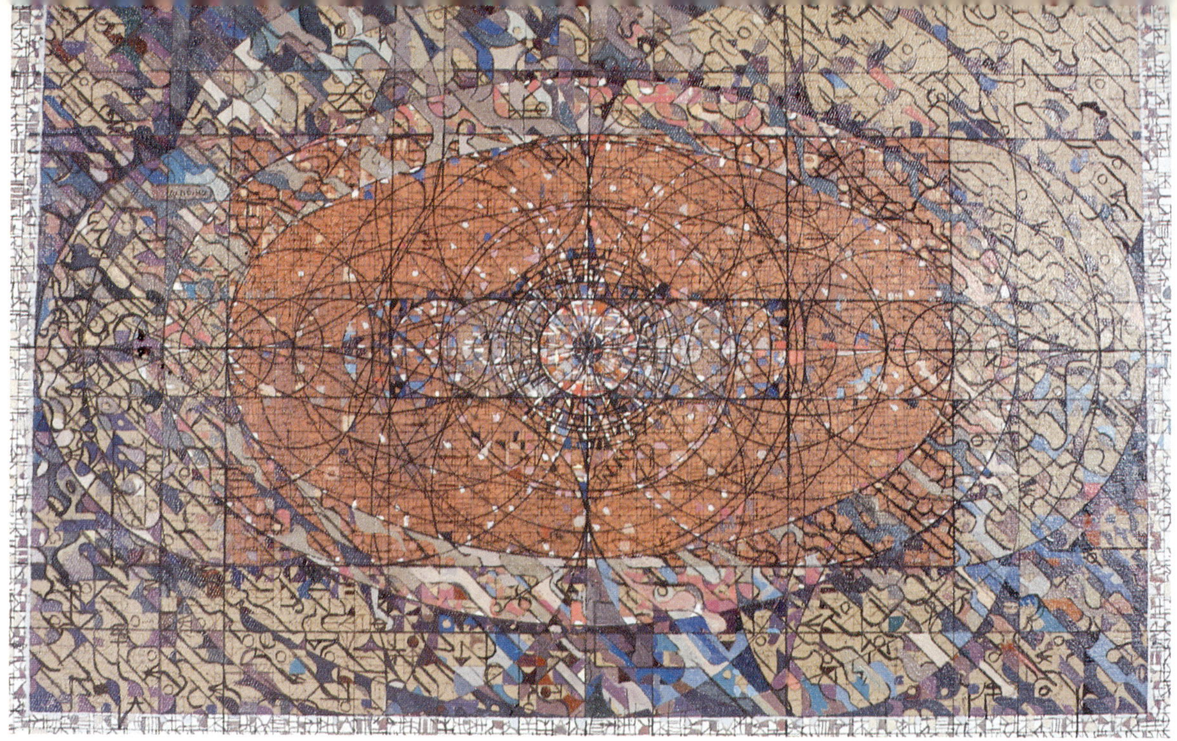

Ioan Chisu
Great Passage
20" x 24" (50.8 cm x 61 cm)
Dutch canvas

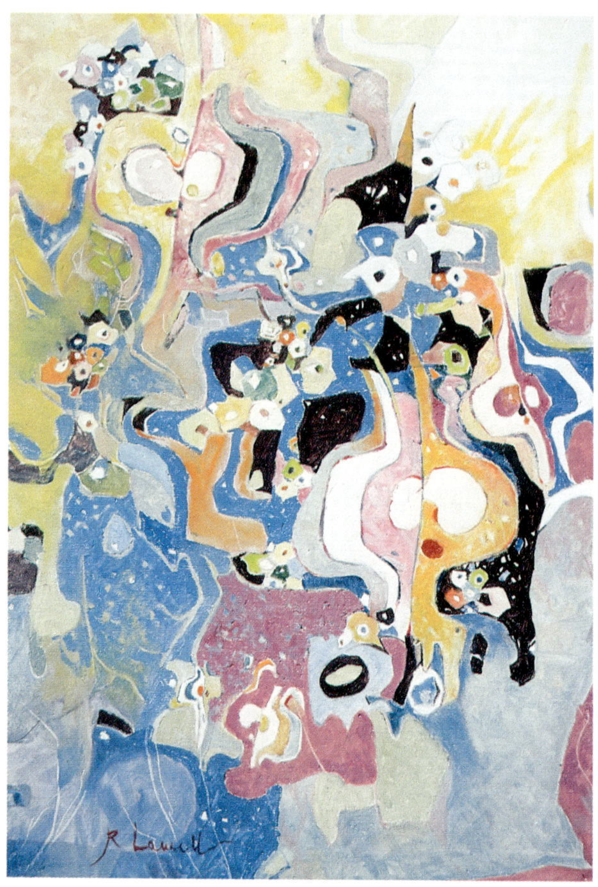

Robert Lamell
The Scent of Jasmine
30" x 24" (76.2 cm x 61 cm)
Canvas

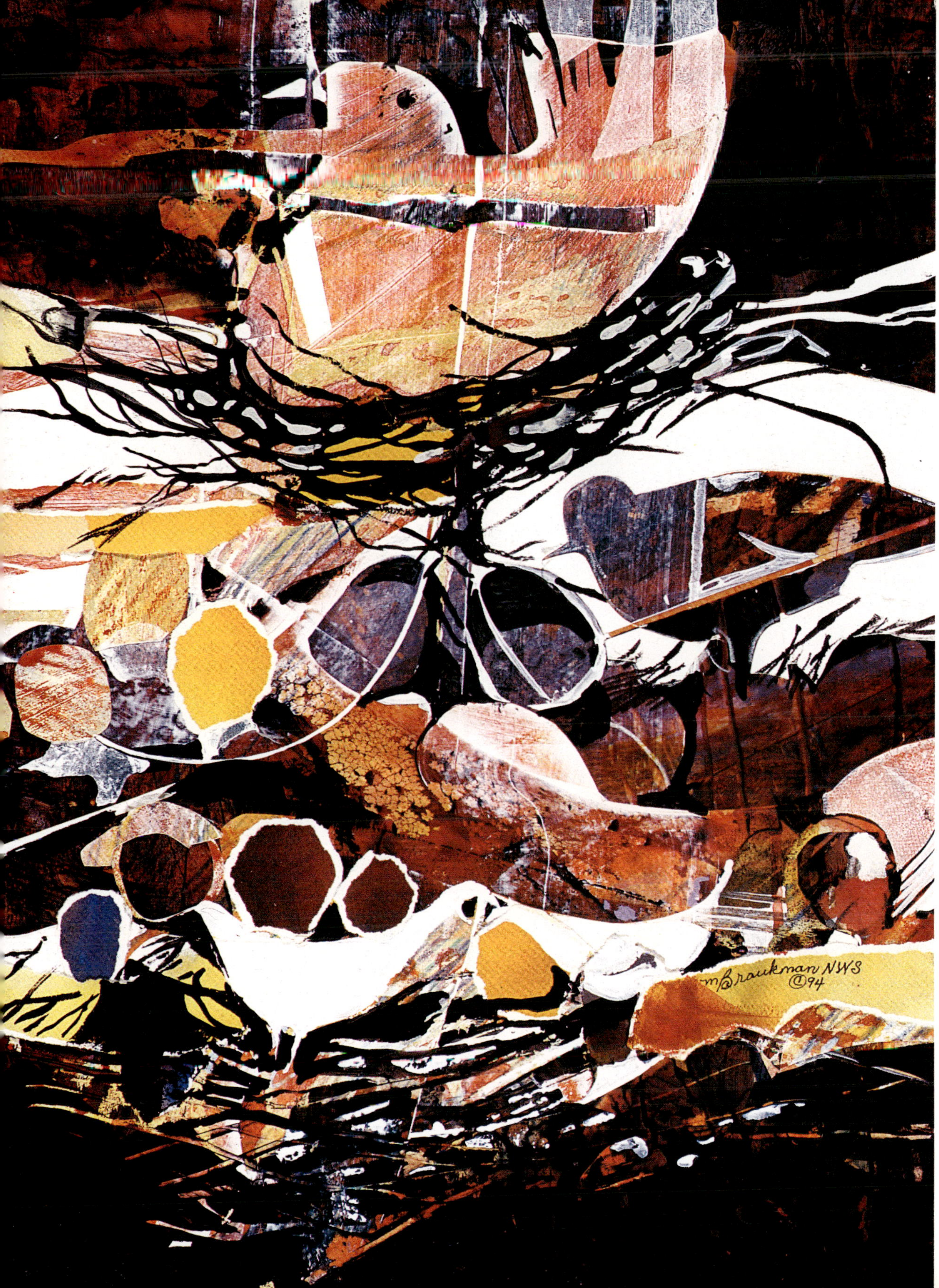

Mary Alice Braukman
Whose Watching My Nest?
19" x 12" (48 cm x 30 cm)
Acrylic with crayon
Strathmore #500 plate surface illustration board

Peggy Brown, A.W.S., N.W.S.
Duet
26" x 40" (66 cm x 101.6 cm)
Rives lightweight
Media: Transparent watercolor, graphite, collage

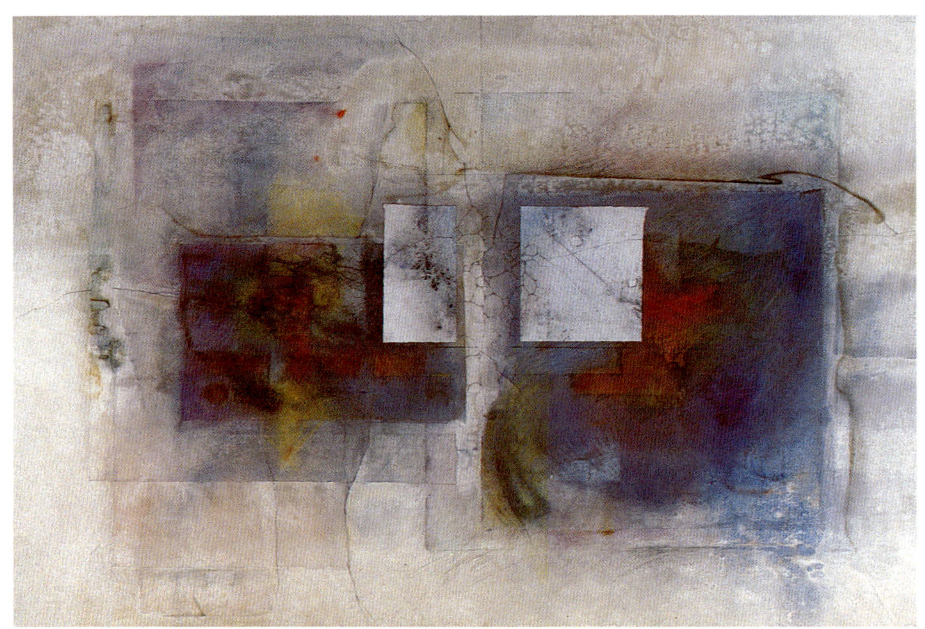

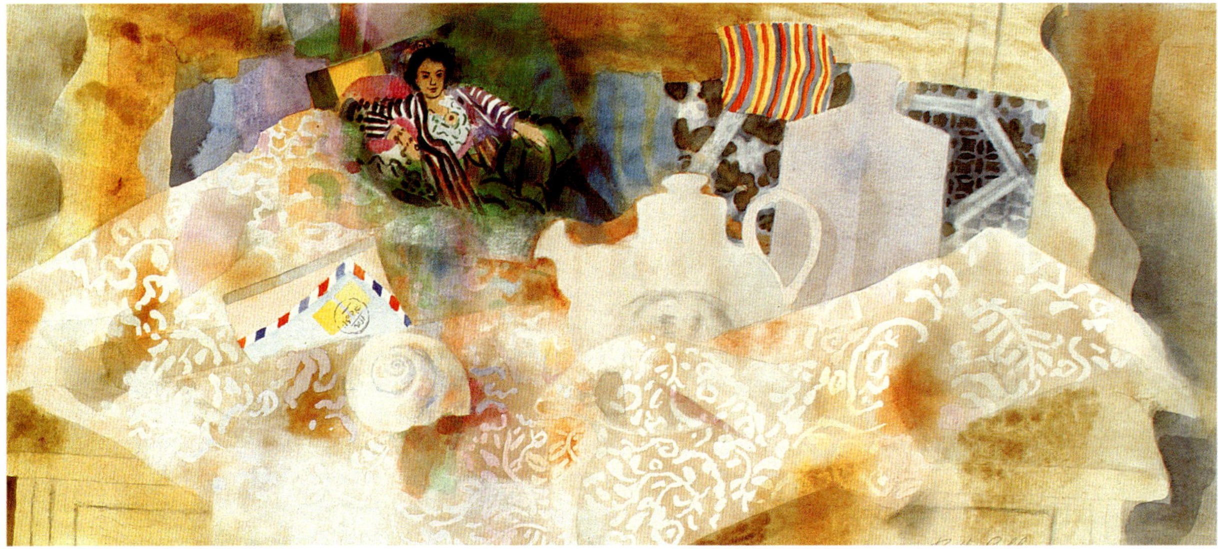

Ruth Cobb
Homage to Matisse
18.5" x 39" (47 cm x 99 cm)
Whatman 133 lb. hot press

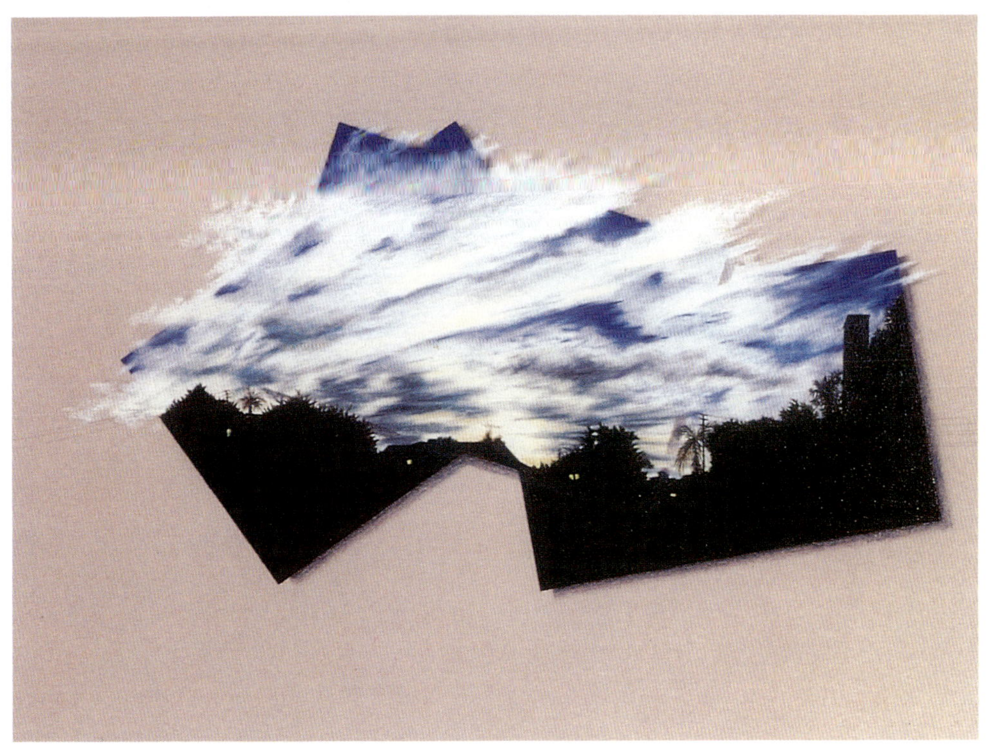

Jane Shibata
Three Snapshots
14" x 18" (36 cm x 46 cm)
Strathmore museum board

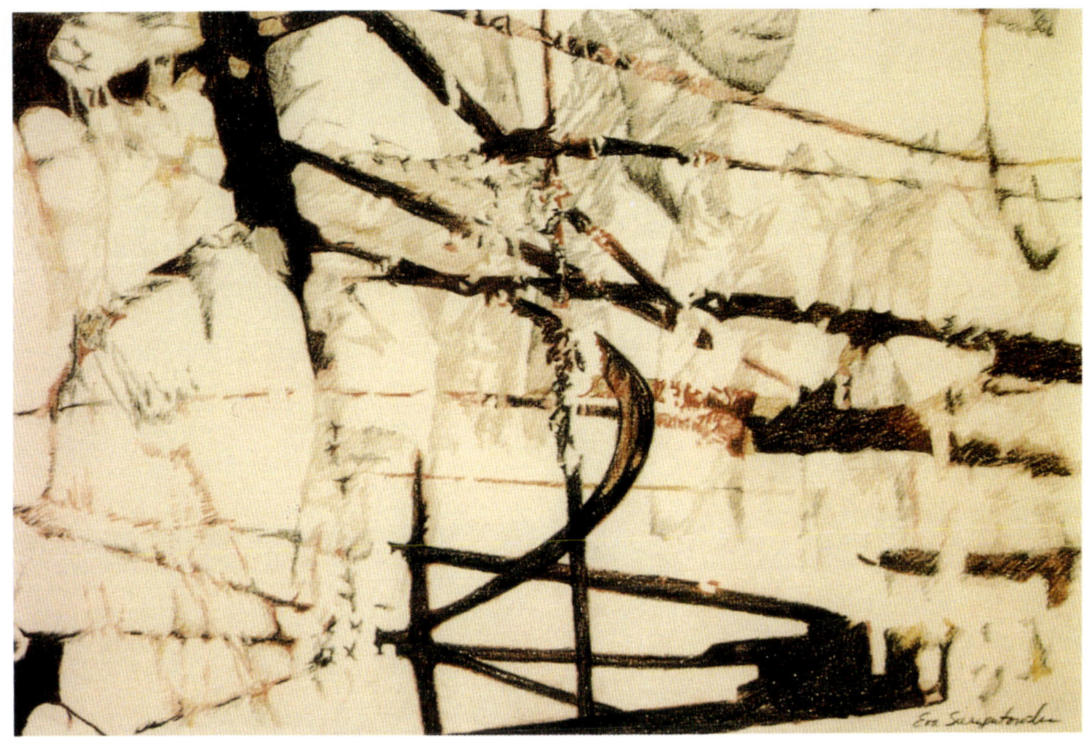

Eva Sierzputowski
Turning Line
15" x 20" (38 cm x 51 cm)
100% rag 2-ply paper

Lloyd Bakan
Celebration
40" x 30" (102 cm x 76 cm)
Arches 140 lb. paper

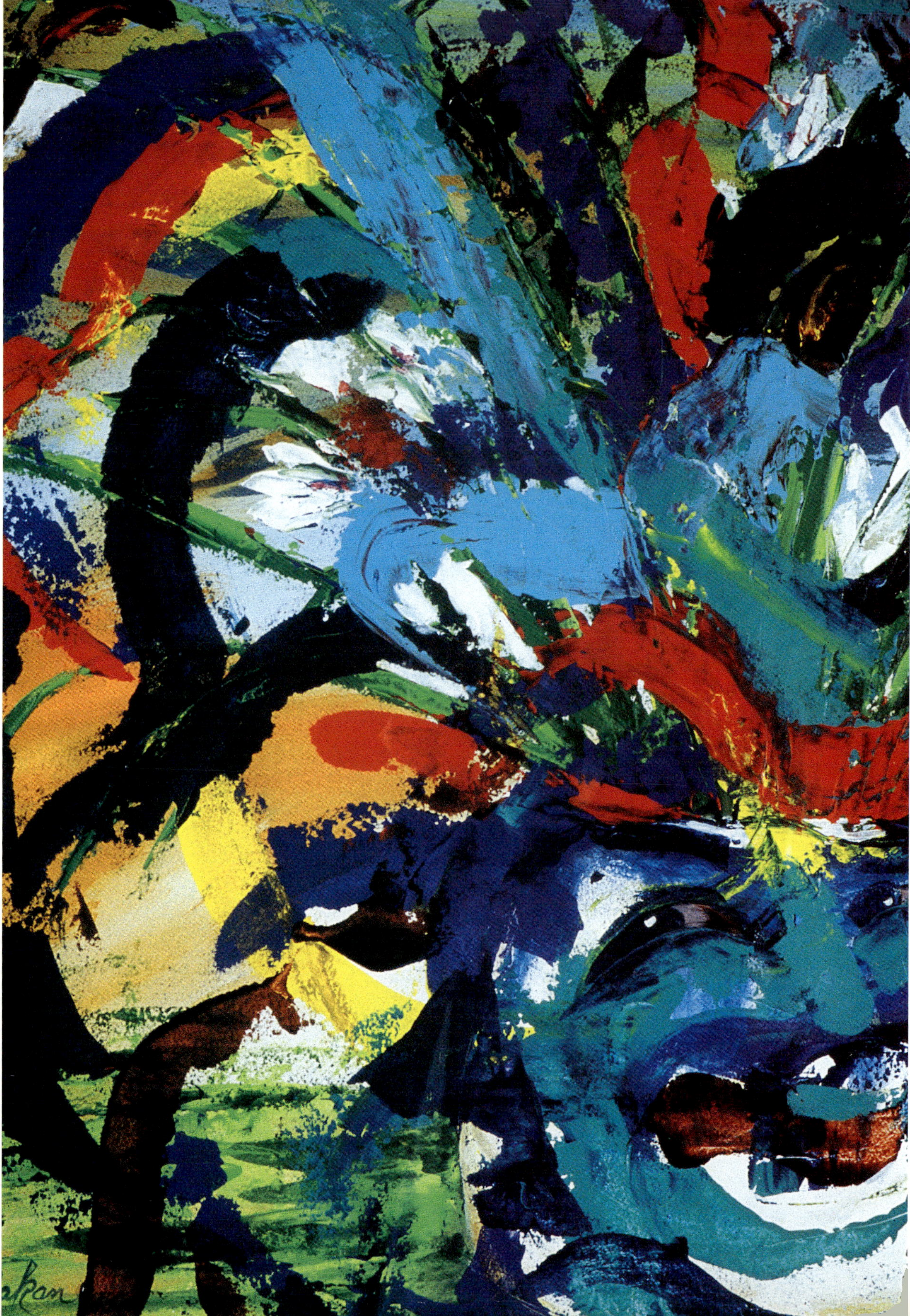

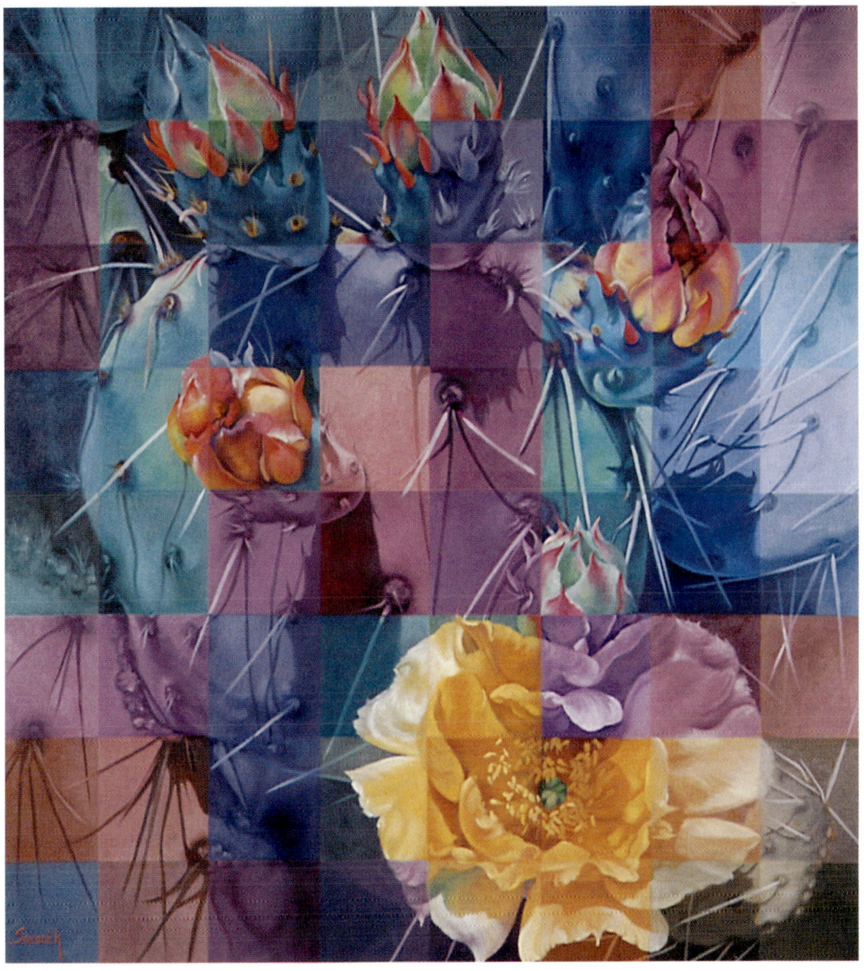

Brenda Semanick
Un Flor Amarillo
40" x 36" (101.6 cm x 91.4 cm)
Canvas

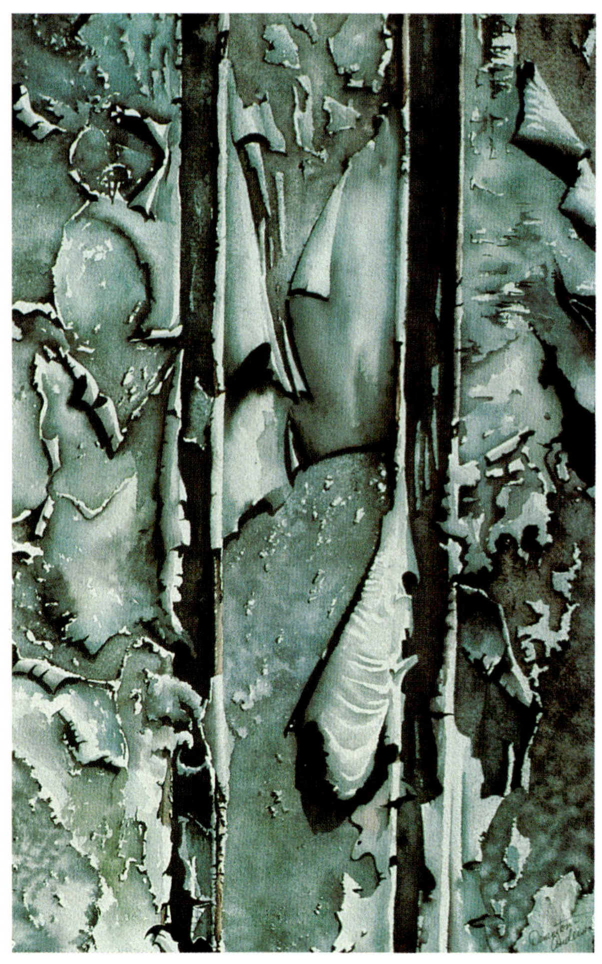

Gayle Denington-Anderson
Stars and Stripes (Almost) Forever
22" x 15" (55.9 cm x 38.1 cm)
Arches 140 lb. rough

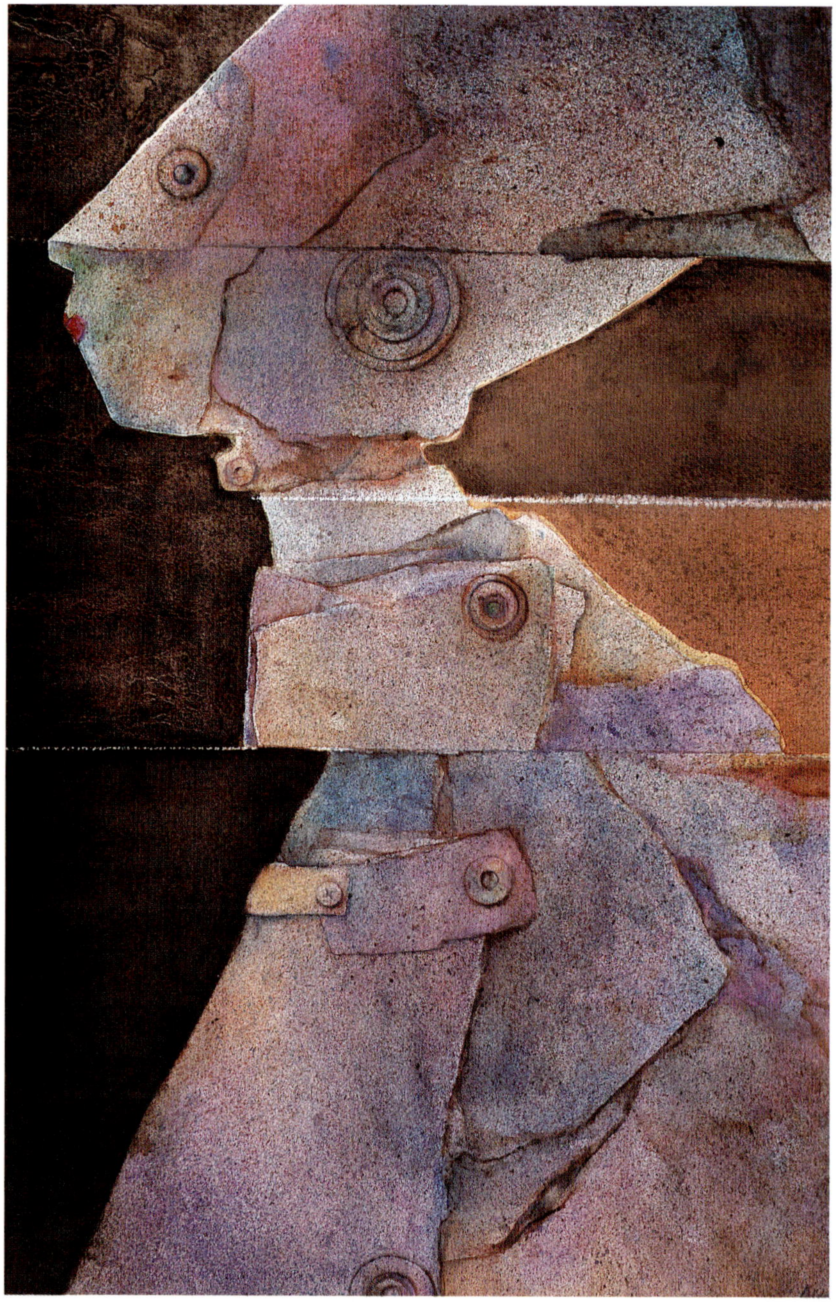

Aida Schneider
Nefertiti - Deconstructed
30" x 22" (76.2 cm x 55.9 cm)
Arches 300 lb. cold press

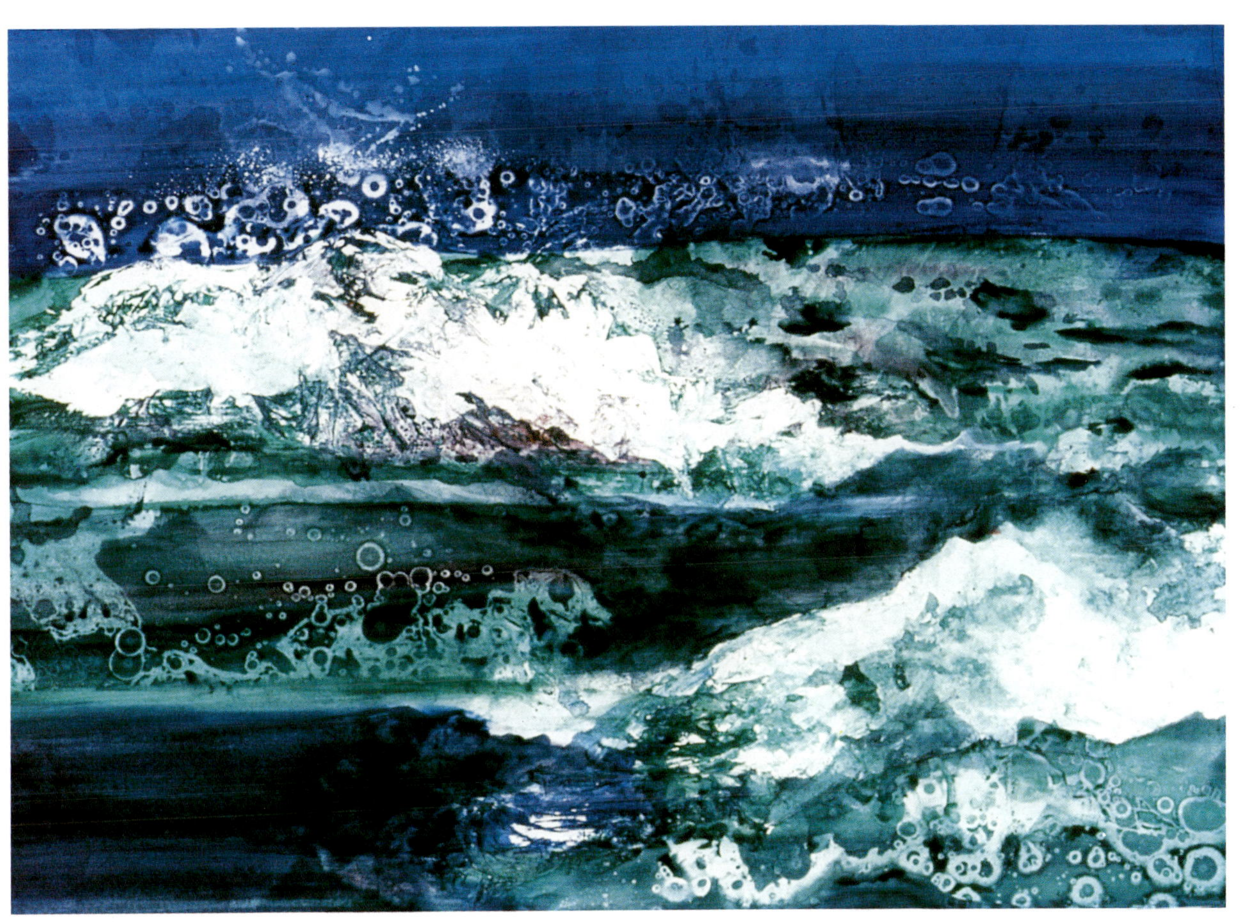

Betsy Gay
The Sea
23" x 29" (58 cm x 74 cm)
Acrylic with alcohol
Strathmore 500

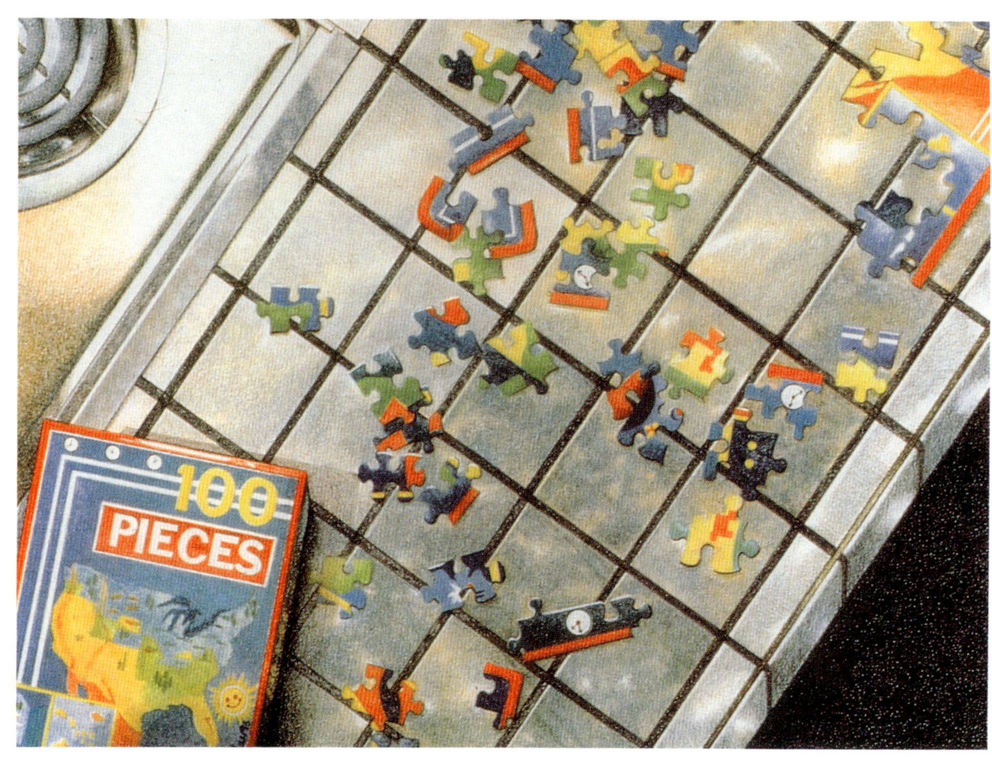

Blair Jackson
One Hundred Pieces
28" x 32" (71 cm x 81 cm)
Crescent illustration board

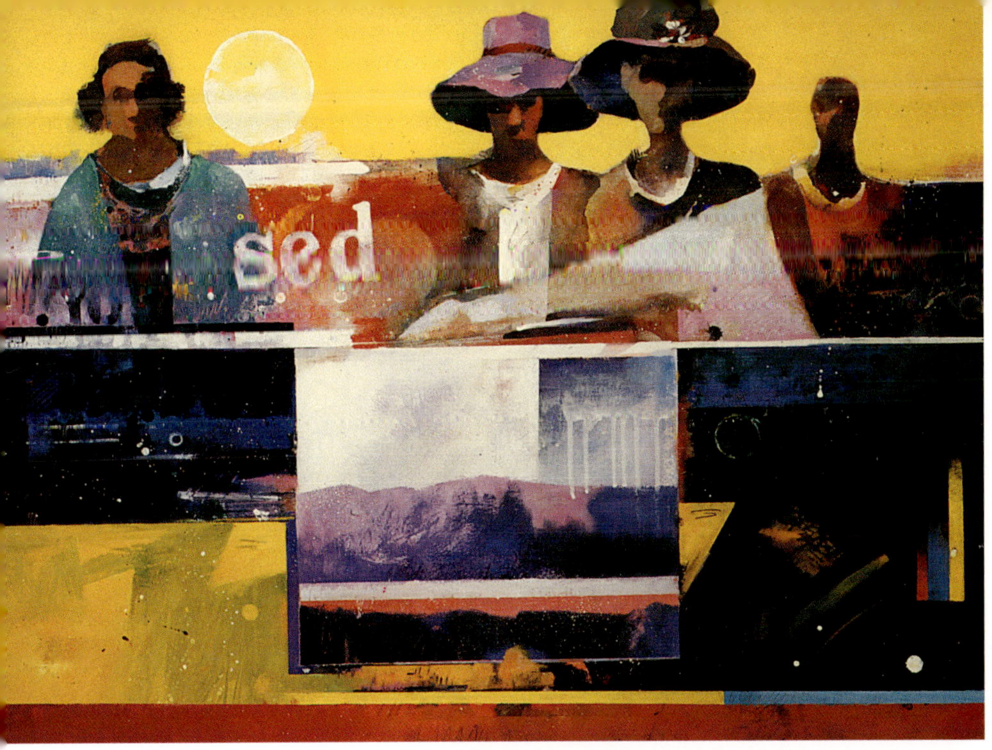

Jorge Bowenforbes
Yesterday's Women
30" x 40" (76 cm x 102 cm)
Illustration board

S. Webb Tregay
I Grew Up Surrounded by Republicans
39" x 49" (99 cm x 125 cm)
Unprimed canvas

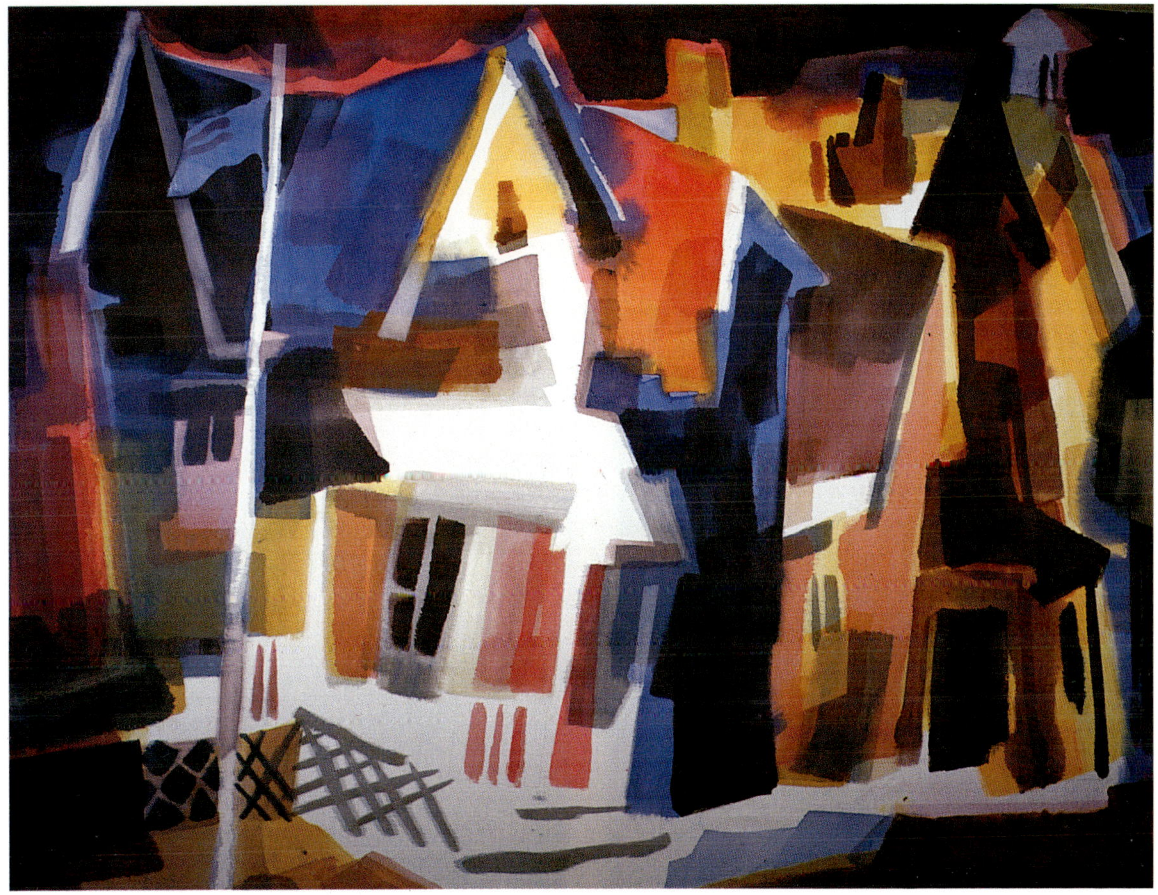

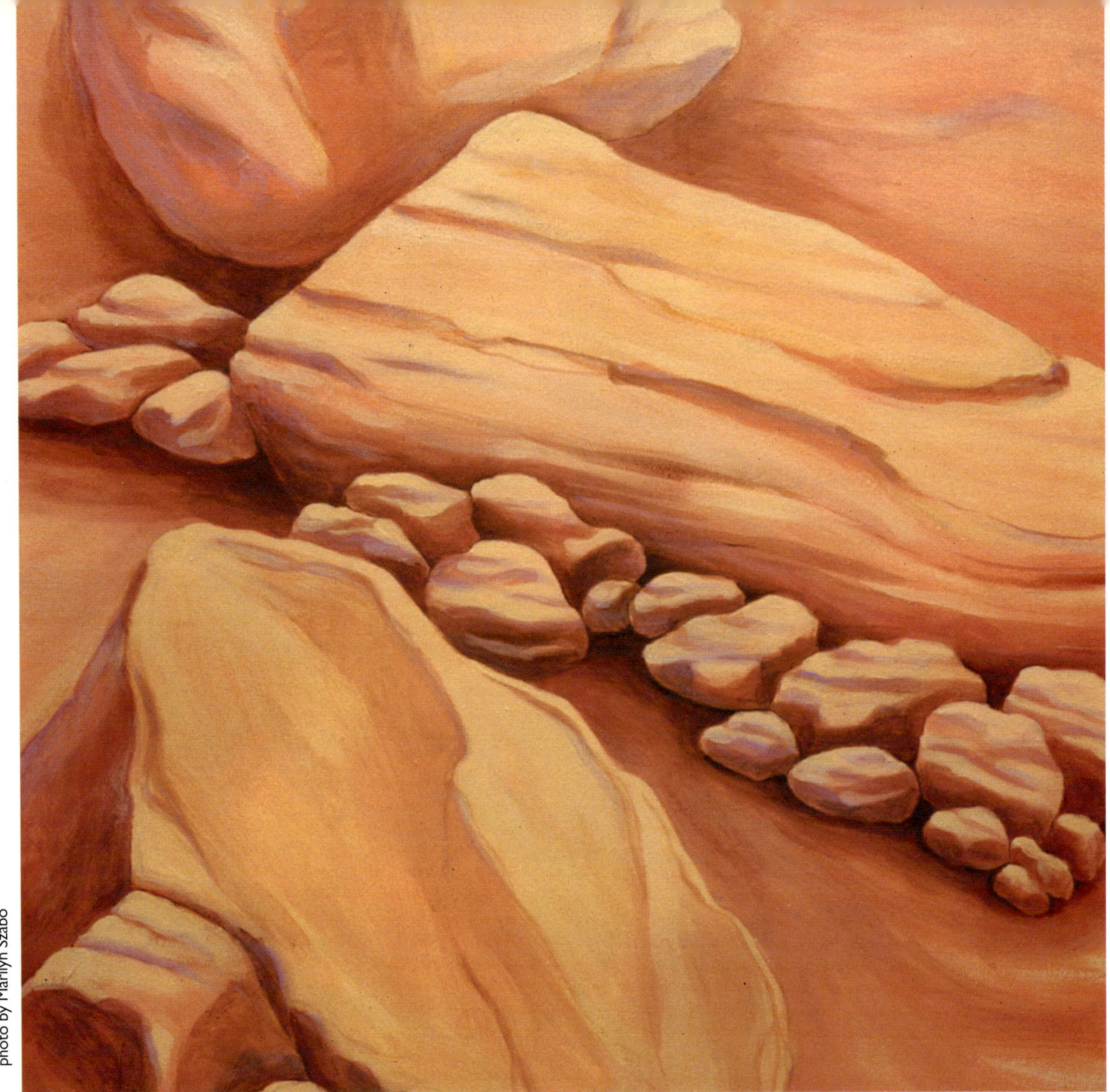

photo by Marilyn Szabo

N. L. Matus
Flux
36" x 36" (91 cm x 91 cm)
Canvas

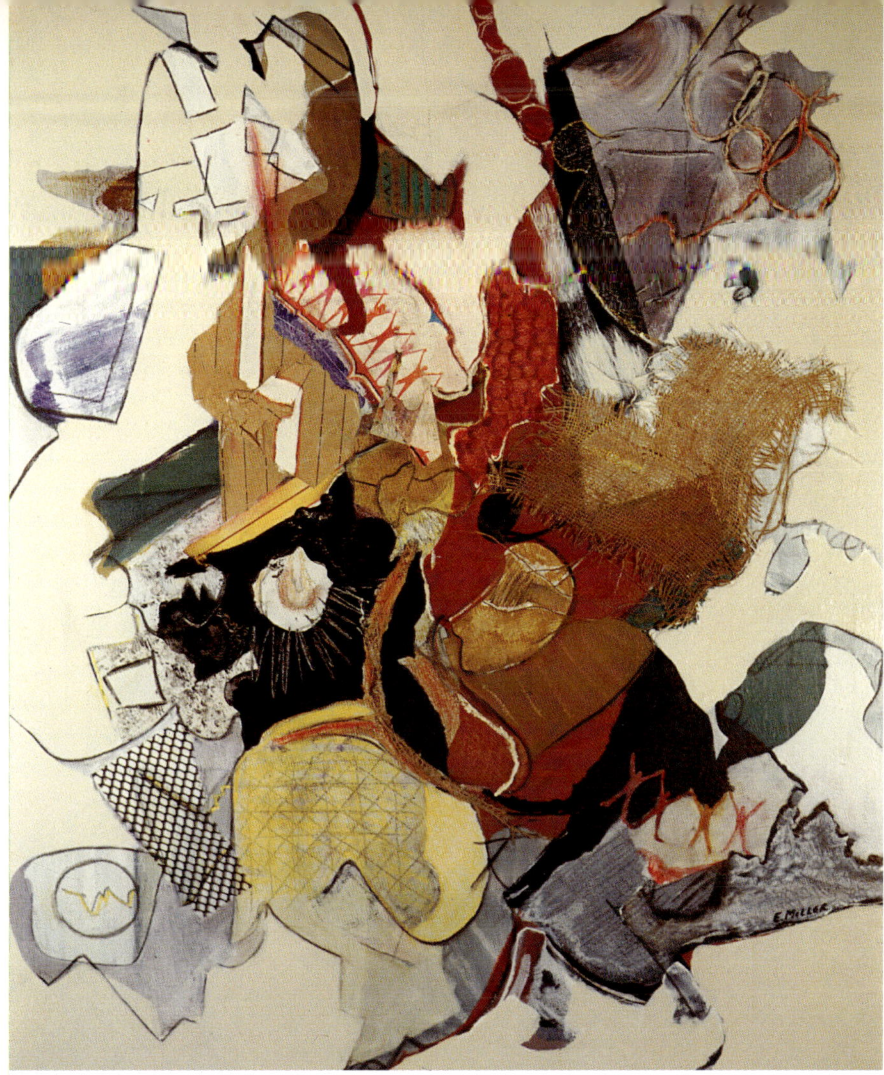

Elaine S. Miller
Unity
41" x 33" (104 cm x 84 cm)
Acrylic with wire mesh, paper, and burlap
Gesso-coated linen canvas

Elaine S. Miller
Chivalry
50" x 40" (127 cm x 102 cm)
Acrylic with plastic mesh
Gesso-coated linen canvas

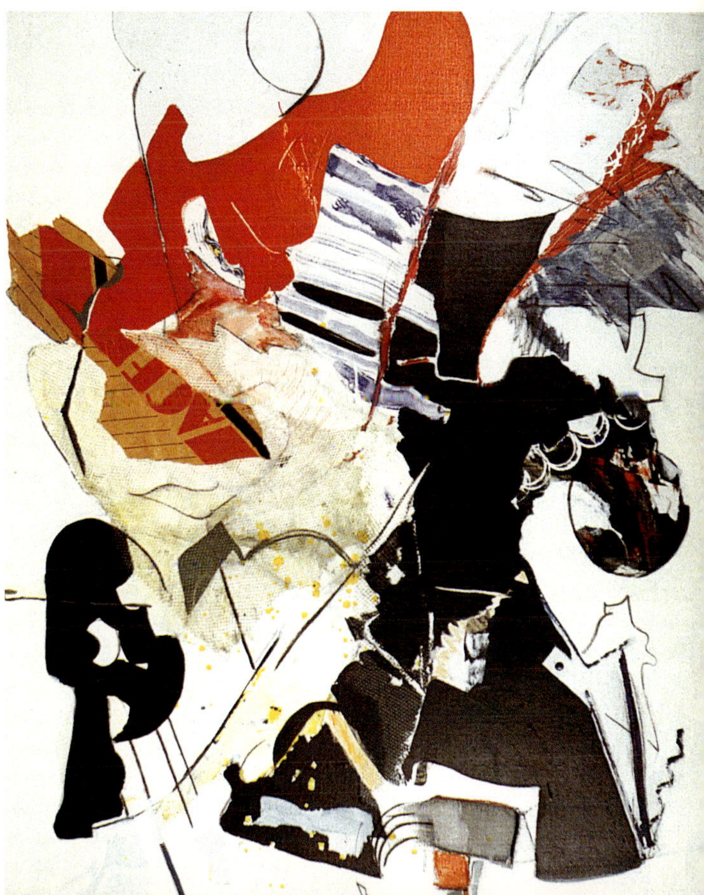

Mike Russell
Undercover
20" x 20" (51 cm x 51 cm)
Crescent illustration board

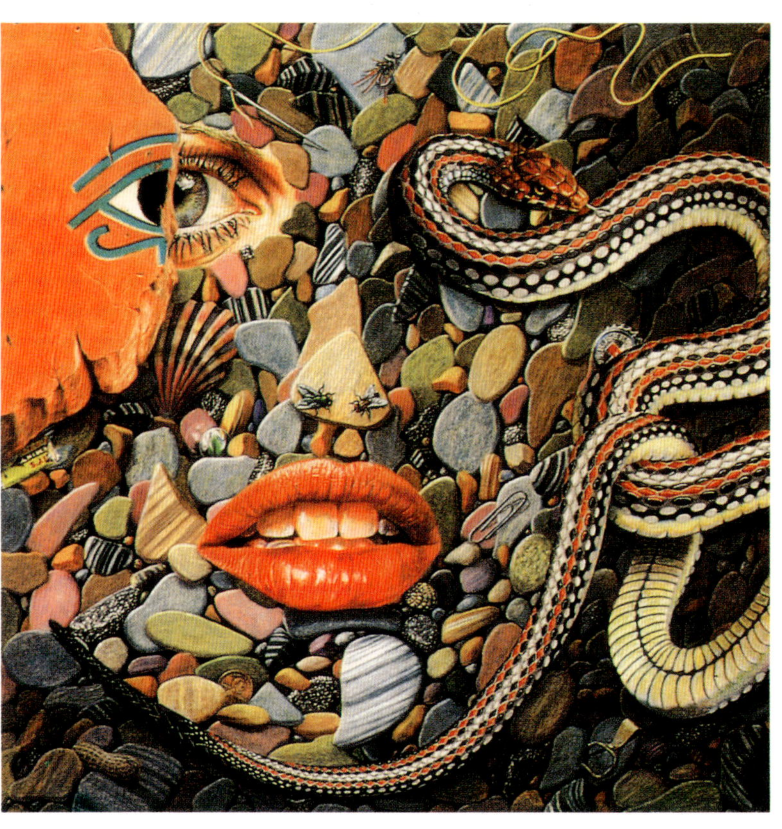

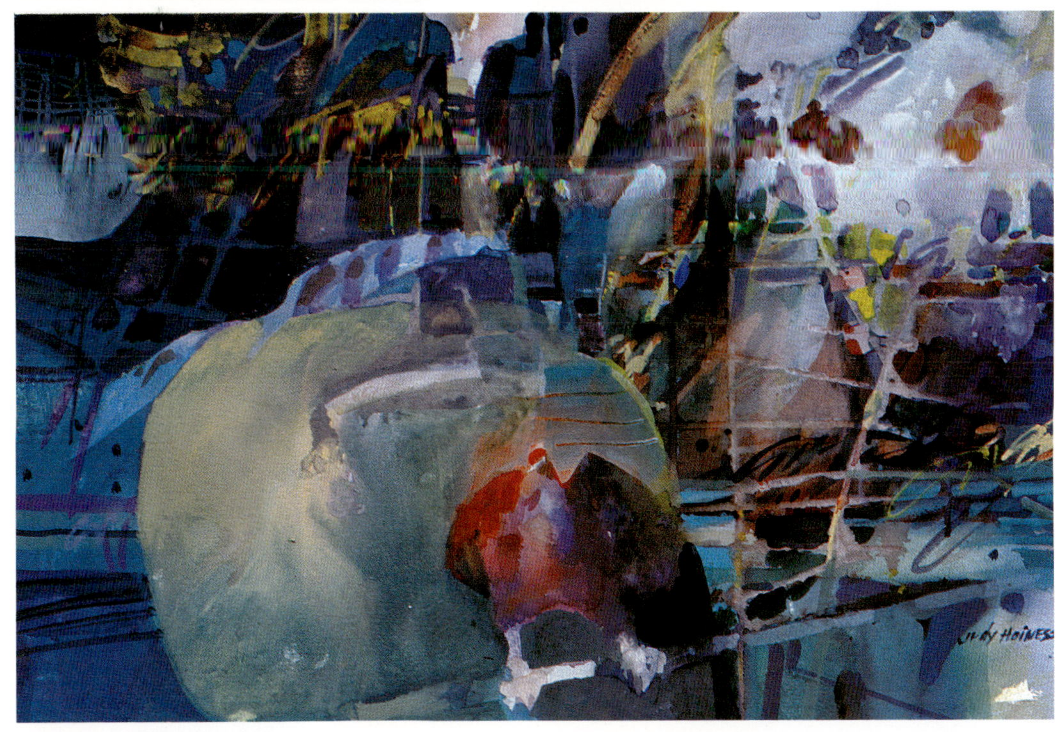

Judy A. Hoiness
Bird and Bouquet
22" x 30" (55.9 cm x 76.2 cm)
300 lb. cold press

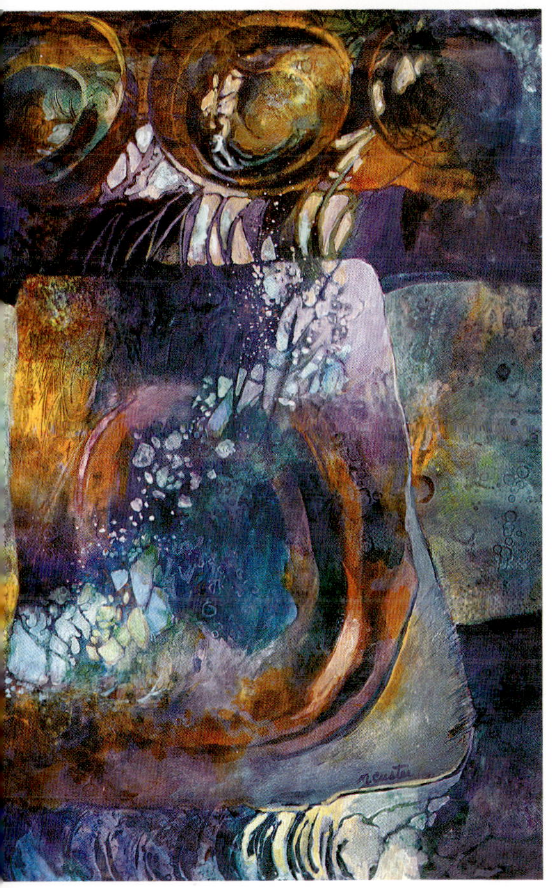

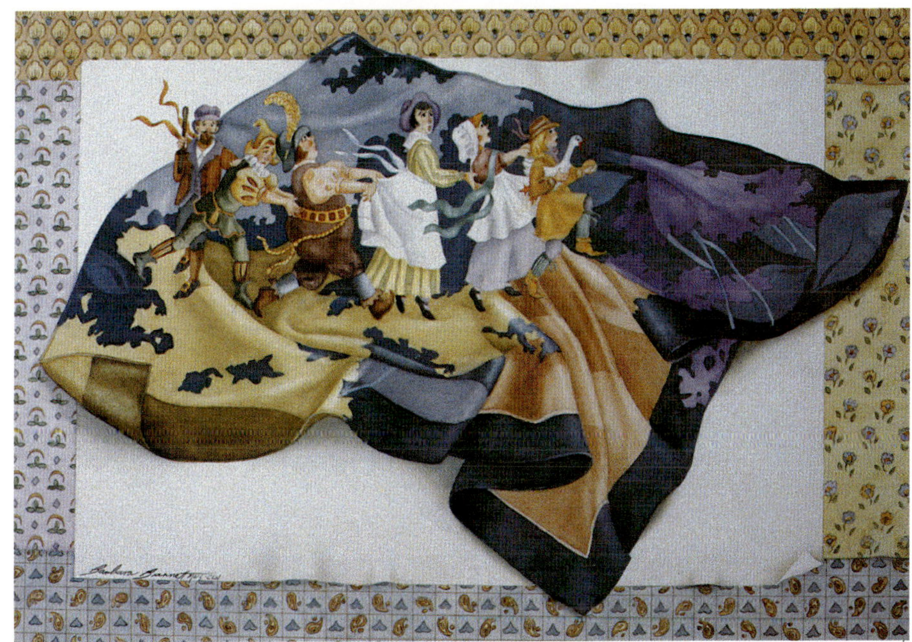

Maxine Custer
Jewels of Discovery
22" x 30" (55.9 cm x 76.2 cm)
Arches 140 lb.
Media: Watercolor, acrylic

Barbara Burnett
Pursuit of the Gold
15" x 21" (38.1 cm x 53.3 cm)
Arches 140 lb. hot press

Atanas Karpeles
Message From Beyond
30" x 23" (76 cm x 59 cm)
Arches 400 lb. paper

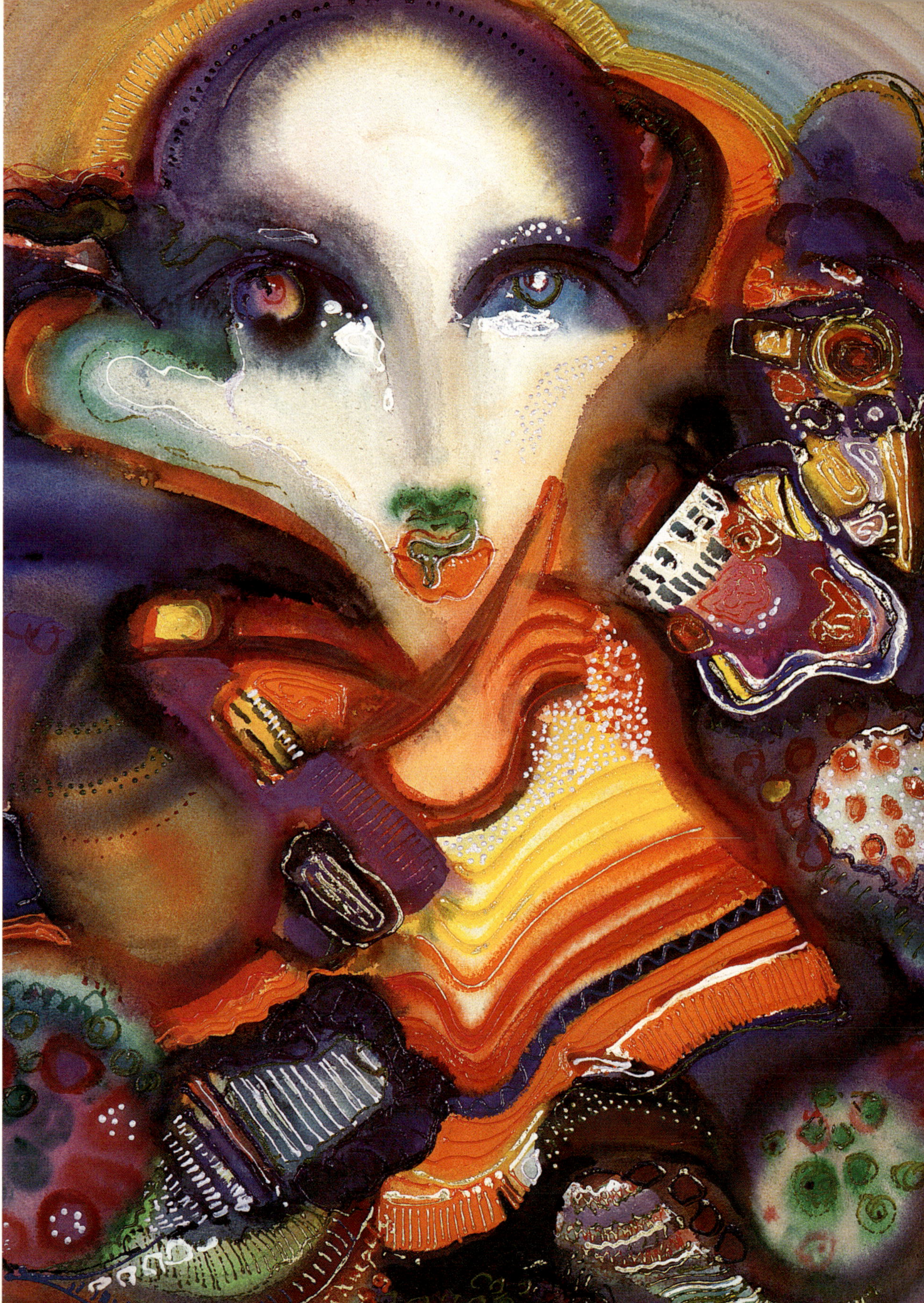

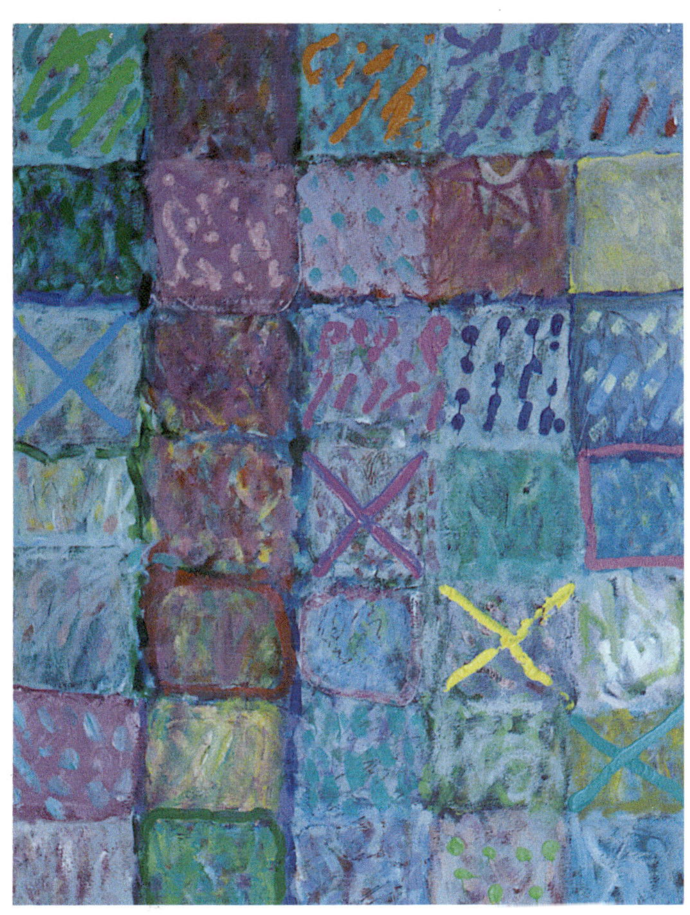

Joan Painter Jones
Hope Quilt #1
30" x 23" (81 cm x 58 cm)
Arches 300 lb. paper

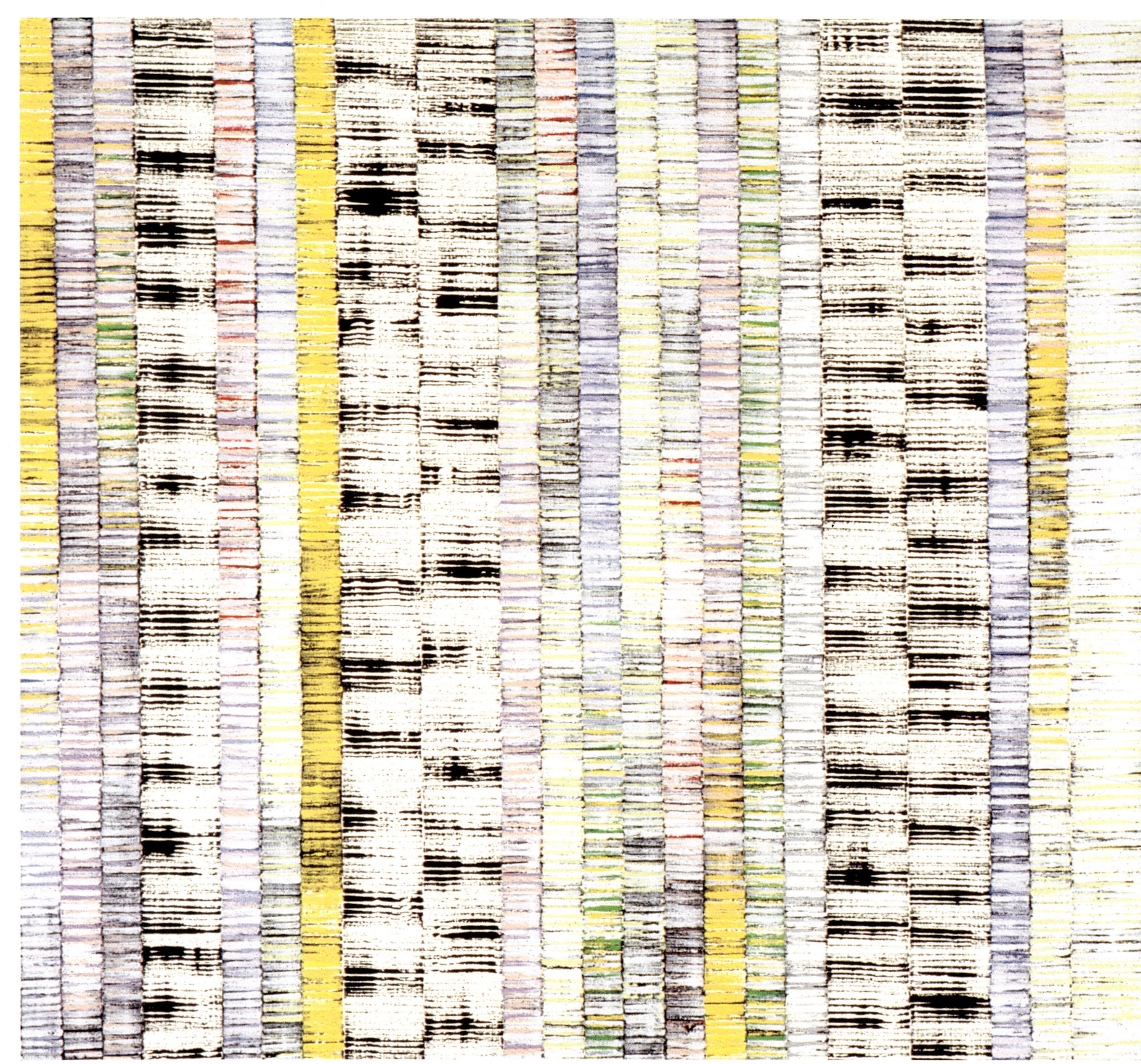

Kathy Stark
A Woman Sitting Comfortably with her Ambivalence
41" x 31" (104 cm x 79 cm)
Canvas

Mary Ann Beckwith
Origin: Dream Caught
30" x 22" (76.2 cm x 55.9 cm)
Arches 140 lb. hot press

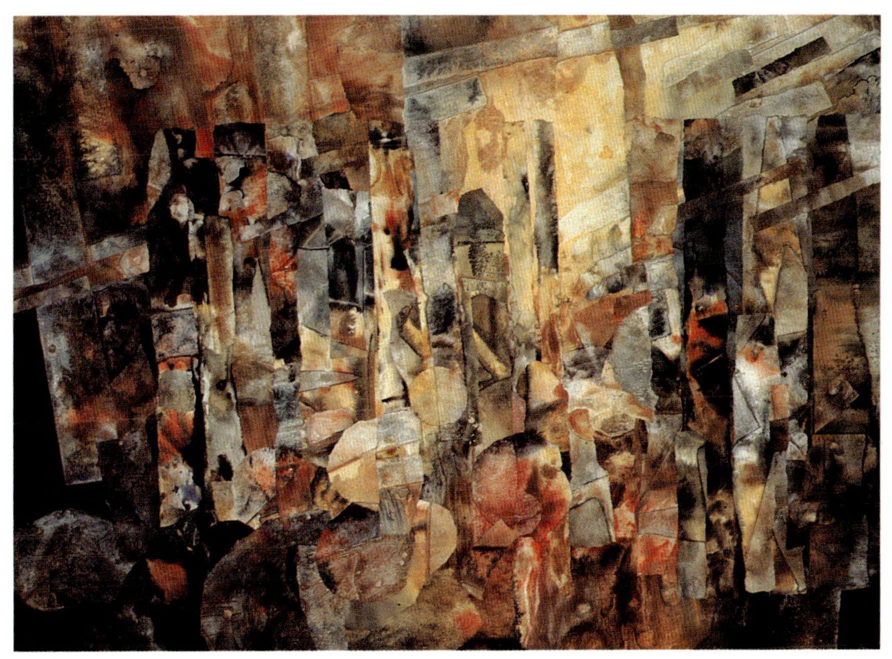

Allan Hill
Suspended Dimension
22.5" x 30" (57.1 cm x 76.2 cm)
Arches 140 lb.

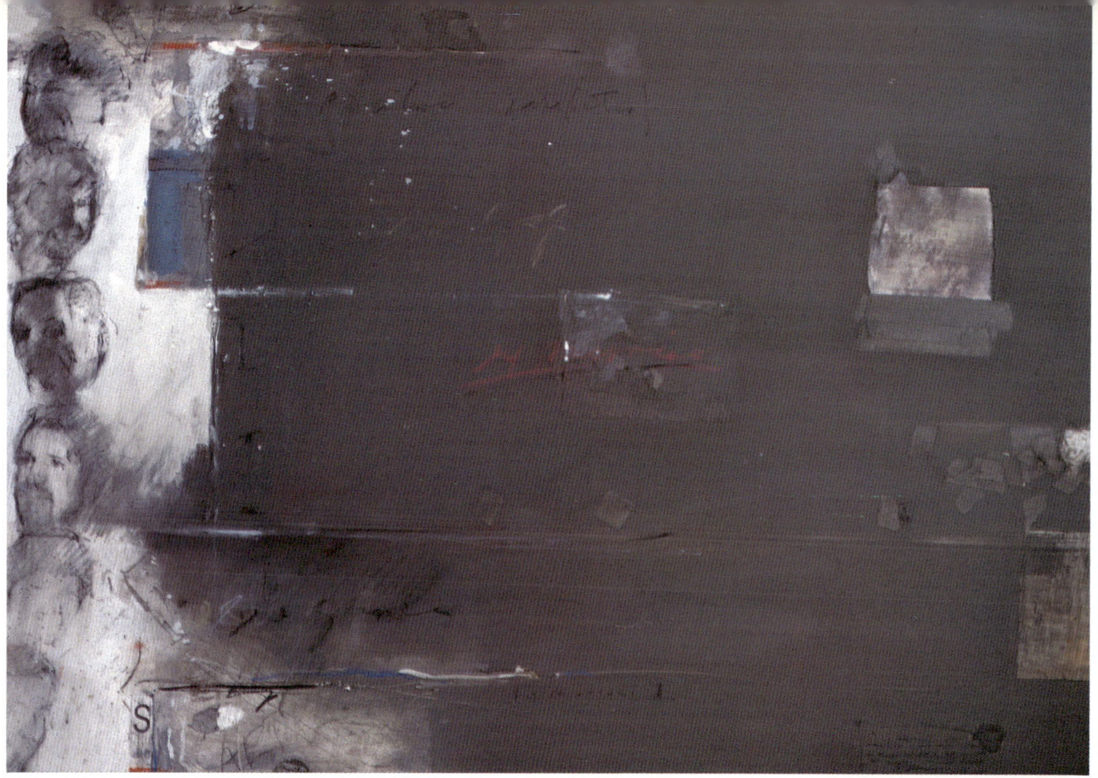

Alex Powers
Art Buddies
30" x 40" (76.2 cm x 101.6 cm)
Strathmore
Media: Gouache, charcoal collage, pastel, watercolor

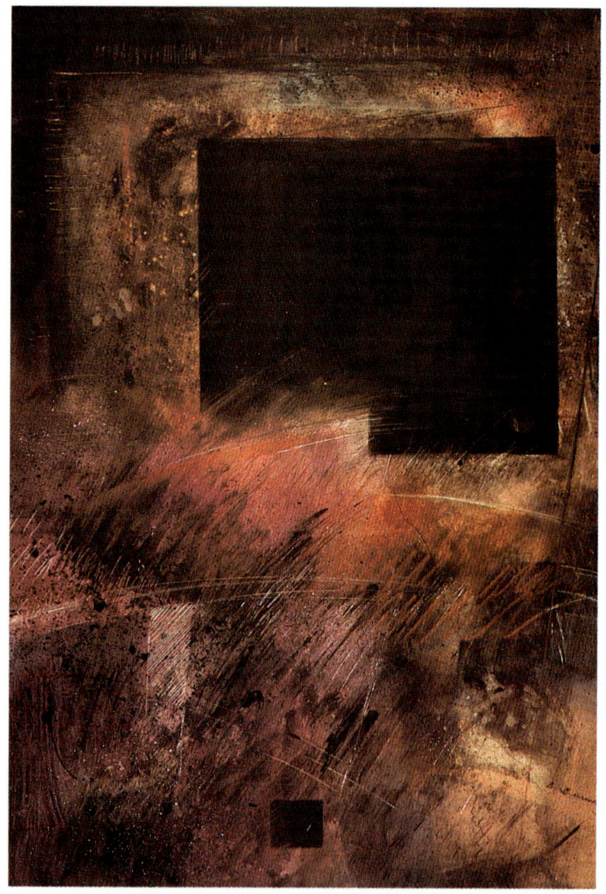

Barbara Burwen
Kiyo
30" x 22" (76.2 cm x 55.9 cm)
140 lb. hot press
Media: Watercolor, charcoal powder, acrylic, watercolor pencils

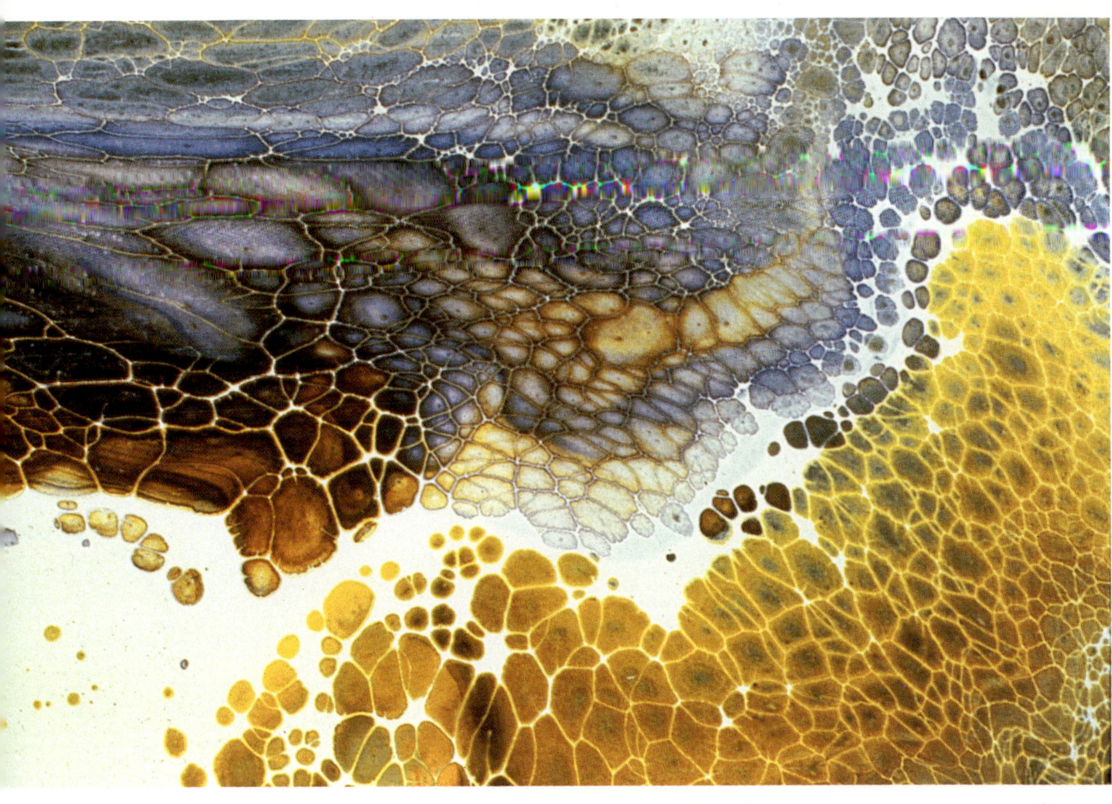

Naomi Marks Cohan
Another Place...Another Time
14.5" x 14.5" (37 cm x 37 cm)
Arches 140 lb. cold press

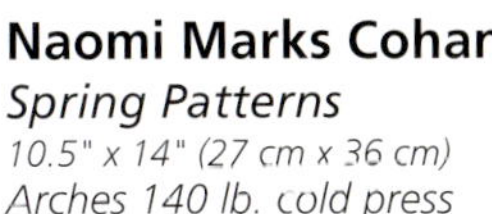

Naomi Marks Cohan
Spring Patterns
10.5" x 14" (27 cm x 36 cm)
Arches 140 lb. cold press

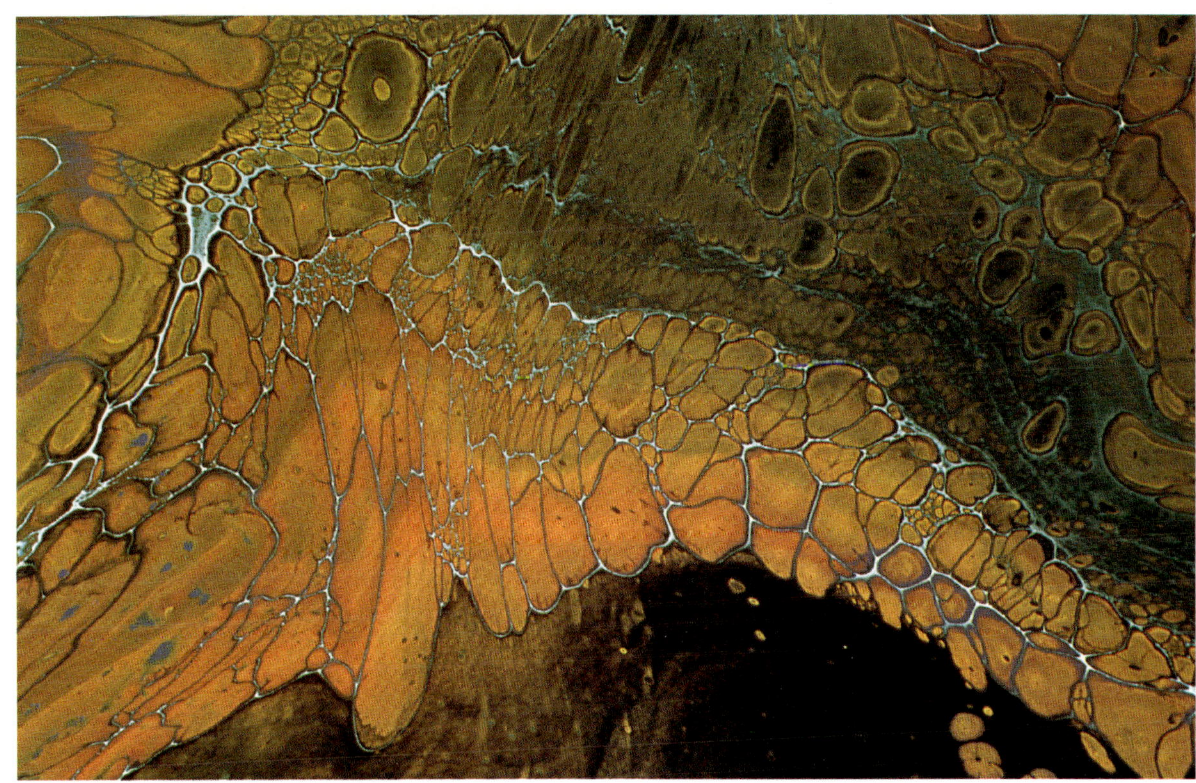

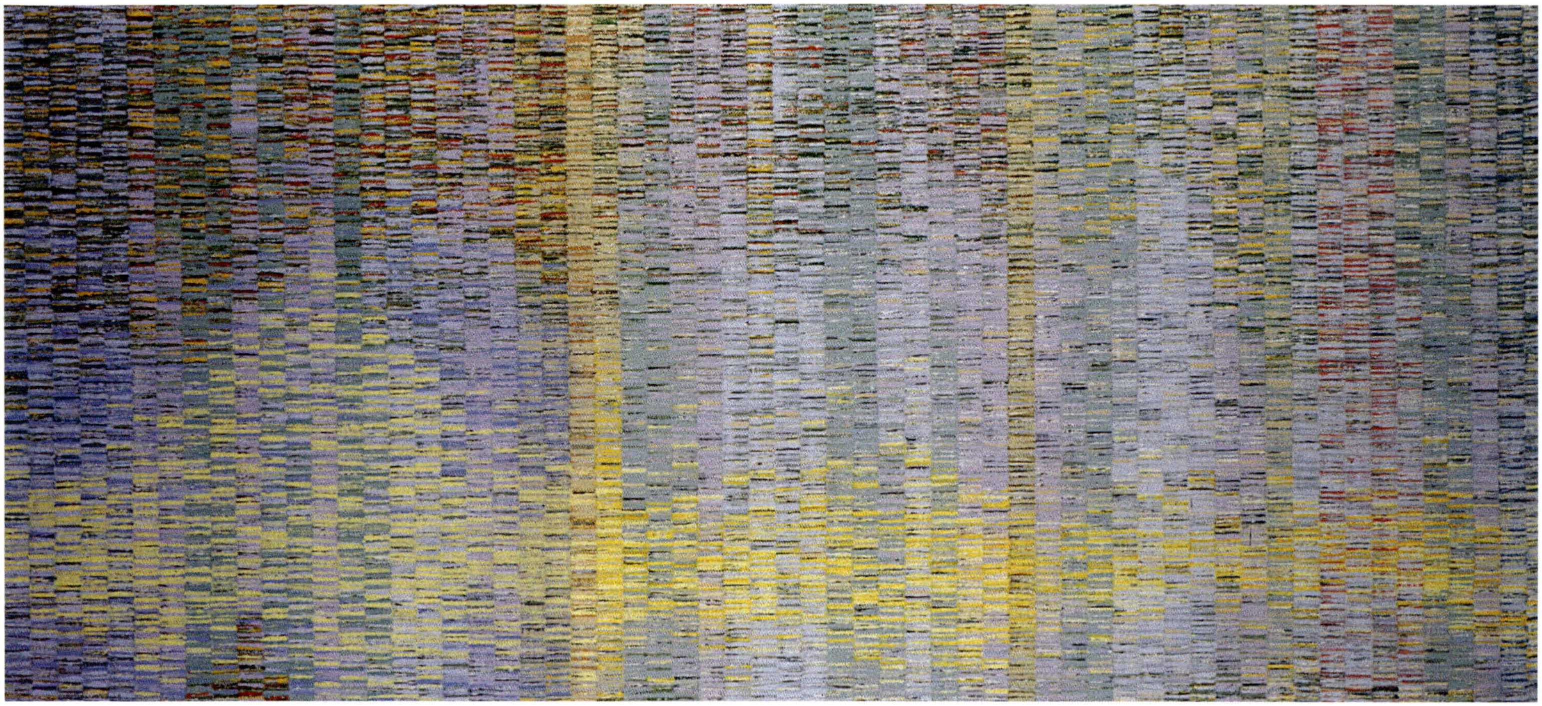

Kathy Stark
Reflections on a Pond
29" x 61" (74 cm x 155 cm)
Canvas

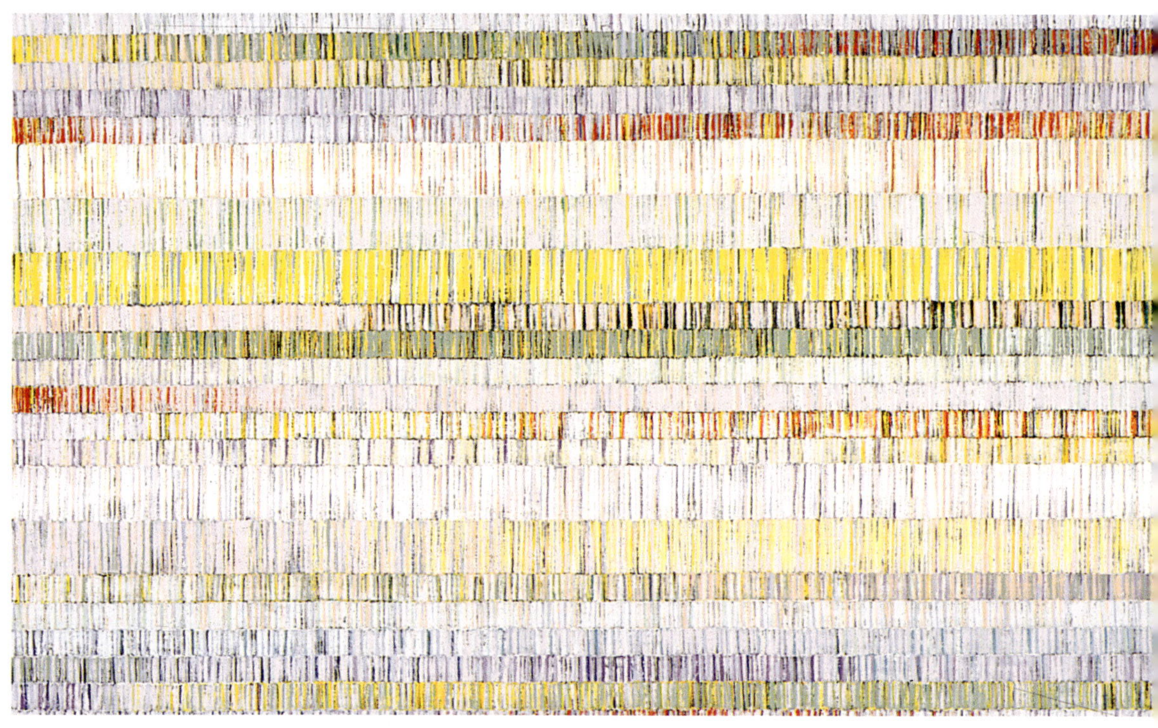

Kathy Stark
An Ever Changing View
27" x 45" (69 cm x 114 cm)
Canvas

Doug Pasek
Searching for Alice Wonderland
36" x 28" (91.4 cm x 71.1 cm)
Strathmore #112
Media: Acrylic, transparent and opaque watercolor

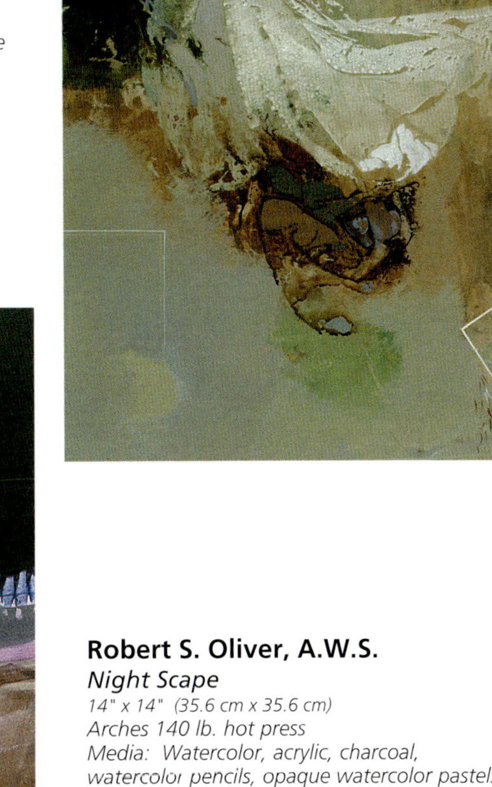

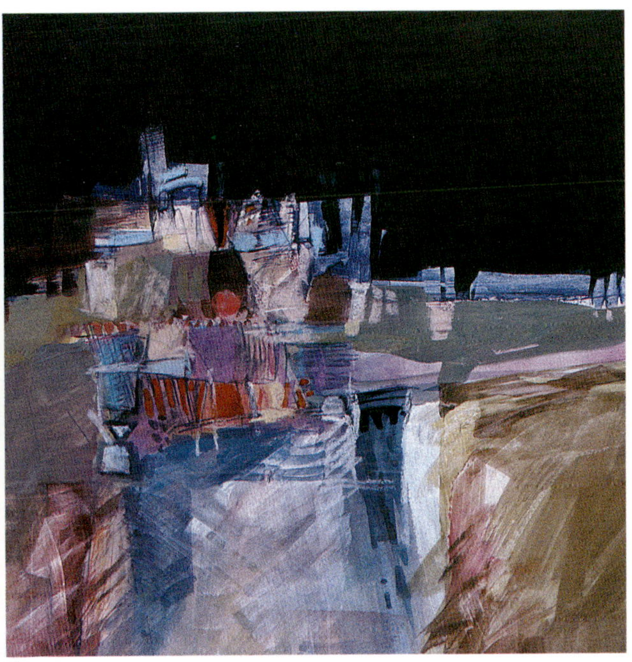

Robert S. Oliver, A.W.S.
Night Scape
14" x 14" (35.6 cm x 35.6 cm)
Arches 140 lb. hot press
Media: Watercolor, acrylic, charcoal, watercolor pencils, opaque watercolor pastels

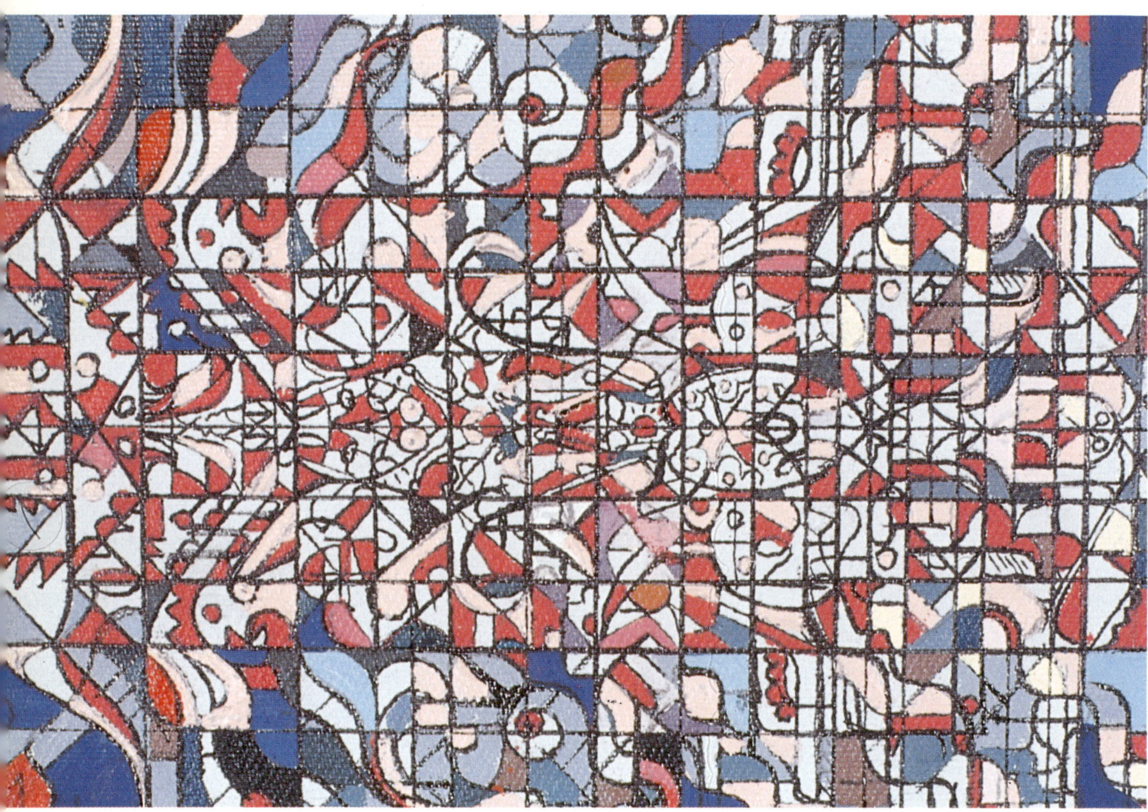

Ioan Chisu
Mad Forest
18" x 22" (430 cm x 46 cm)
Canvas

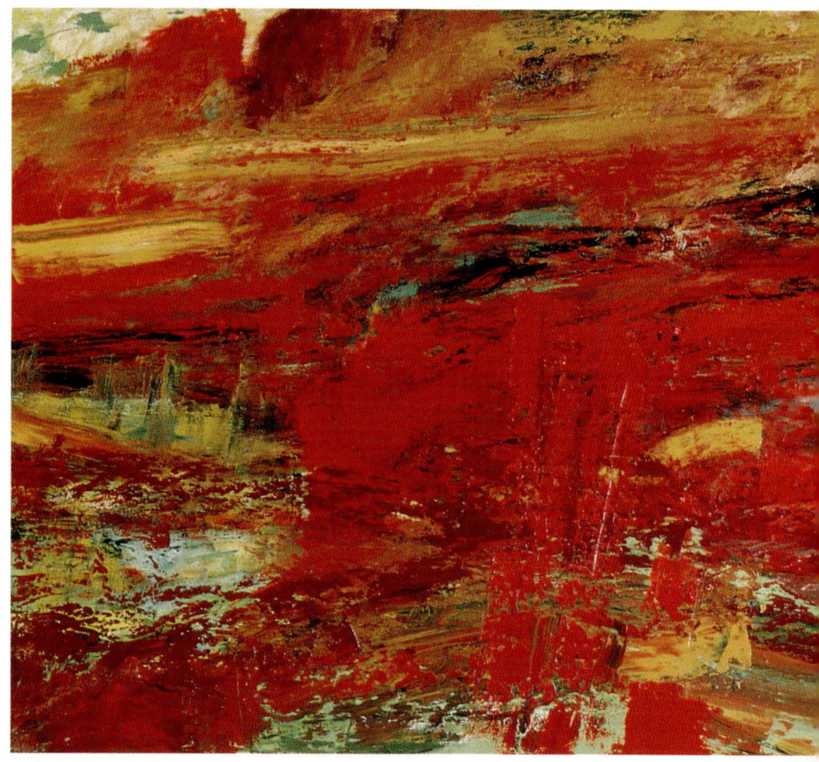

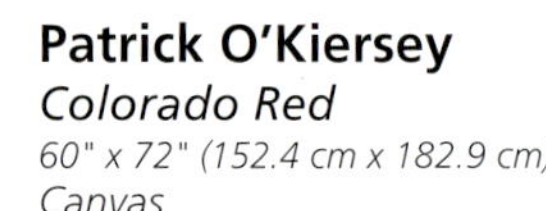

Patrick O'Kiersey
Colorado Red
60" x 72" (152.4 cm x 182.9 cm)
Canvas

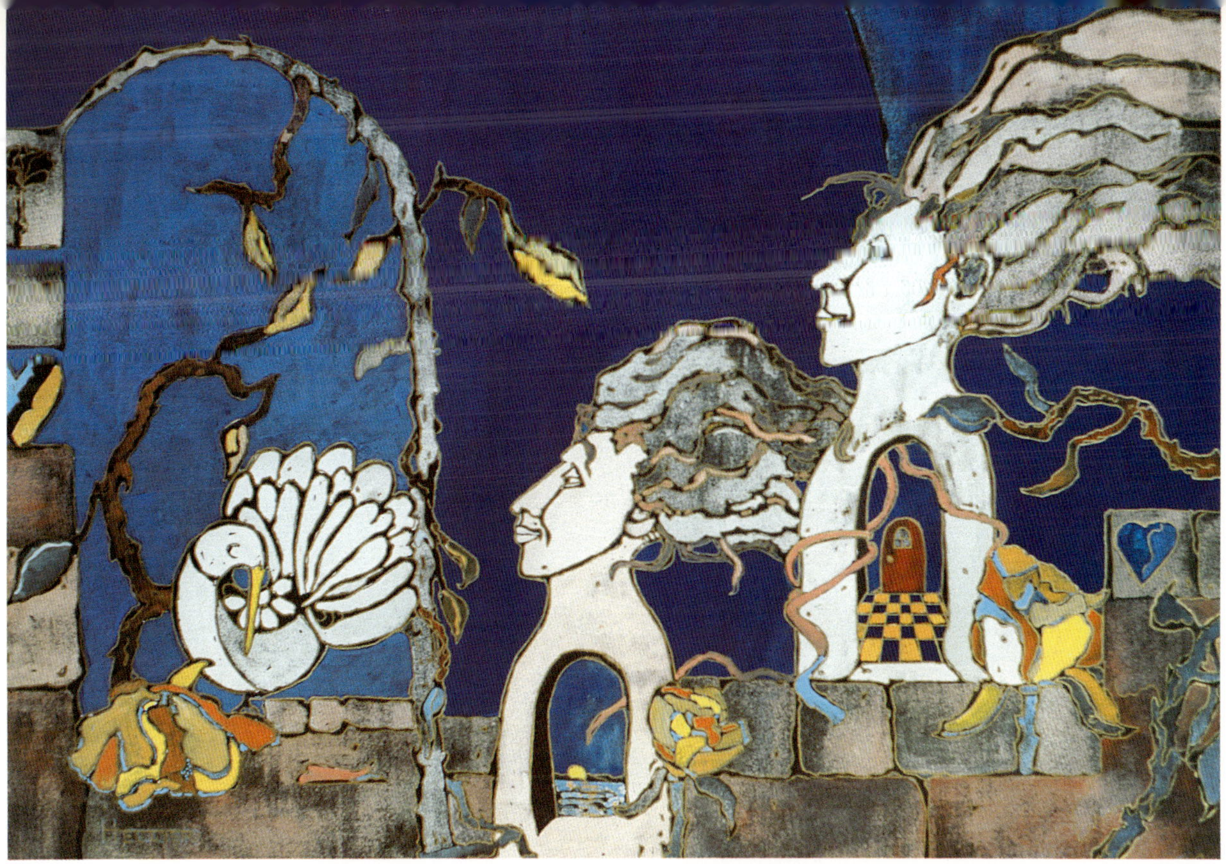

Phyllis Hellier, F.W.S., G.W.S., K.W.S.
Doorway To Beyond
22" x 30" (55.9 cm x 76.2 cm)
Arches 300 lb. cold press
Media: Gouache, ink resist, acrylic

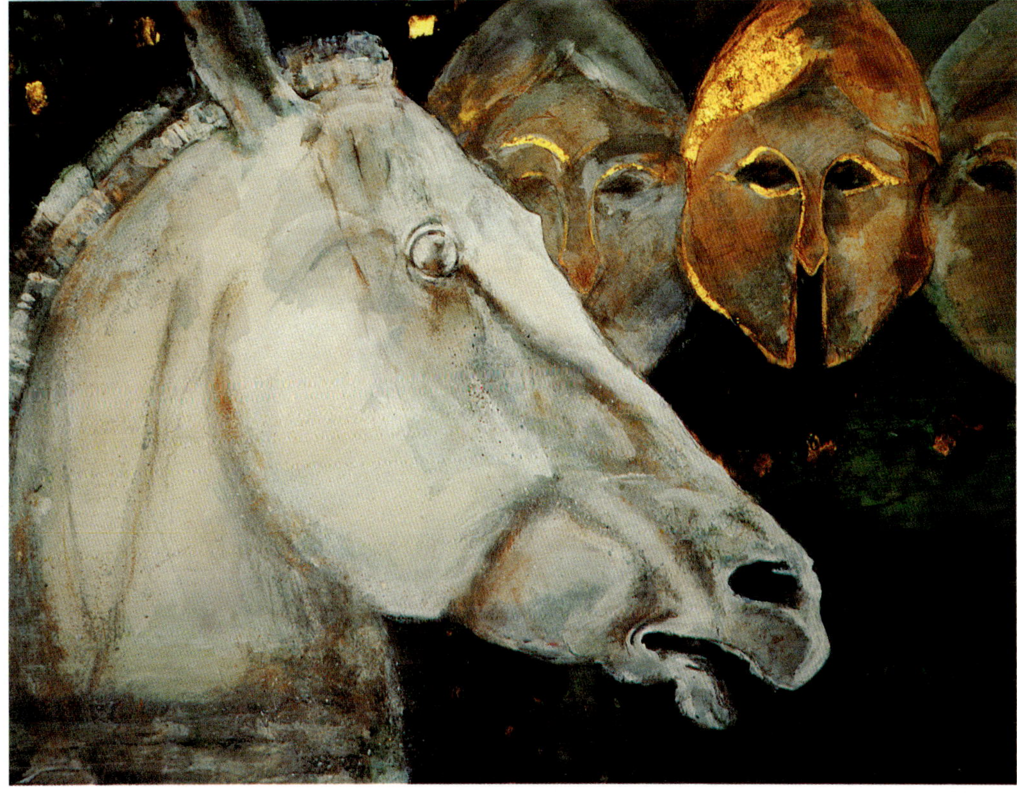

Pat Regan
Horse of the Goddess of the Moon
22" x 30" (55.9 cm x 76.2 cm)
Arches 140 lb. cold press
Media: Watercolor, acrylic, gold leaf

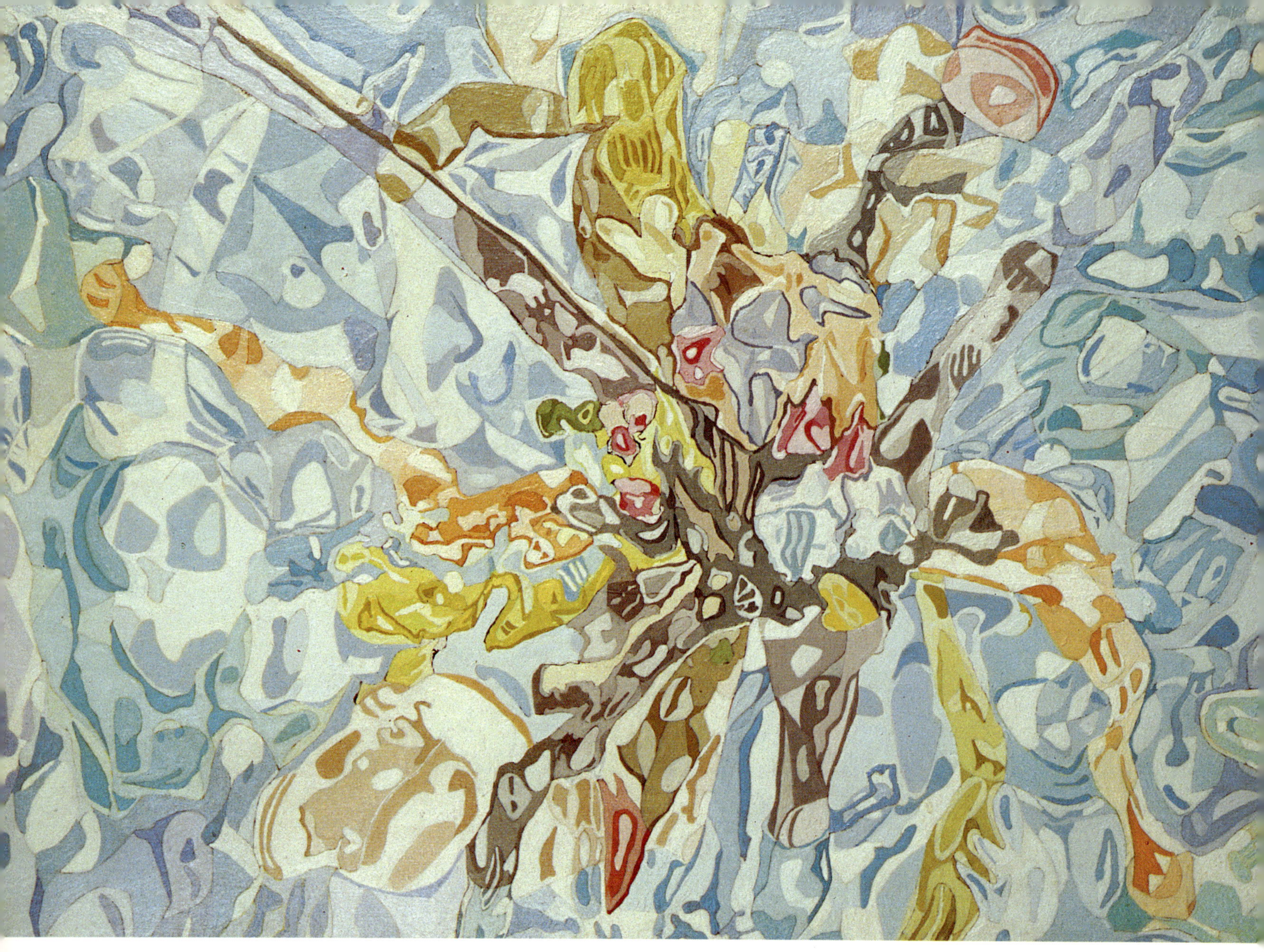

Denise Carey
The Bud
18" x 24" (46 cm x 61 cm)
Masonite 100% rag rice paper-covered gesso-coated panel

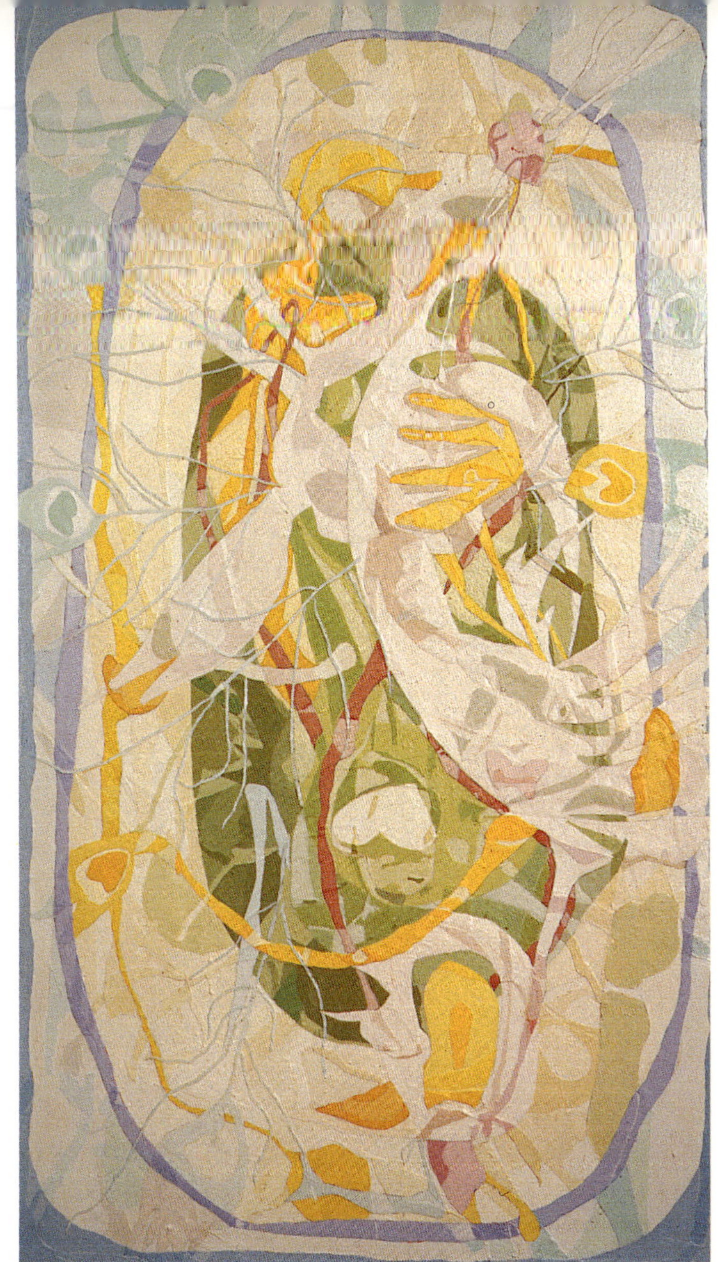

Denise Carey
Slaying of the Peacock
36" x 20" (91 cm x 51 cm)
Masonite 100% rag rice paper-covered board

Edith Socolow
Night on Salt Island
29" x 36" (74 cm x 91 cm)
Canvas

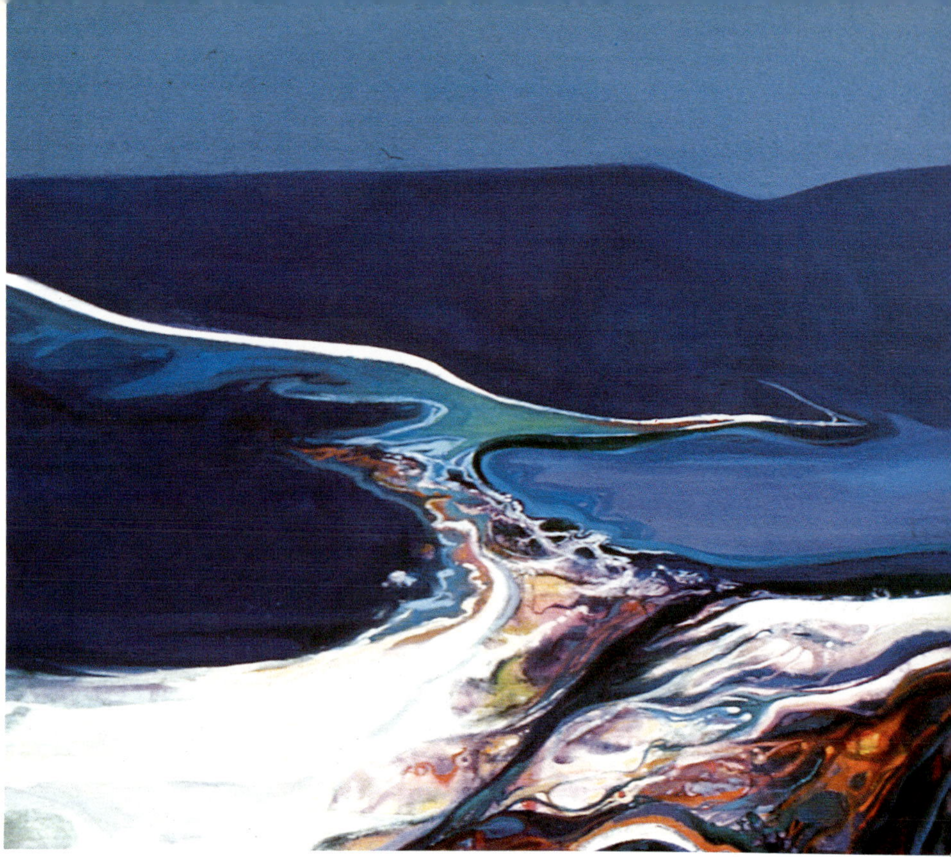

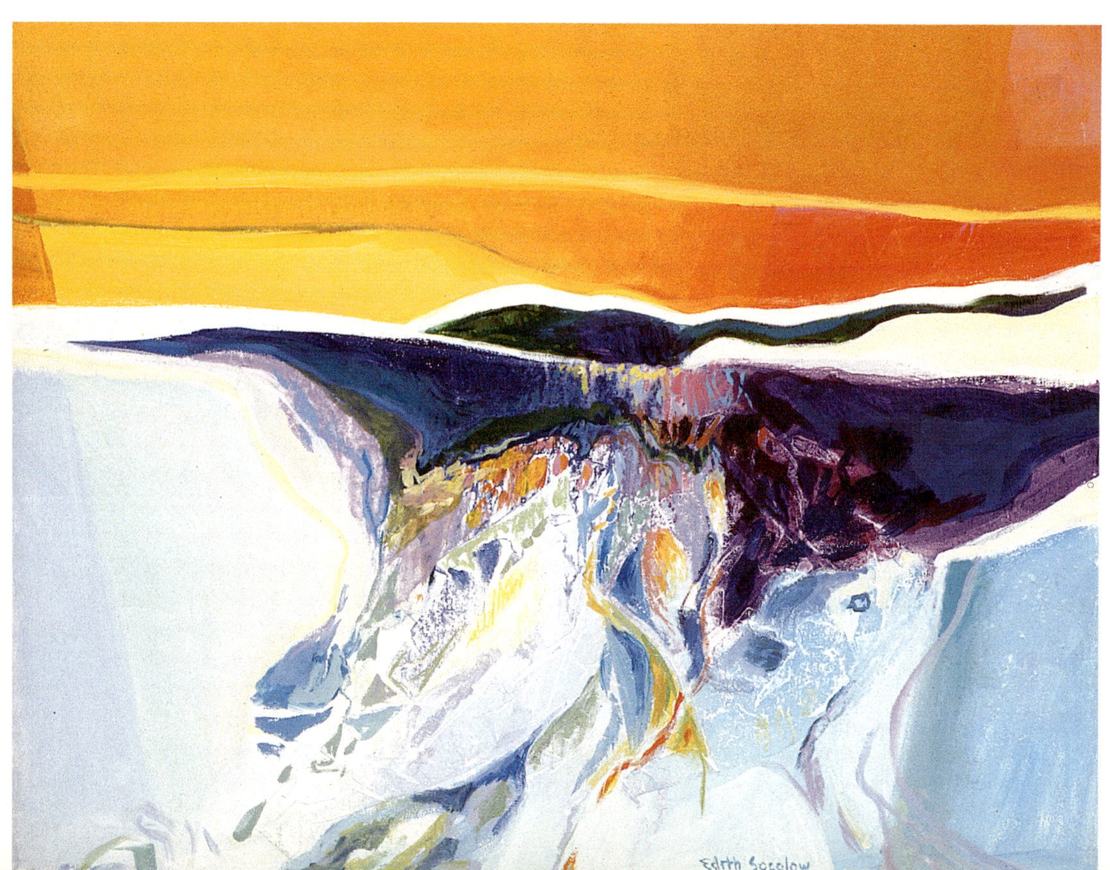

Edith Socolow
Receding Tides
21" x 25" (54 cm x 64 cm)
Canvas

Fredi Taddeucci
River's Crest
21.25" x 28.75" (54 cm x 73 cm)
Arches 140 lb. cold press
Media: Watercolor, acrylic, colored pencil

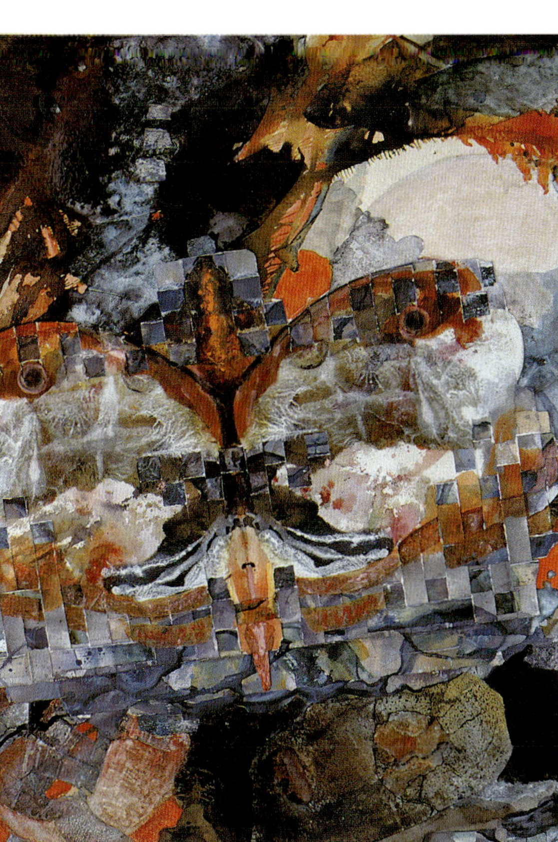

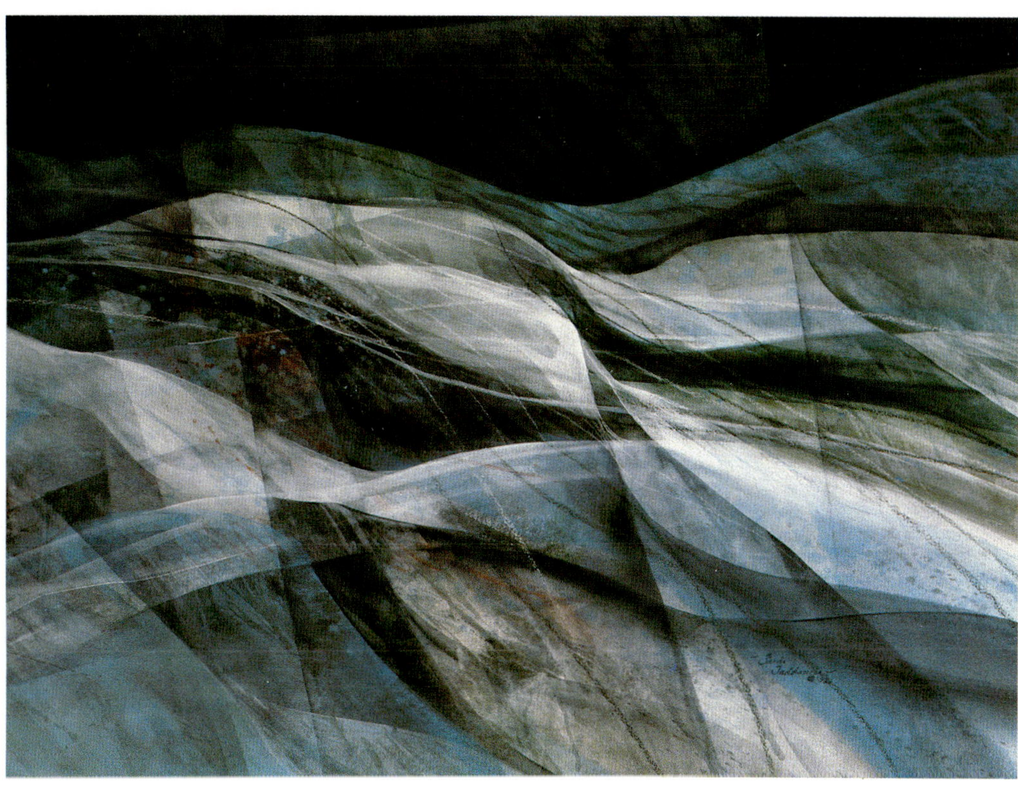

Margaret C. Manter
Firebug
30.25" x 23.5" (76.8 cm x 59.7 cm)
Arches 140 lb. cold press,
Strathmore Aquarius II 90 lb.
Media: Watercolor, Golden and
Grumbacher acrylic, Pelikan ink

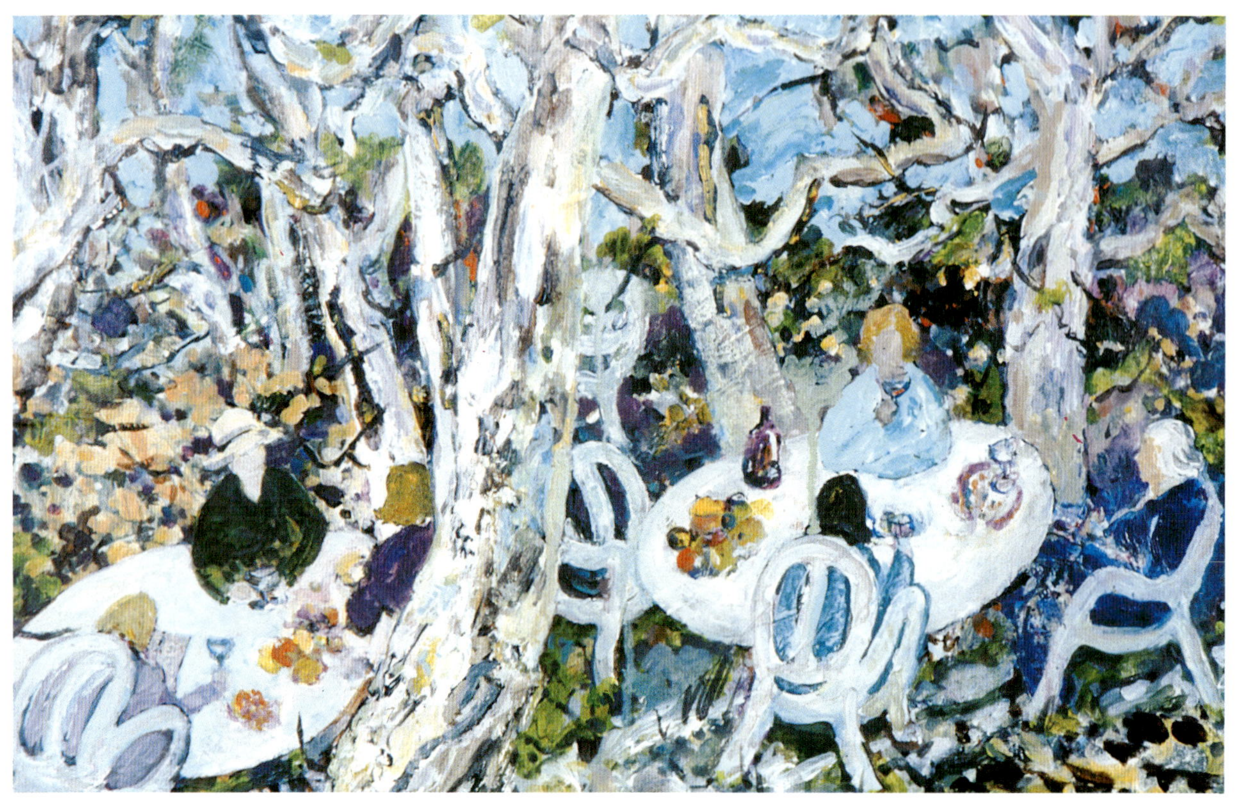

Leona Sherwood
Le Déjeuner—La Napoule
20.5" x 27.75" (52.1 cm x 70.5 cm)
Arches 140 lb. cold press (unstretched)
Media: Watercolor, gouache

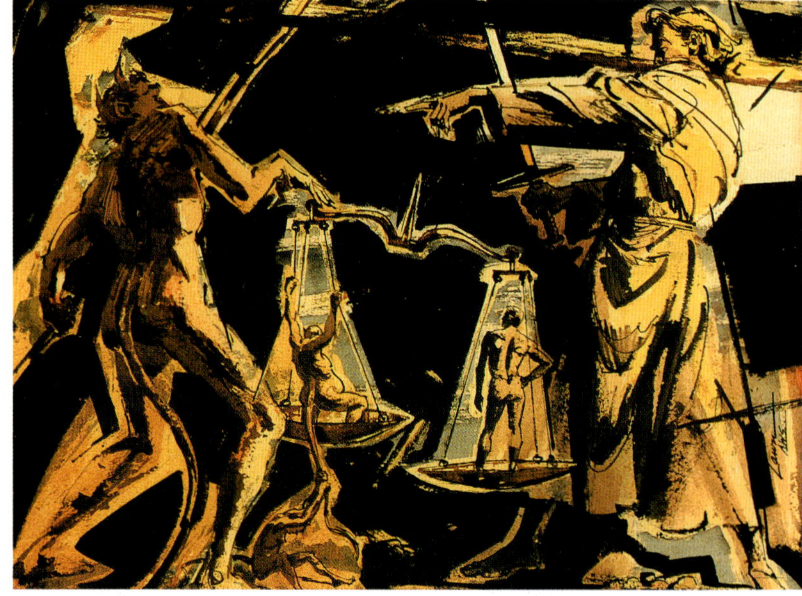

John A. Lawn, A.W.S.
Go To Hell
16" x 20" (40.6 cm x 50.8 cm)
Arches 140 lb.
Media: Watercolor, acrylic, diluted water, proof black ink

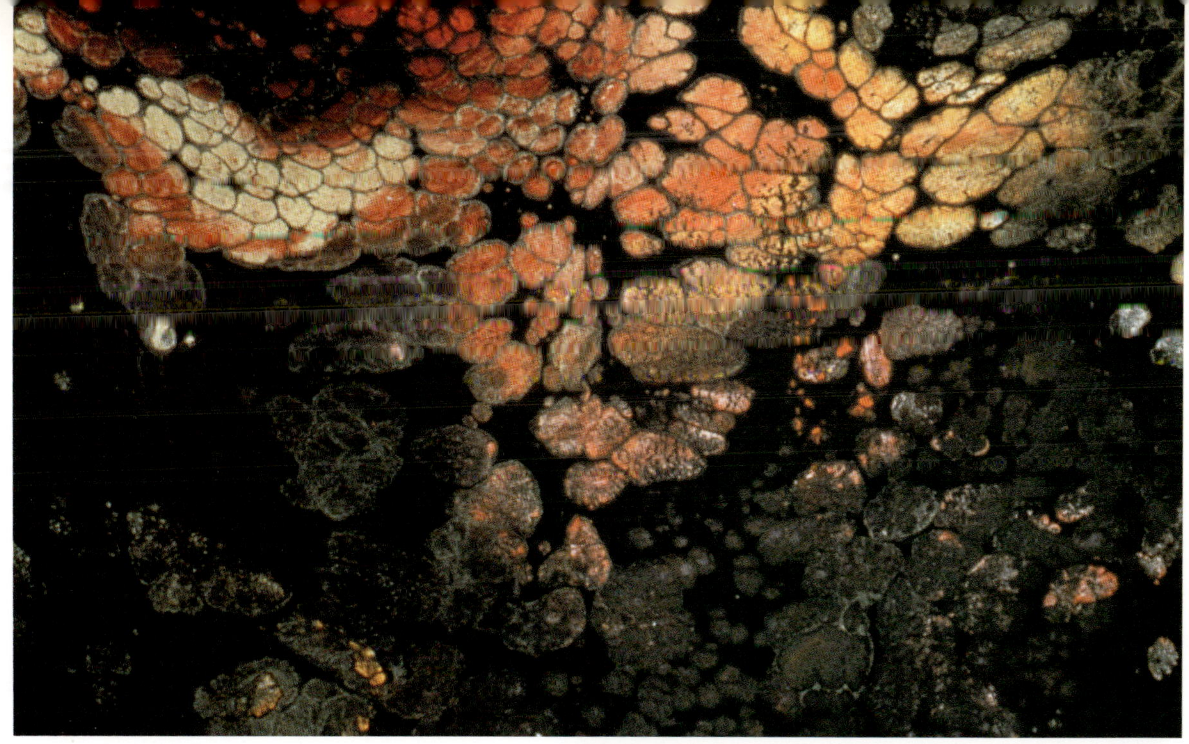

Naomi Marks Cohan
Suspended Flowers II
14" x 14" (36 cm x 36 cm)
Arches 140 lb. cold press

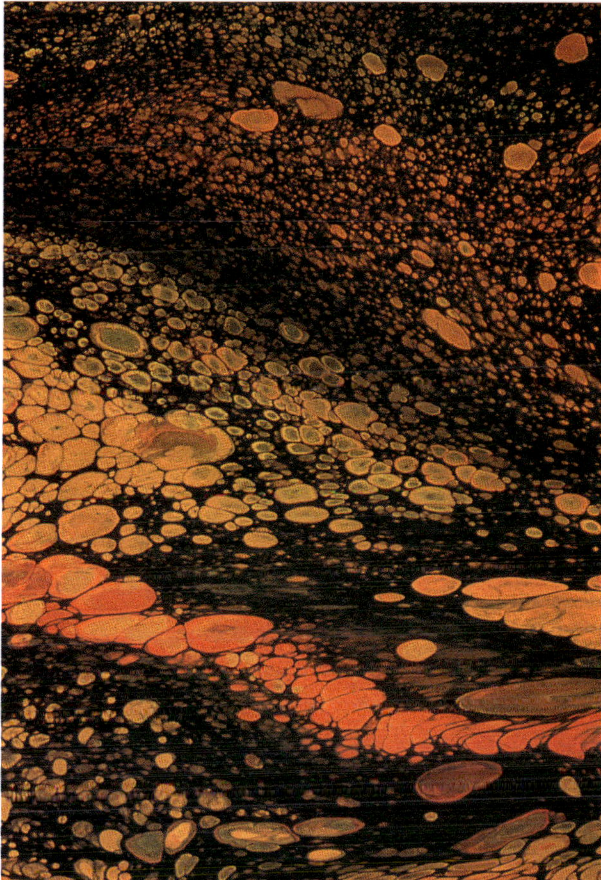

Naomi Marks Cohan
Autumn Twilight
13.5" x 12.5" (34 cm x 32 cm)
Arches 140 lb. cold press

Atanas Karpeles
Symmetry
30" x 23"
(76 cm x 59 cm)
Arches 300 lb. paper

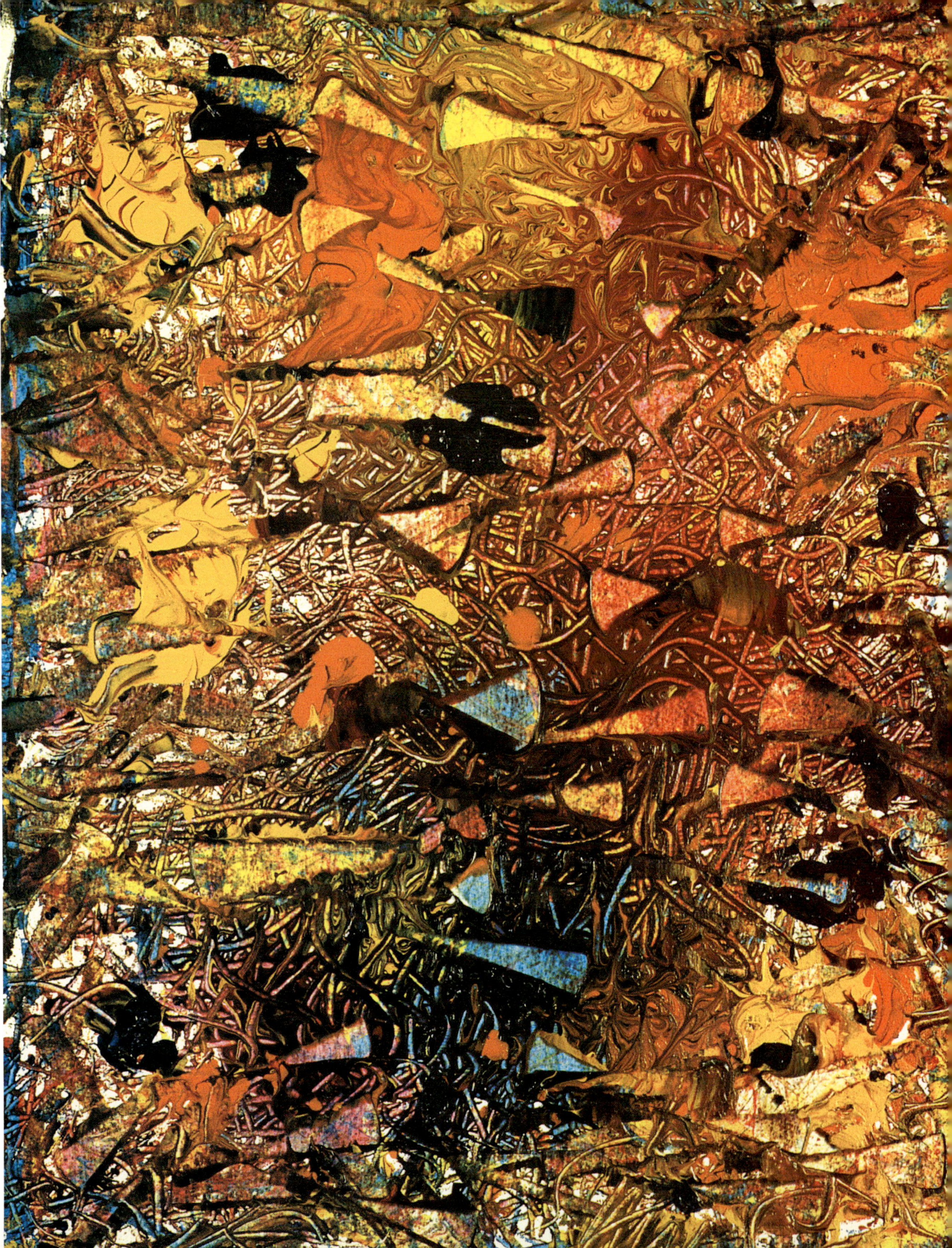

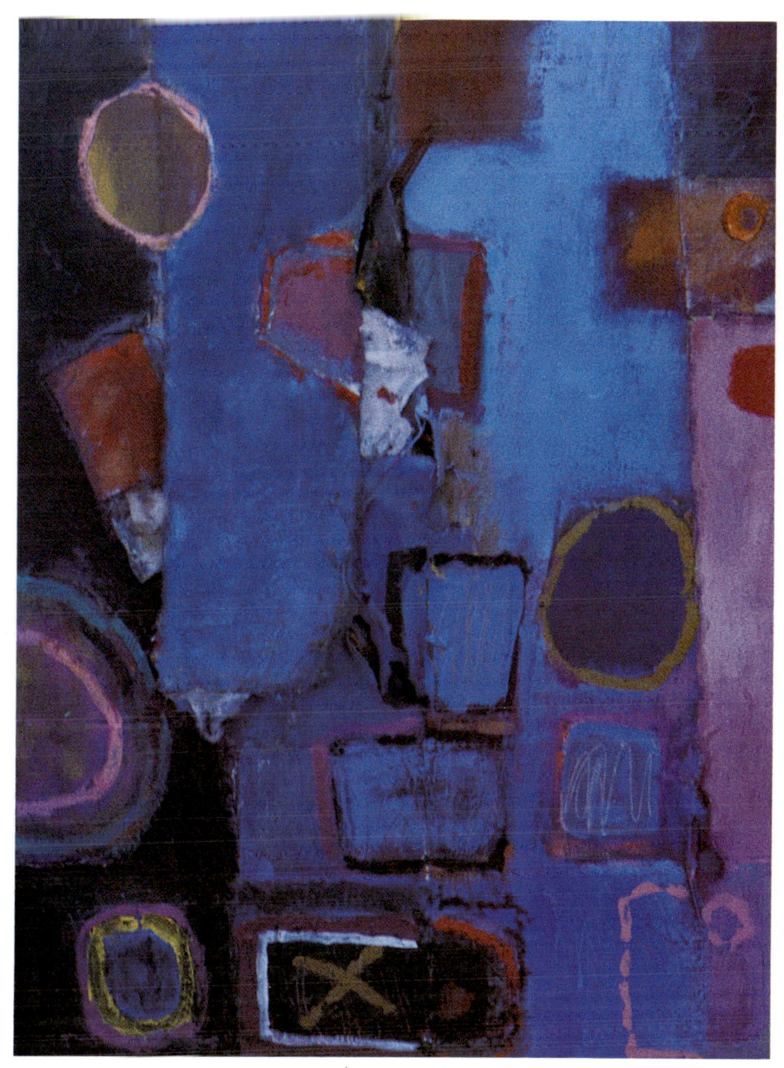

Joan Painter Jones
Torn Quilt #2
25" x 19" (63 cm x 48 cm)
Acrylic with cloth and wood
Canvas

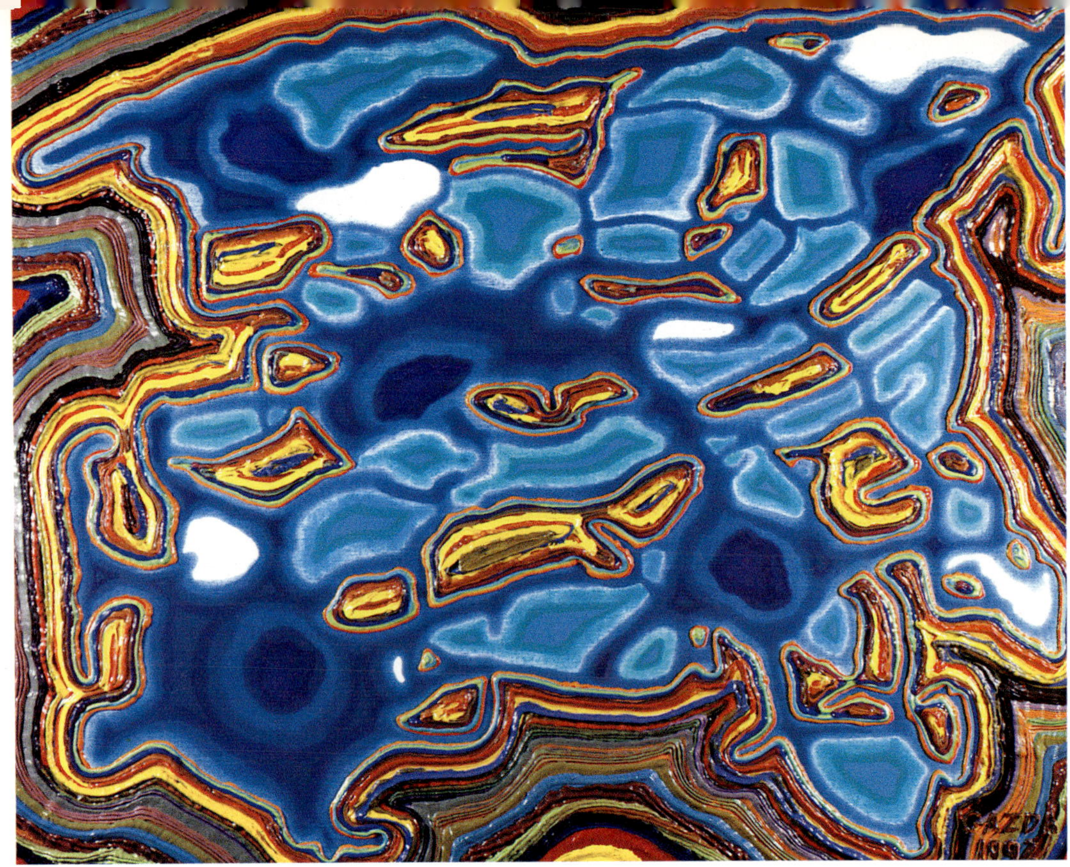

Paul Gazda
Archipelago
18" x 22" (45 cm x 55 cm)
Canvas

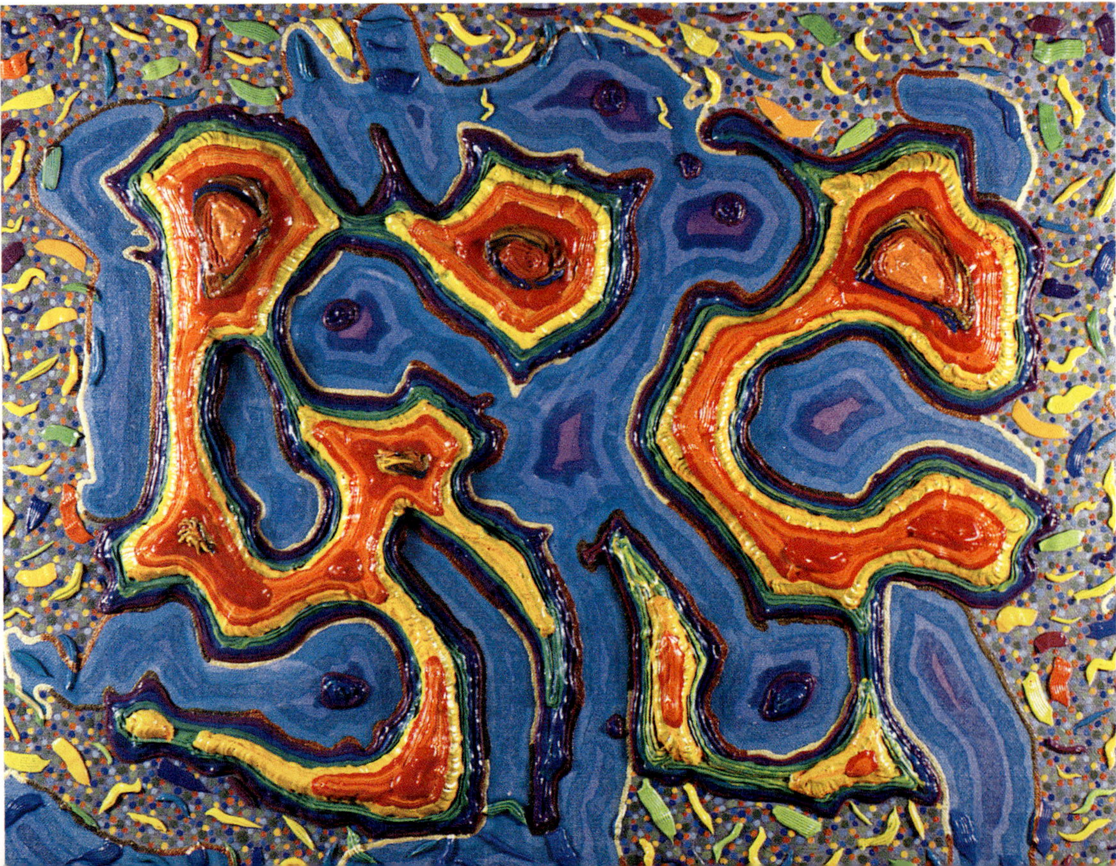

Paul Gazda
Overhead View
14" x 18" (35 cm x 45 cm)
Acrylic with modeling paste and glaze
Canvas

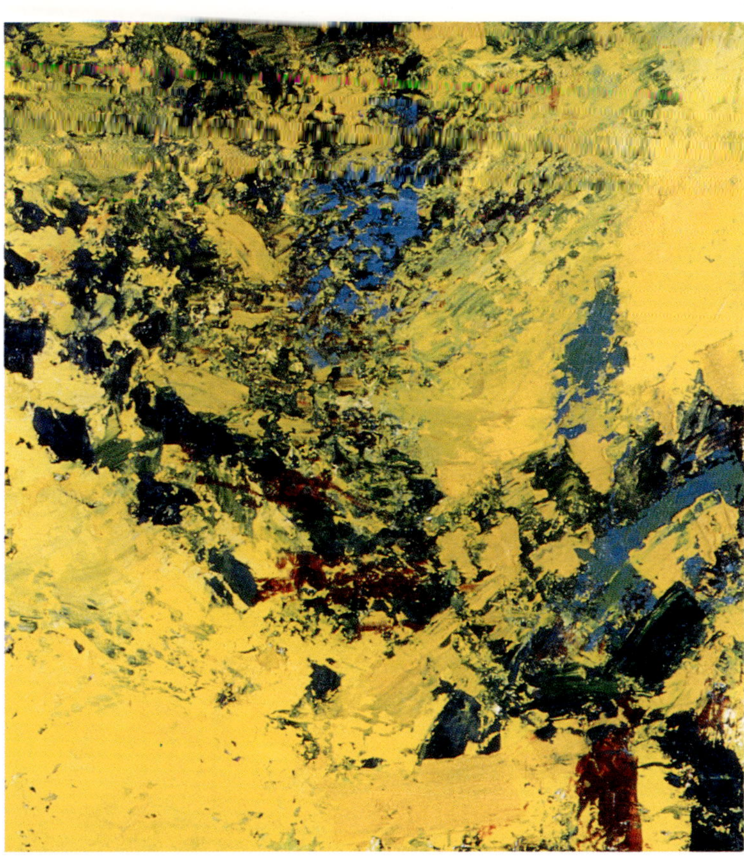

Patrick O'Kiersey
June Noon
36" x 32" (91.4 cm x 81.3 cm)
Canvas

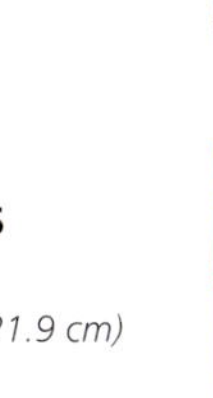

Atanas Karpeles
Below As Above
48" x 48" (121.9 cm x 121.9 cm)
Cotton canvas

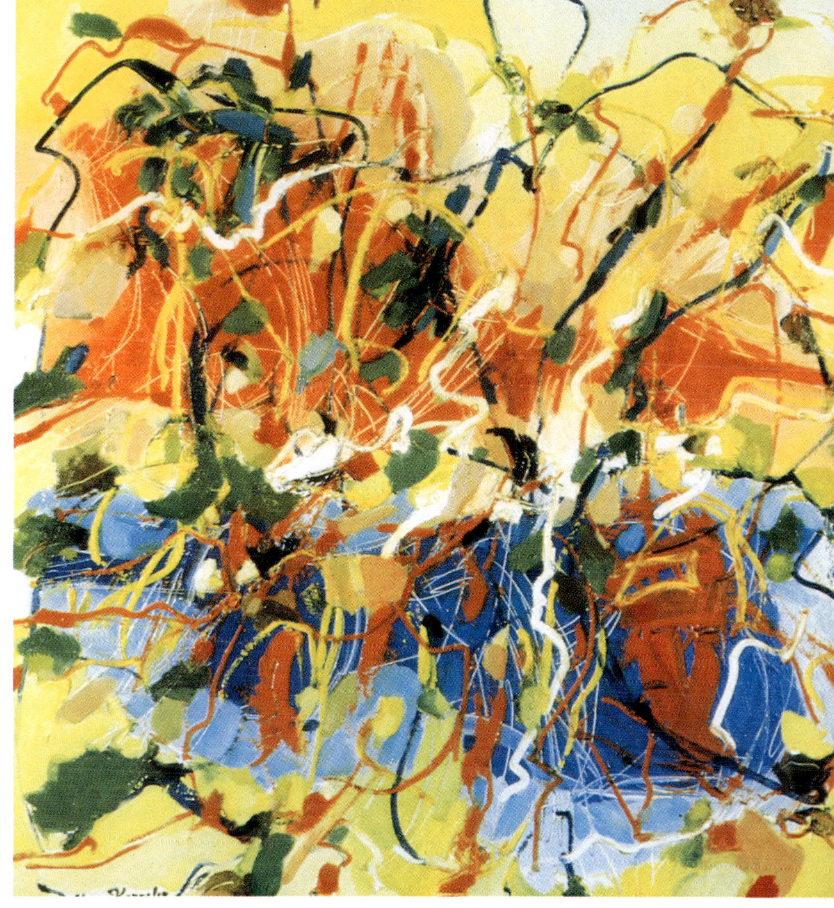

Mary Ellen Andren, F.W.S.
Rx: One Daily
28" x 30" (71.1 cm x 76.2 cm)
Strathmore 114 lb.
Media: Watercolor, colored pencil, acrylic, crayon

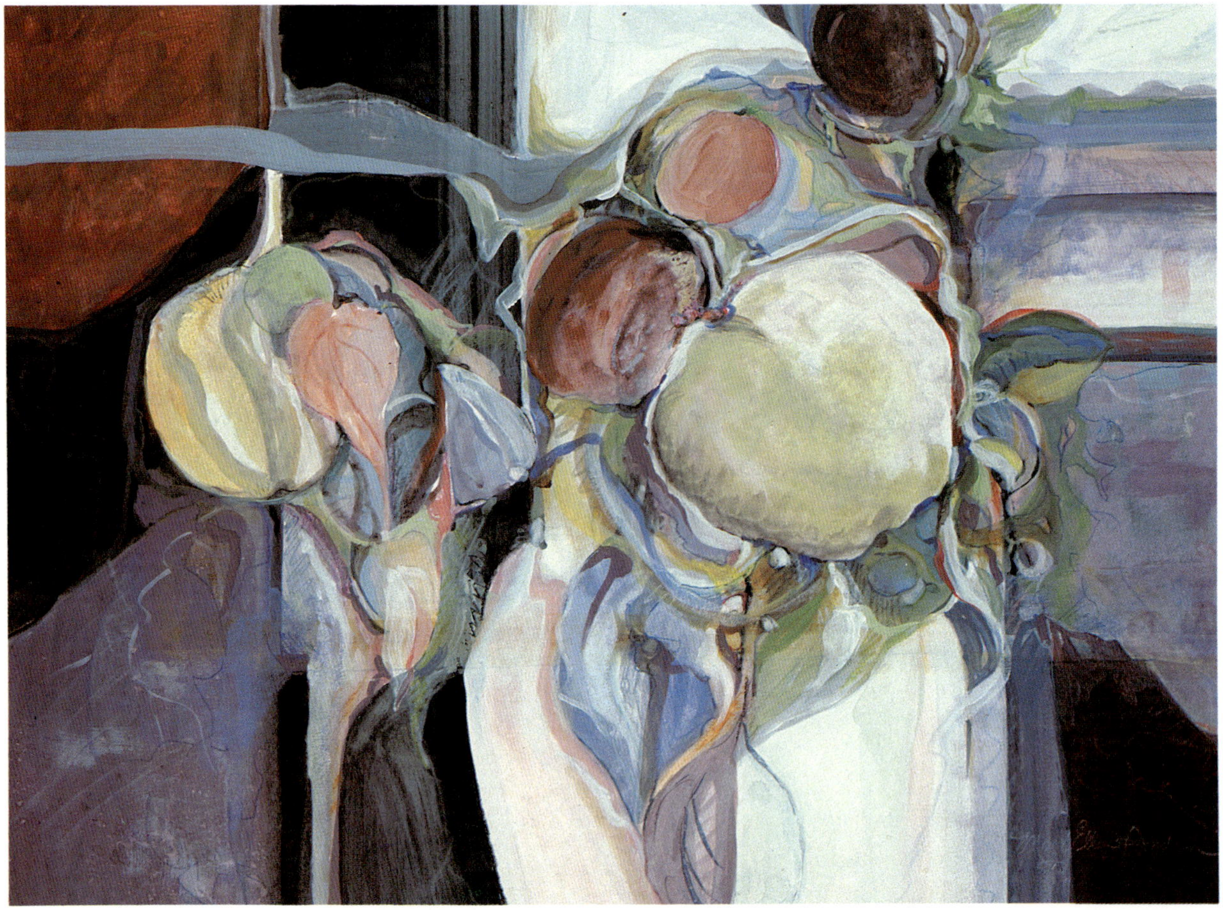

Sybil Moschetti
Wrapped & Riveted
30" x 42" (76.2 cm x 106.7)
Arches 300 lb. cold press

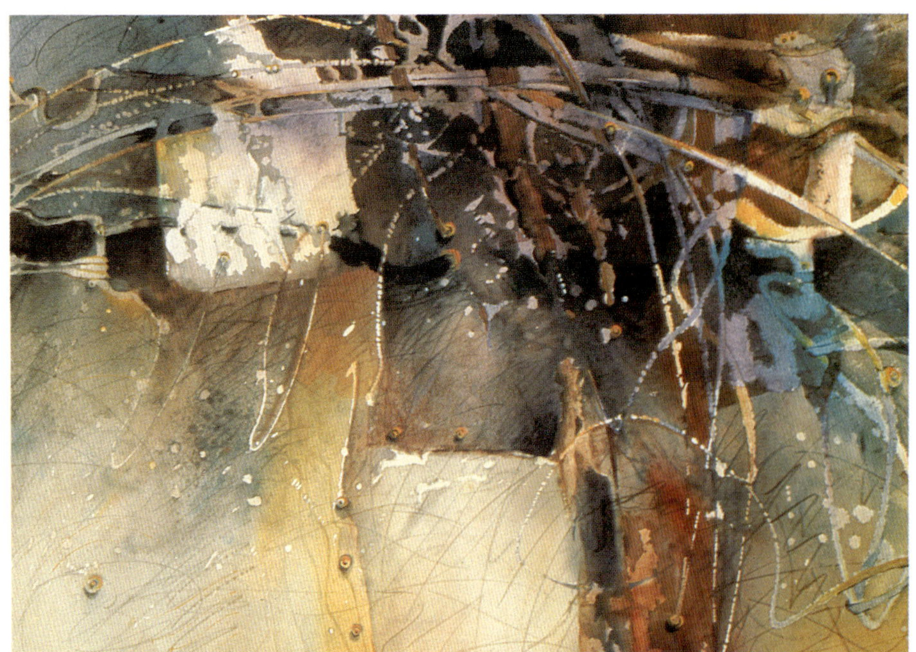

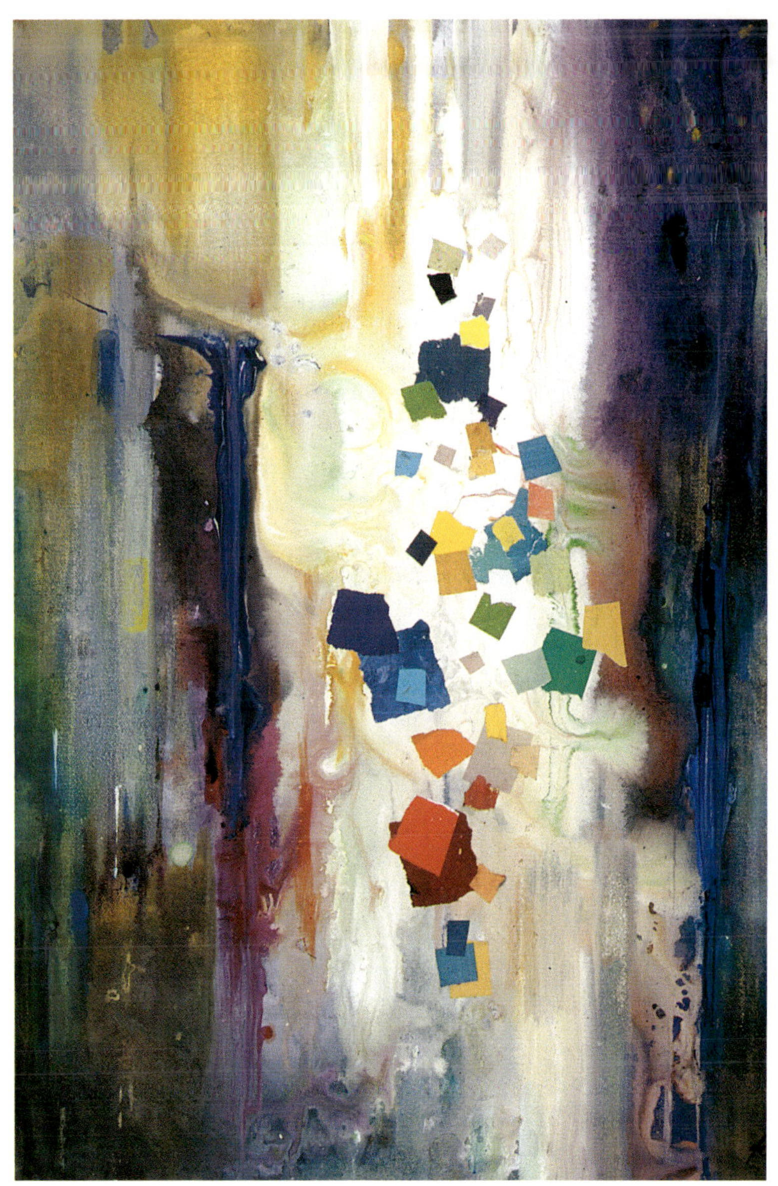

Nydia Preede
Positive Approach to Color Integration
24" x 18" (61 cm x 46 cm)
Canvas

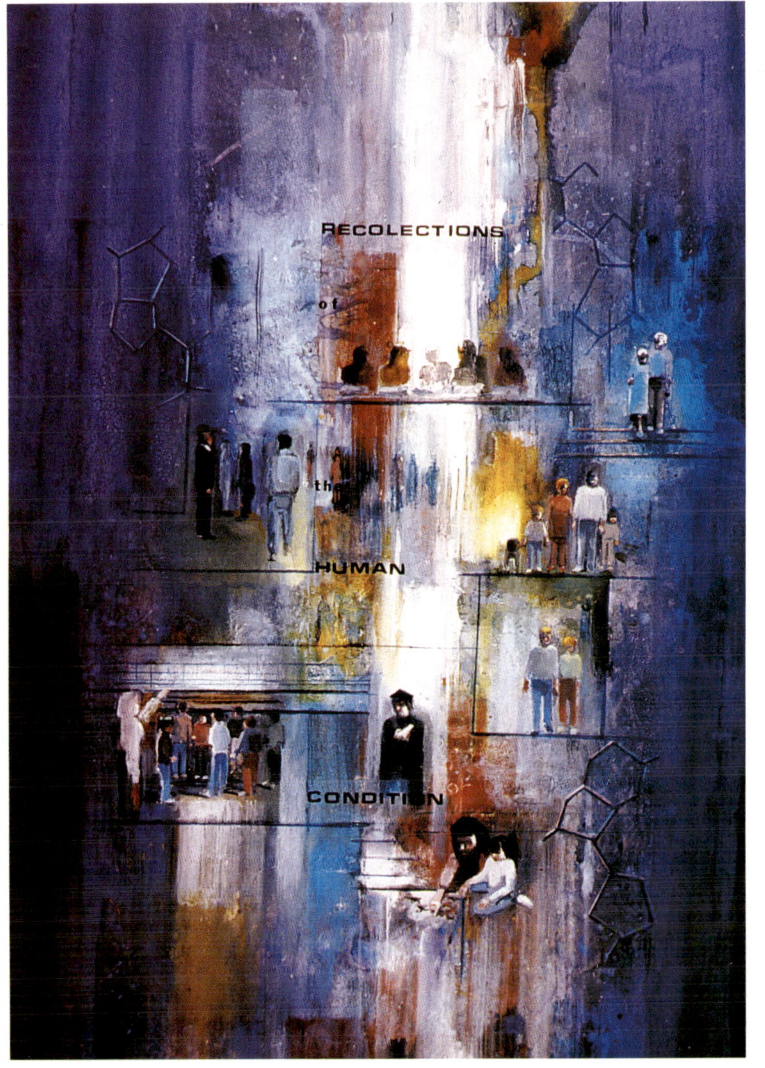

Nydia Preede
Recollections of the Human Condition
40" x 30" (102 cm x 76 cm)
Board

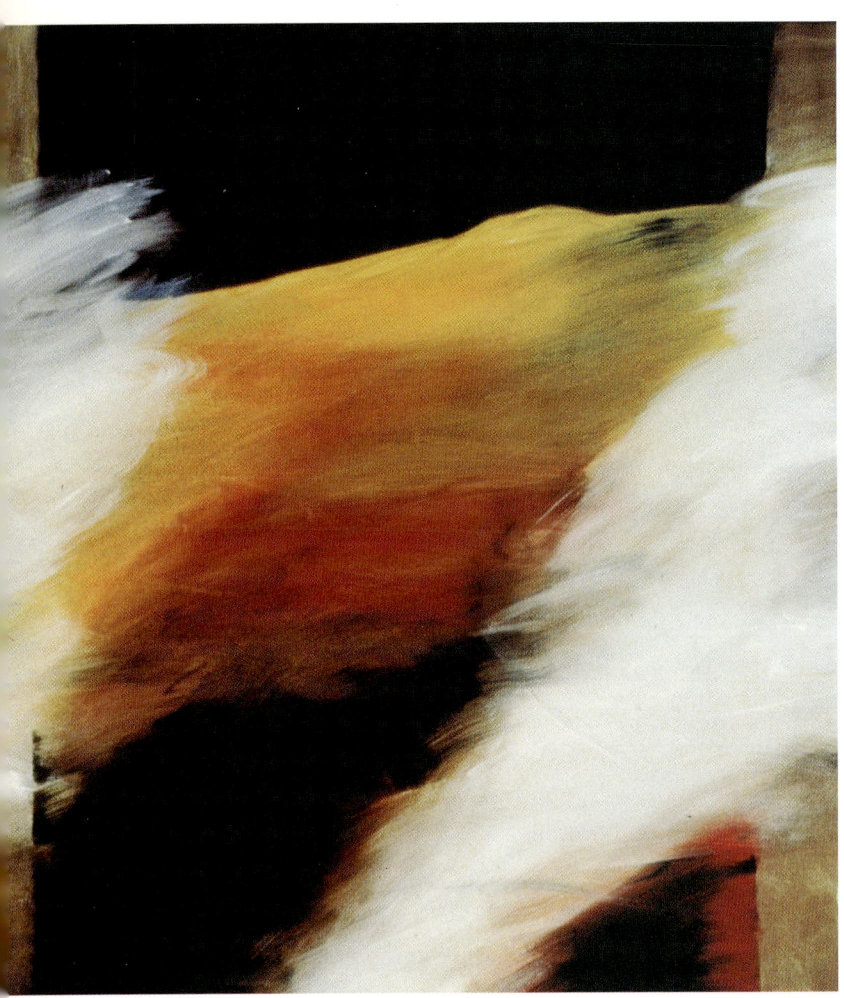

Maxine Warren
In My End Is My Beginning
(Private Words for T.S. Eliot Series)
48" x 44" (121.9 cm x 111.8 cm)
Canvas on stretchers

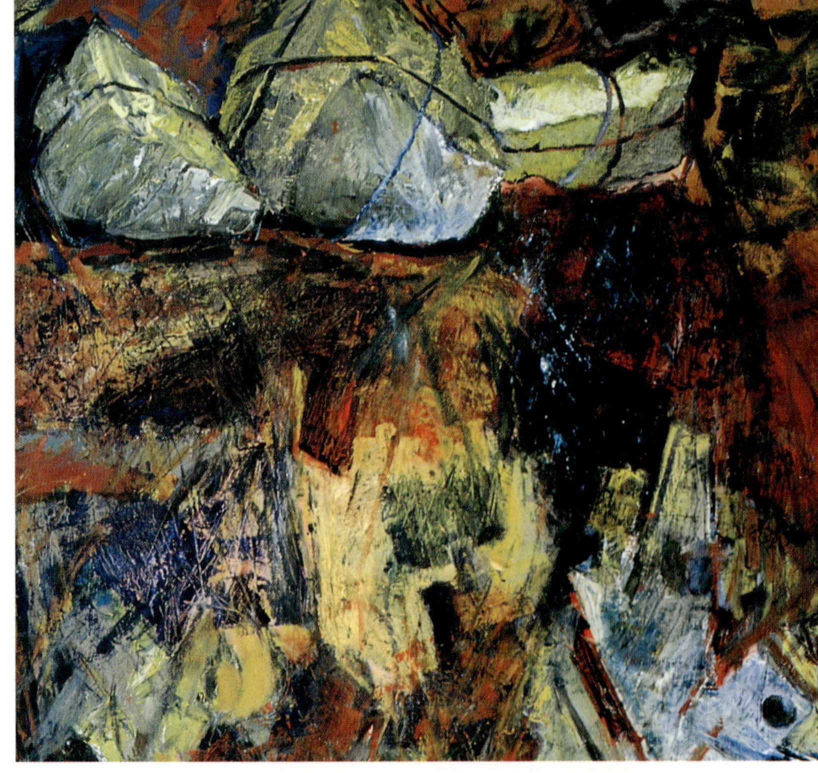

Gloria B. Blades
Stones Tied Together to Keep the House Safe
39" x 45" (99.1 cm x 114.3 cm)
Canvas

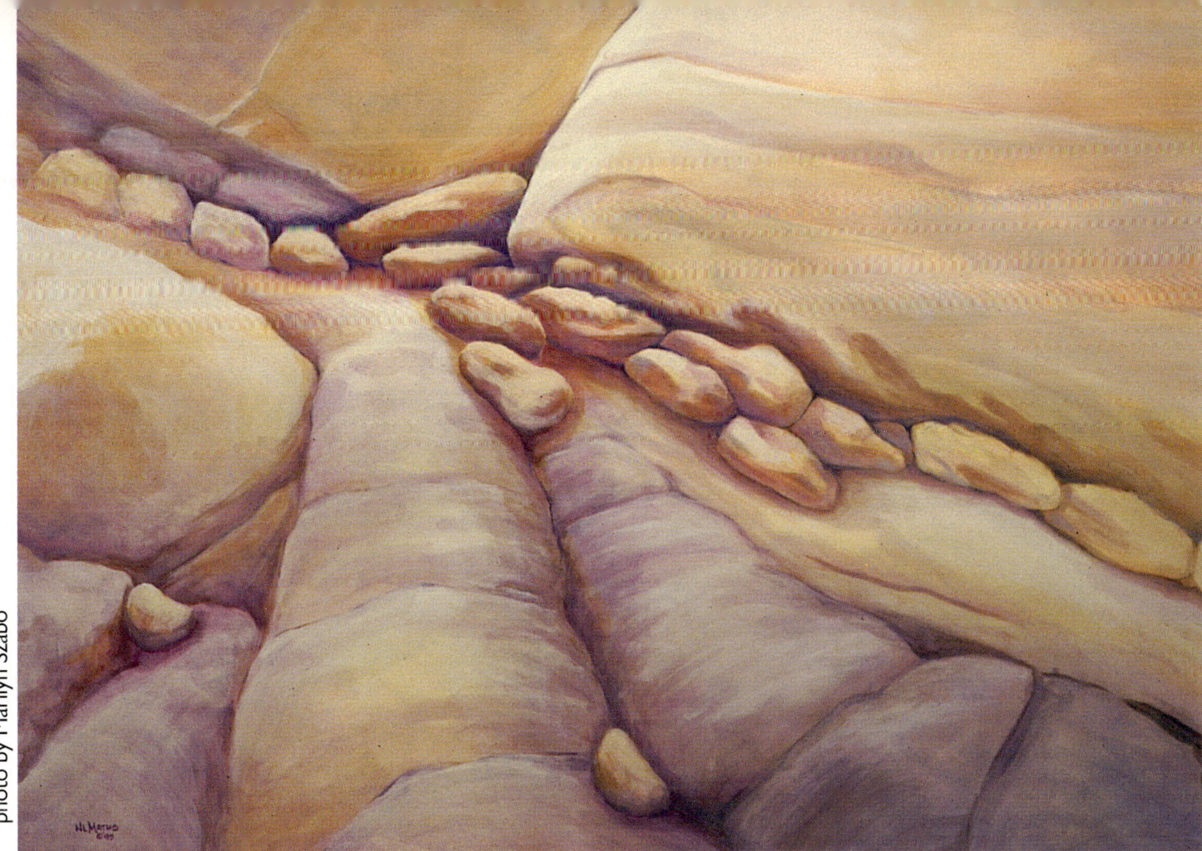

photo by Marilyn Szabo

N. L. Matus
Terra III
36" x 48" (91 cm x 122 cm)
Canvas

N. L. Matus
Sanctuary
10" x 20" (25 cm x 51 cm)
Canvas

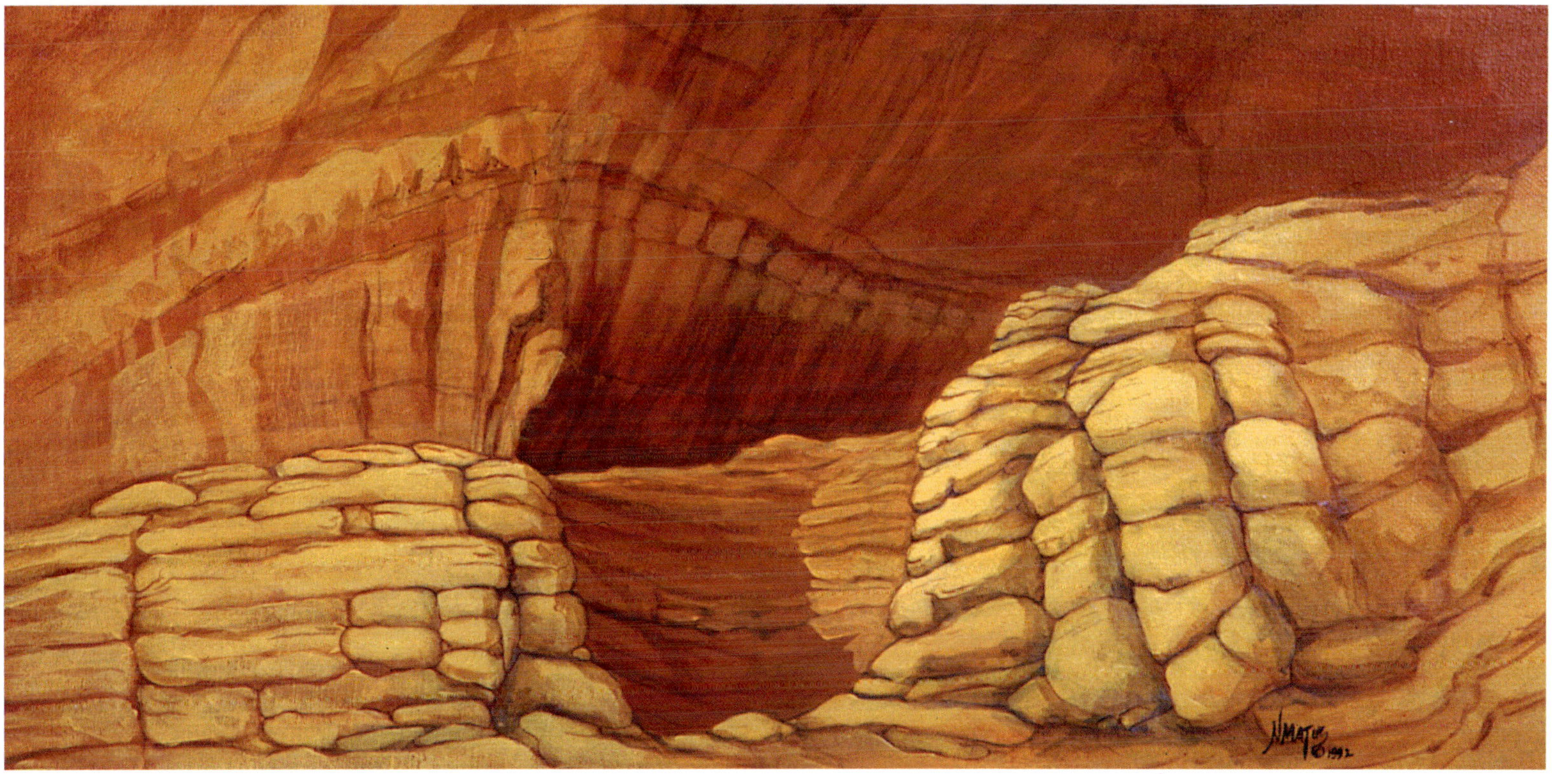

photo by Marilyn Szabo

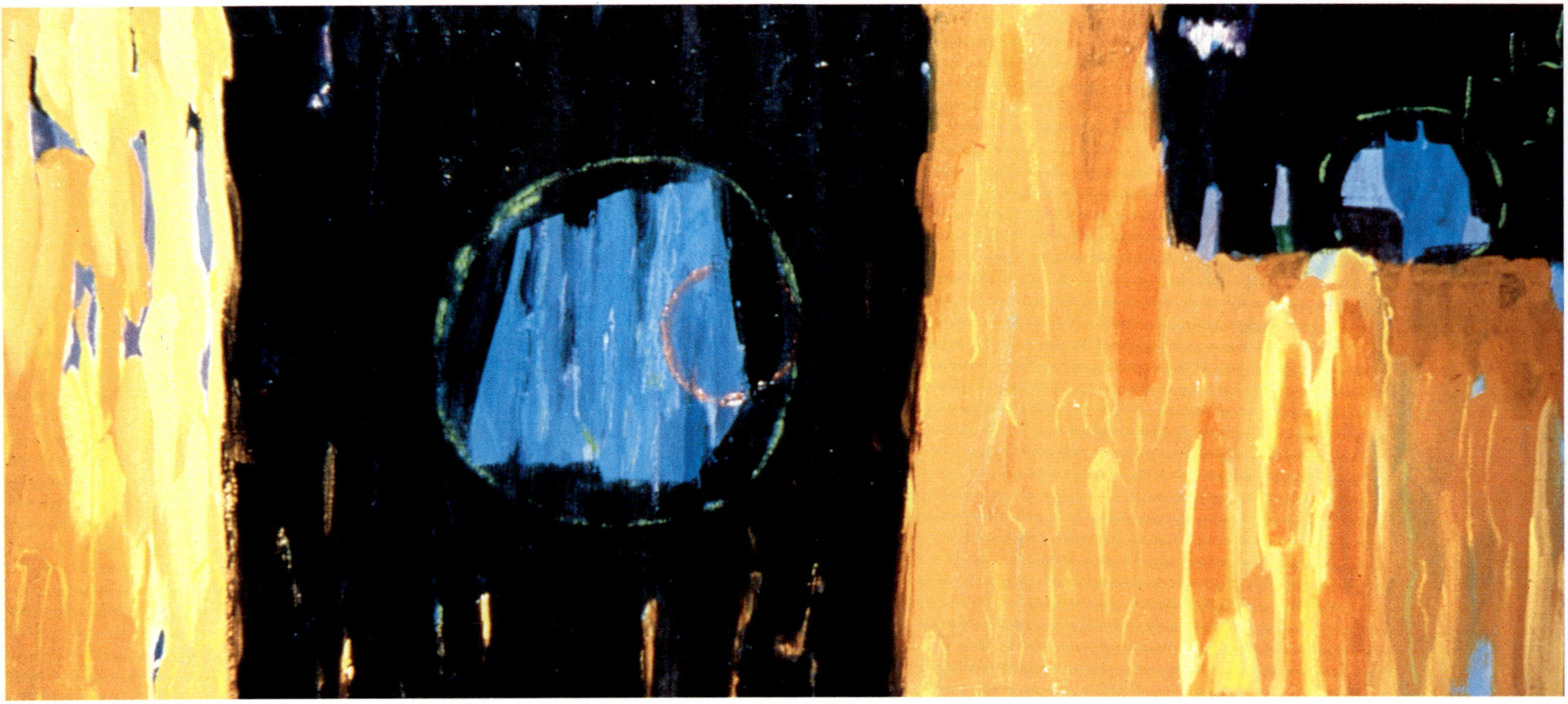

Claffy Williams
Night Grasses
30" x 66" (76 cm x 168 cm)
Canvas

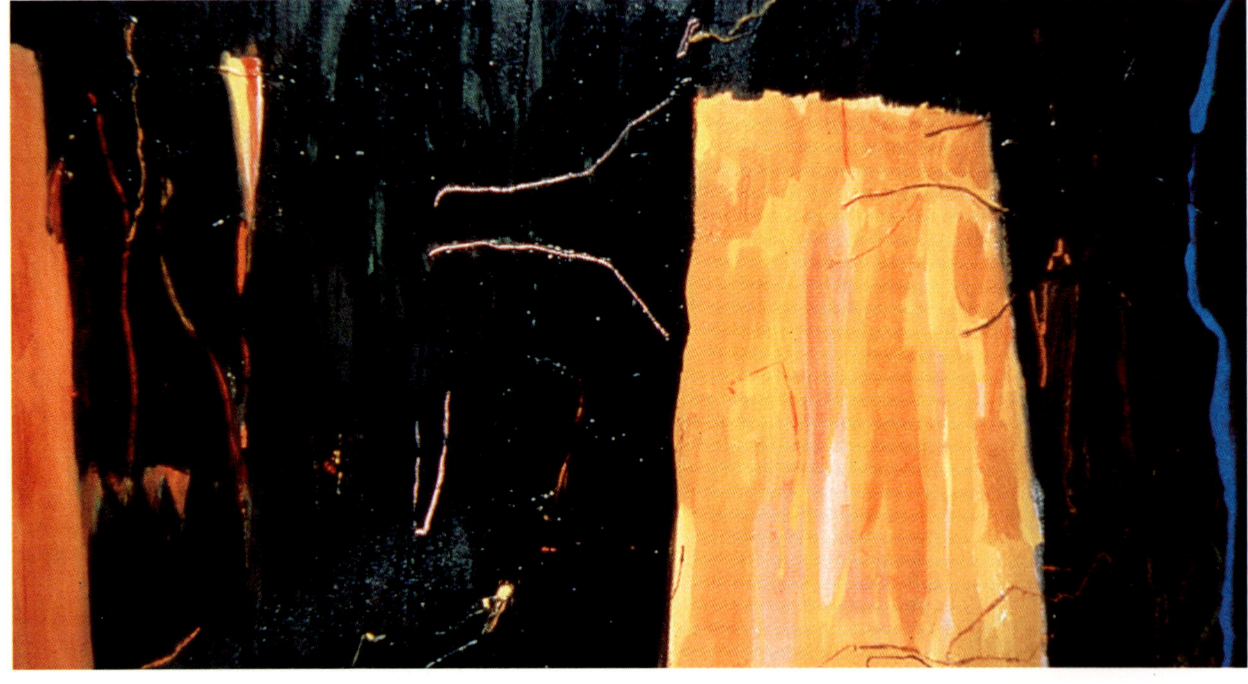

Claffy Williams
Kala
(A Weather God in India)
36" x 66" (91 cm x 168 cm)
Canvas

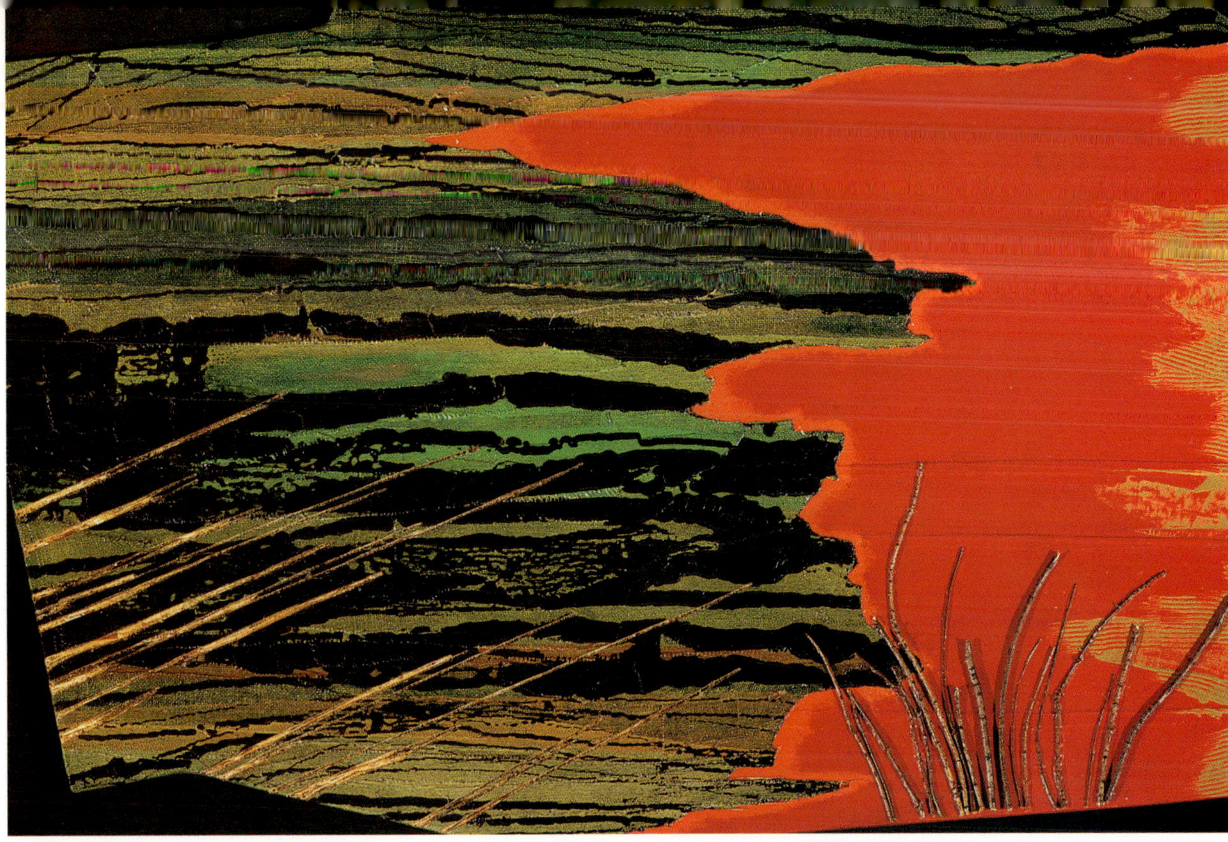

Ed Brodkin
Millstone Valley
38" x 58" (97 cm x 148 cm)
Acrylic with polyurethane
Burlap and canvas on
wood panel

Claffy Williams
Waka
(Goddess of
Food in Japan)
28" x 54" (71 cm x 137 cm)
Canvas

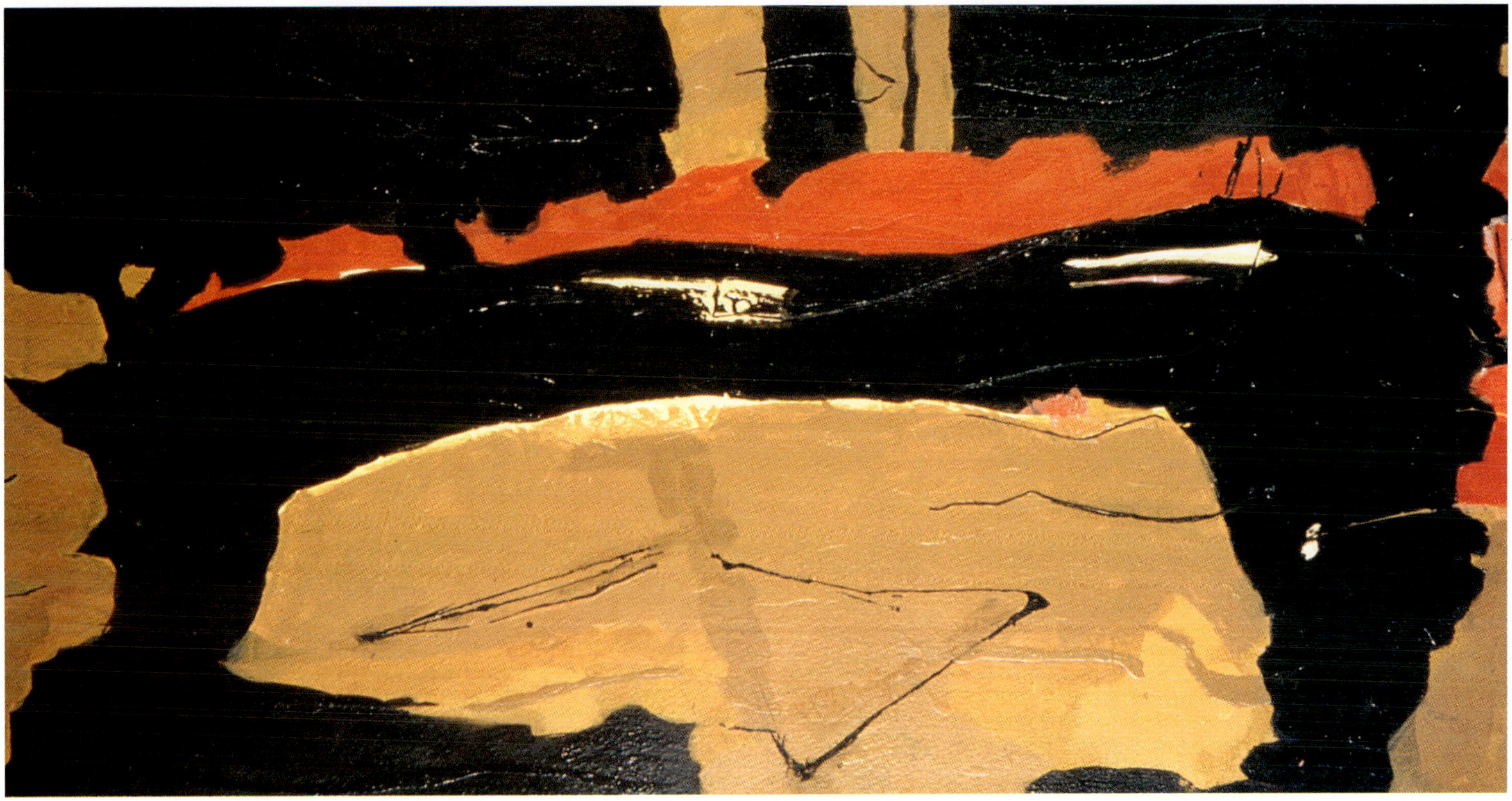

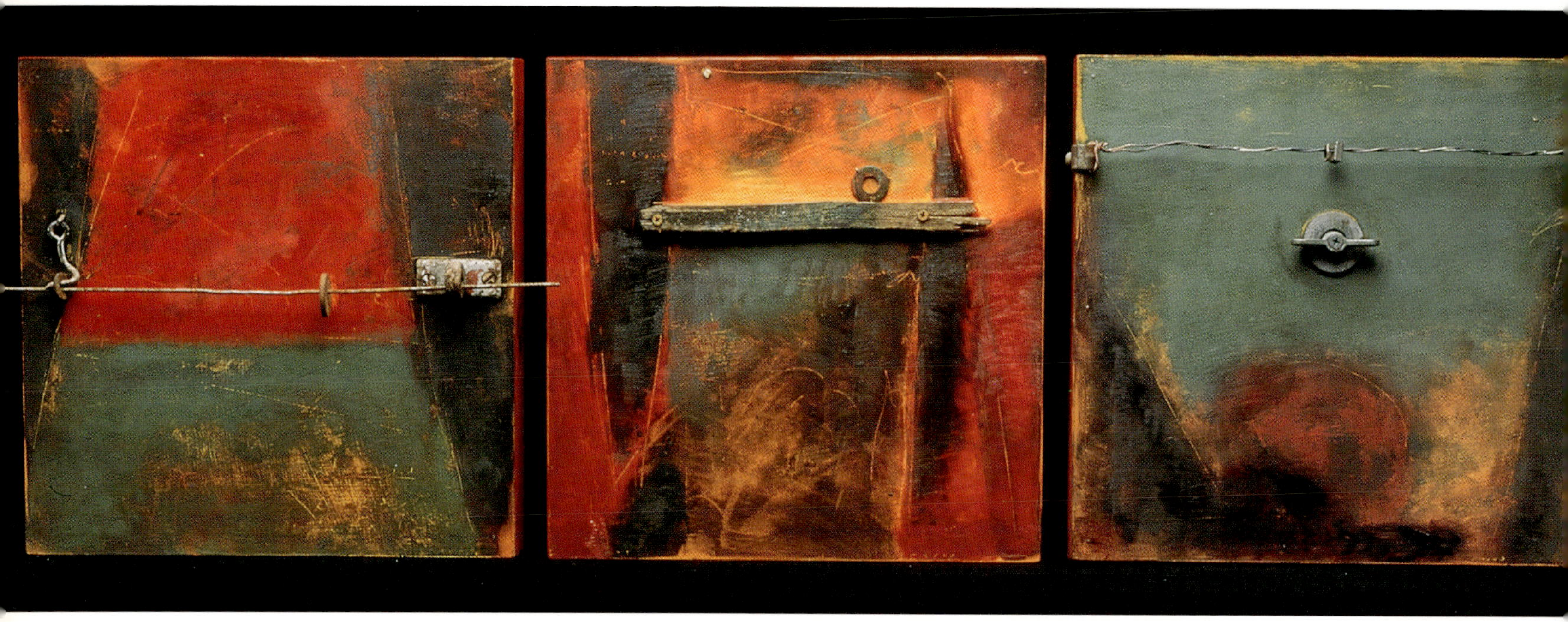

Kathryn Frund
Fin-de-Siecle II (Triptych)
10" x 10" each panel
(25.4 cm x 25.4 cm each panel)
Oil with found objects and metal
Panel..

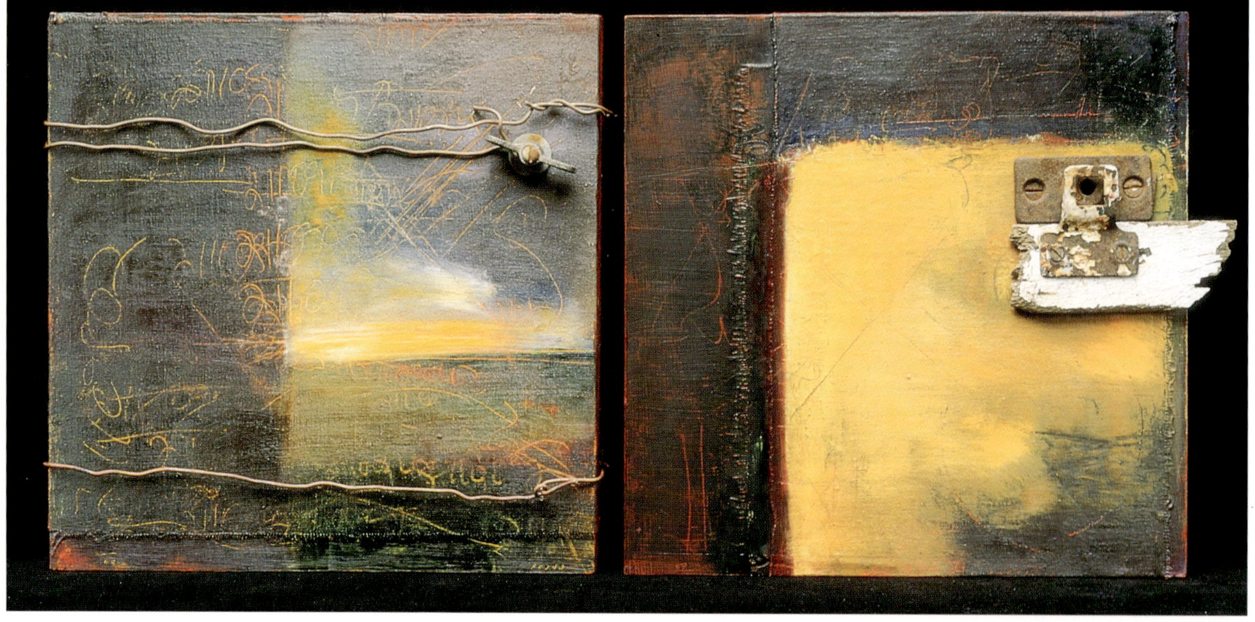

Kathryn Frund
Heaven & Earth (Diptych)
11" x 11" each panel
(27.9 cm x 27.9 cm each panel)
Canvas

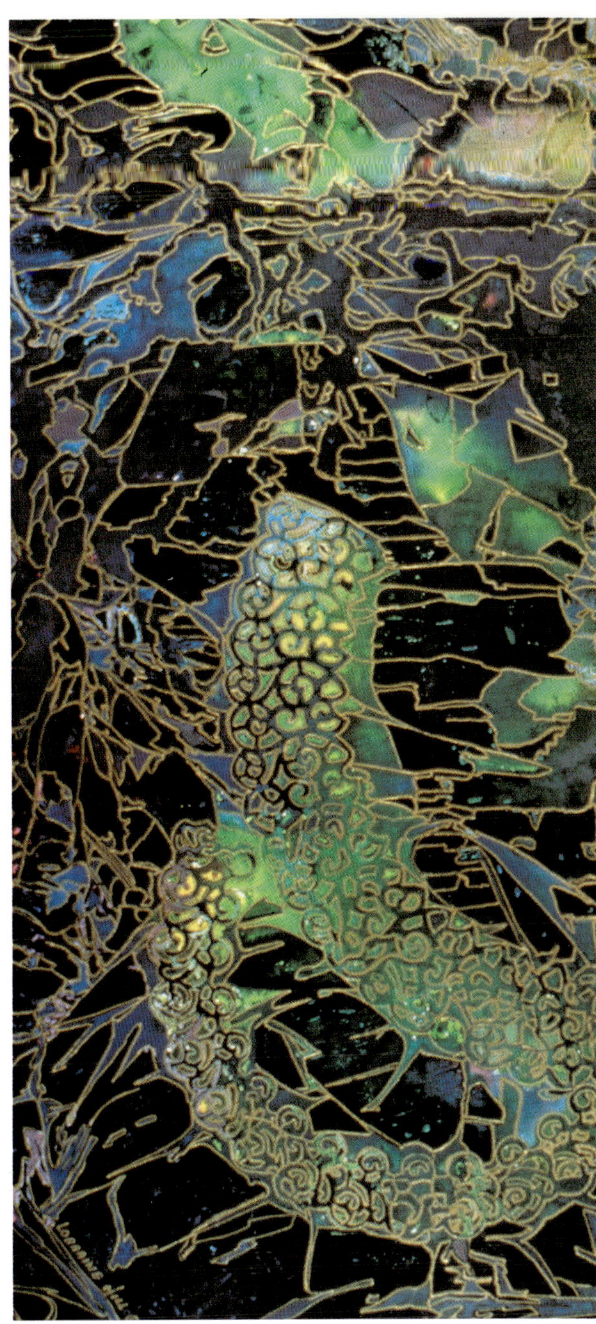

Lorraine Hill, S.E.A.
Intricate Patterns
9" x 21" (22.9 cm x 53.3 cm)
Bainbridge
Media: Premixed ink, watercolor, acrylic, gold pen

Willena Jeane Belden
Momentary Vision
12" x 18" (30.5 cm x 45.7 cm)
140 lb. cold press

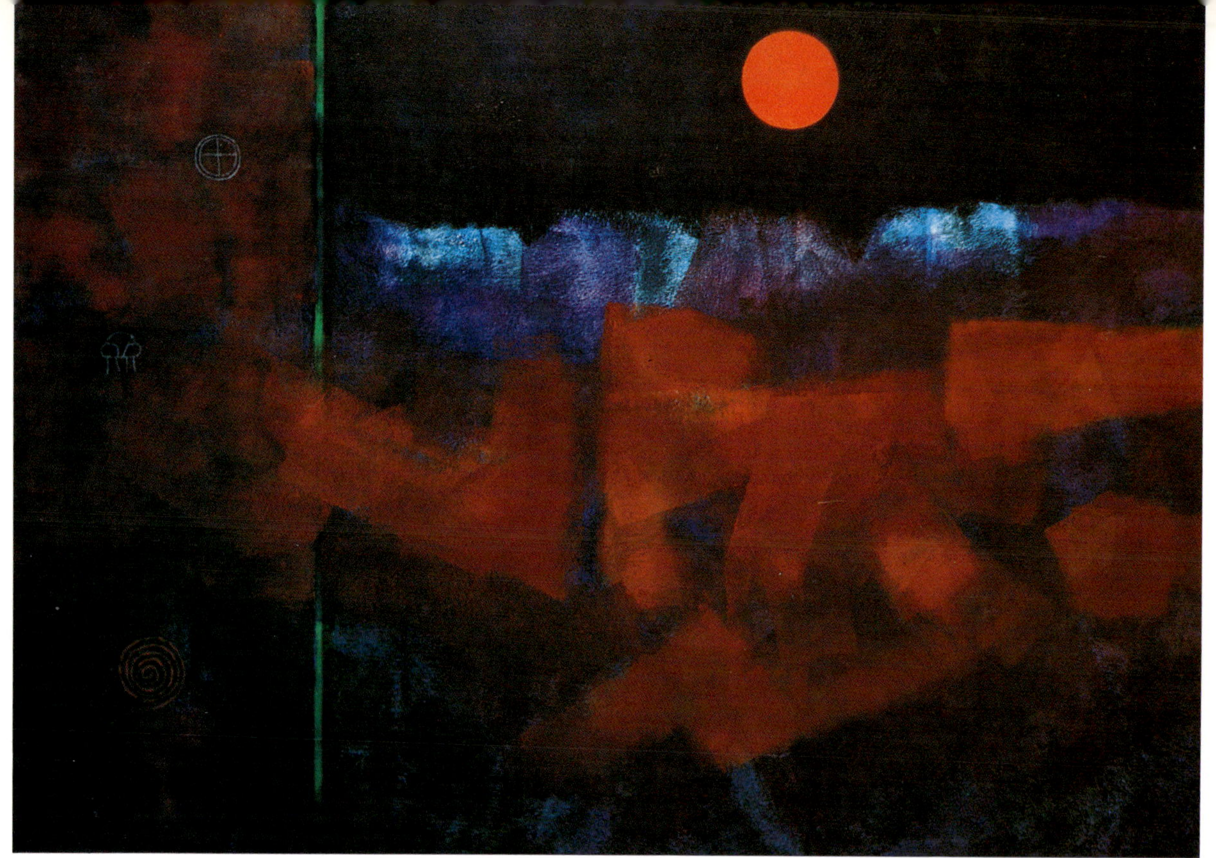

John Casey
Kylotsmovi
36" x 48" (92 cm x 121 cm)
Board

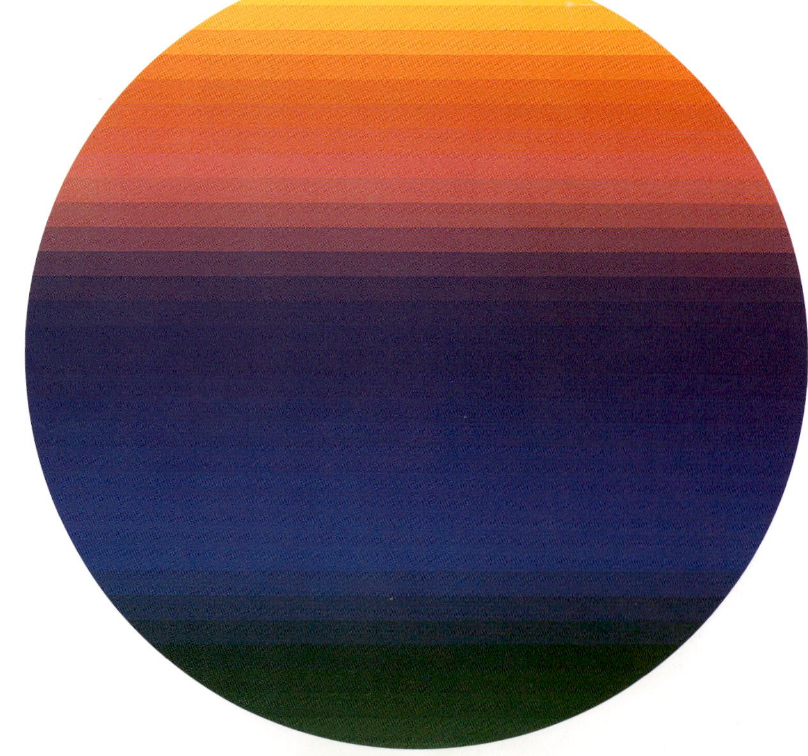

Andy Syrbick
Gledene
33" x 33" (84 cm x 84 cm)
Luan .25" plywood

Sharon Teabo
They Share The Tree
18" x 24" (46 cm x 61 cm)
Bristol 2-ply

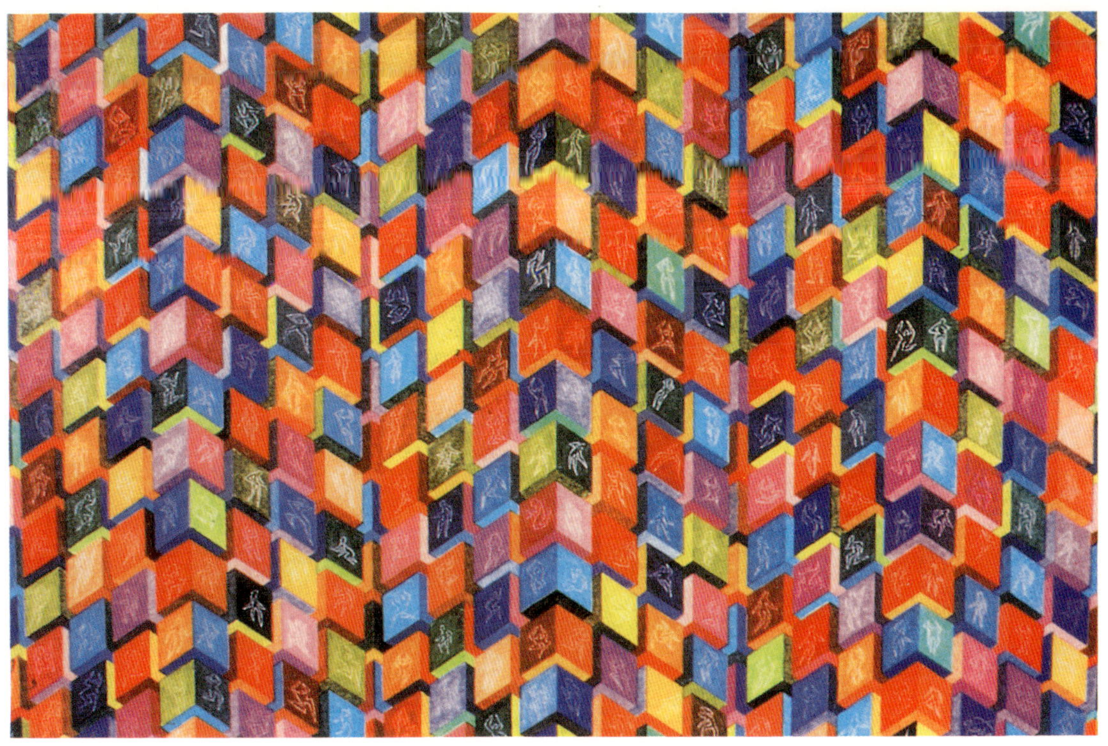

Timothy Santoirre
The Painter's Muse
19" x 16" (48 cm x 41 cm)
Canson Mi-Tientes

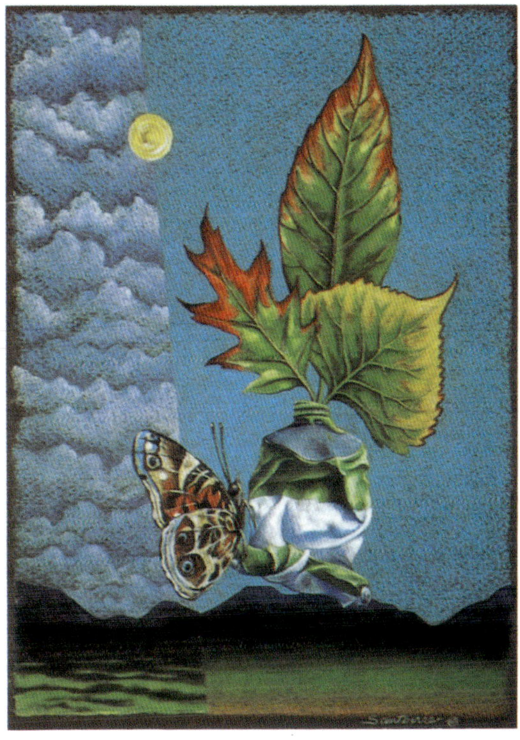

Marsh Nelson
Greener Fields
31" x 39" (79 cm x 99 cm)
Two-ply museum board

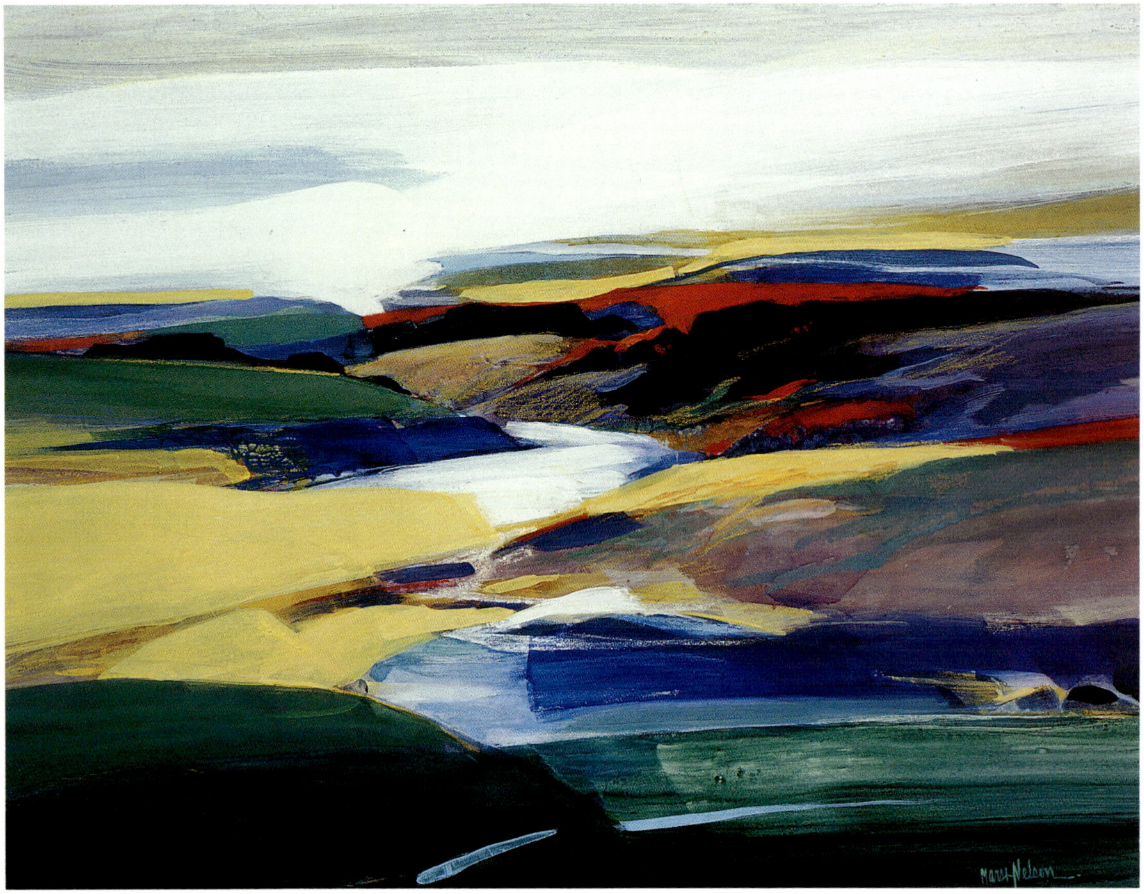

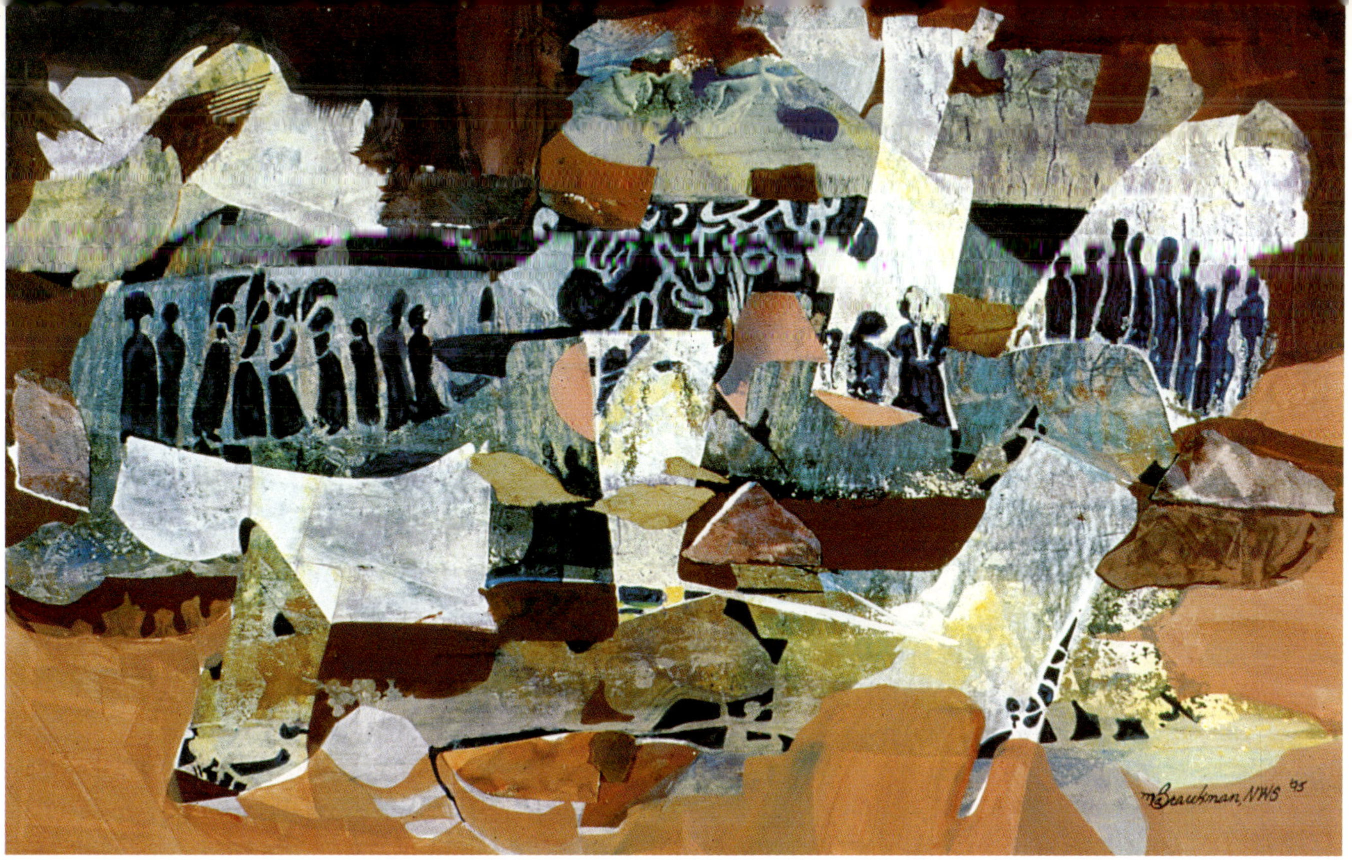

Mary Alice Braukman
Kindred Creatures
22" x 30" (56 cm x 76 cm)
Acrylic with pastel
T.H. Saunders 300 lb.
cold press paper

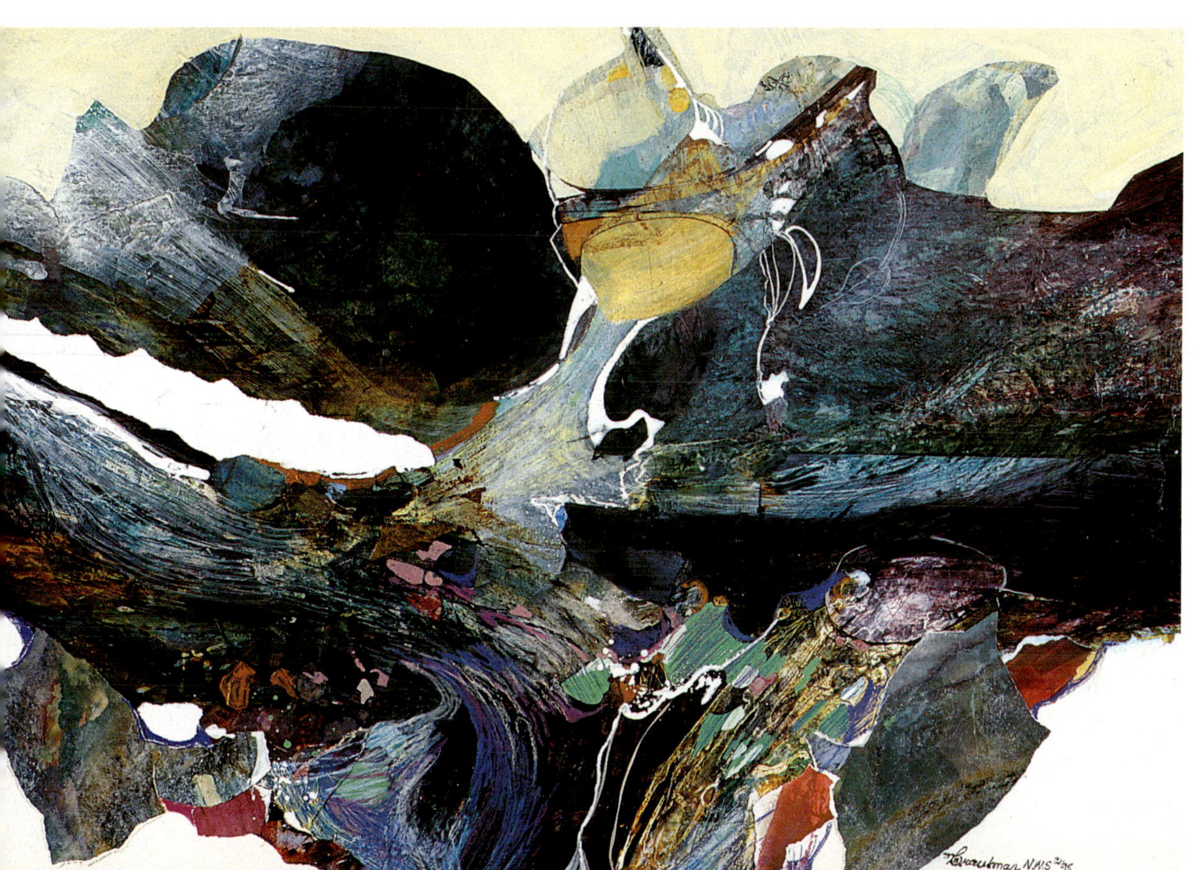

Mary Alice Braukman
Eroded Rocks
22" x 30" (56 cm x 76 cm)
Acrylic with gesso, inks, watercolor
pencil, and watercolor crayon
Fabriano 300 lb. hot press

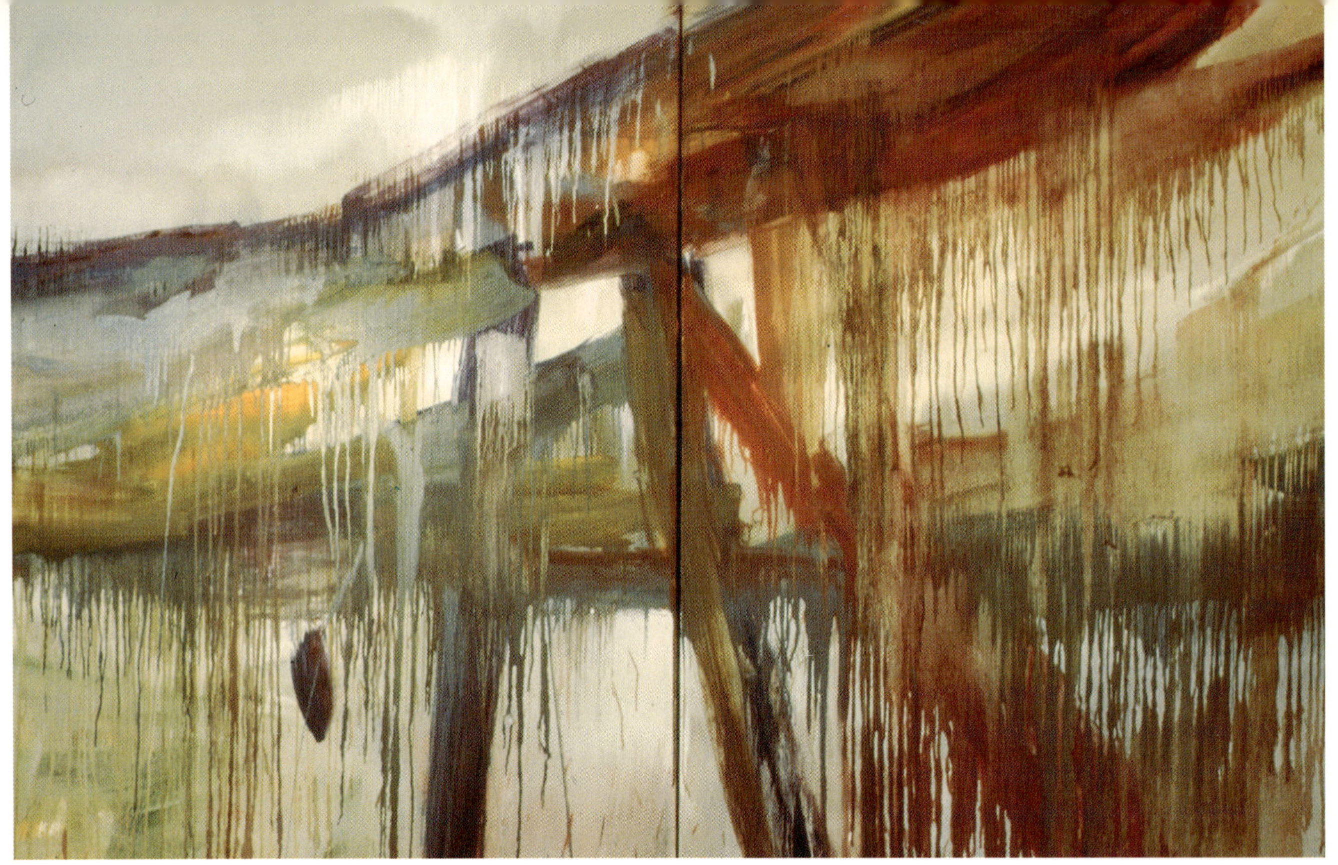

Margaret Arthur
Magic
68" x 100" (172.7 cm x 254 cm)
Linen canvas

Esther Levy
Deep Purple
52" x 63" (132.1 cm x 160 cm)
Canvas

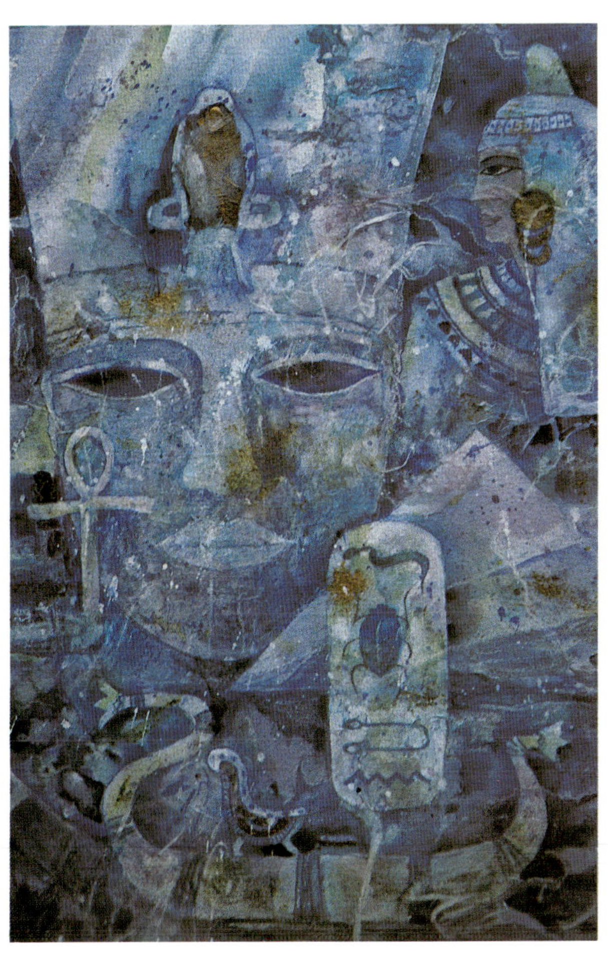

Mary Unterbrink
Land of the Pharaohs
13" x 18" (33 cm x 45.7 cm)
Arches 140 lb. cold press

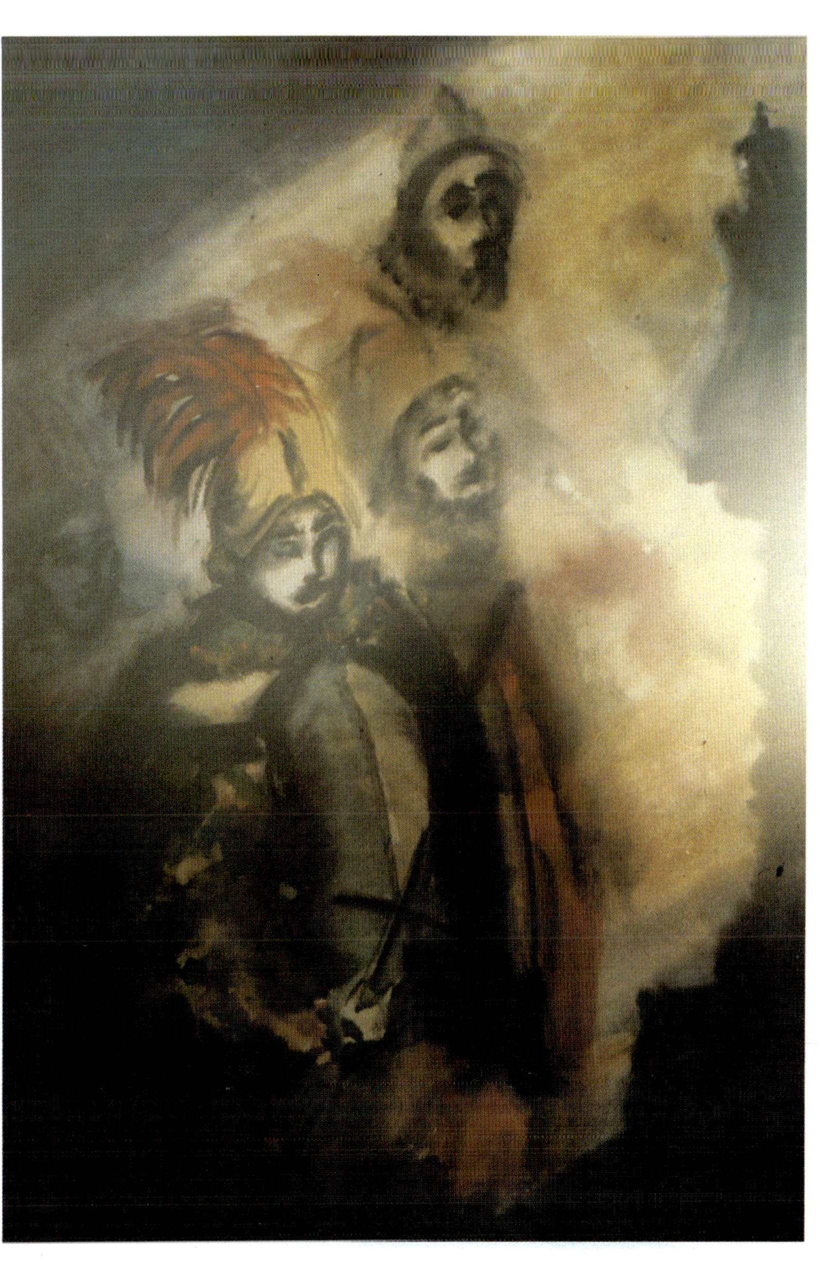

Lois Duitman
Don Diego De Vargas
18" x 24" (45.7 cm x 60.9 cm)
140 lb. cold press rough

Dennis Green
Mixed Signals
30" x 24" (75 cm x 60 cm)
Paper on wood

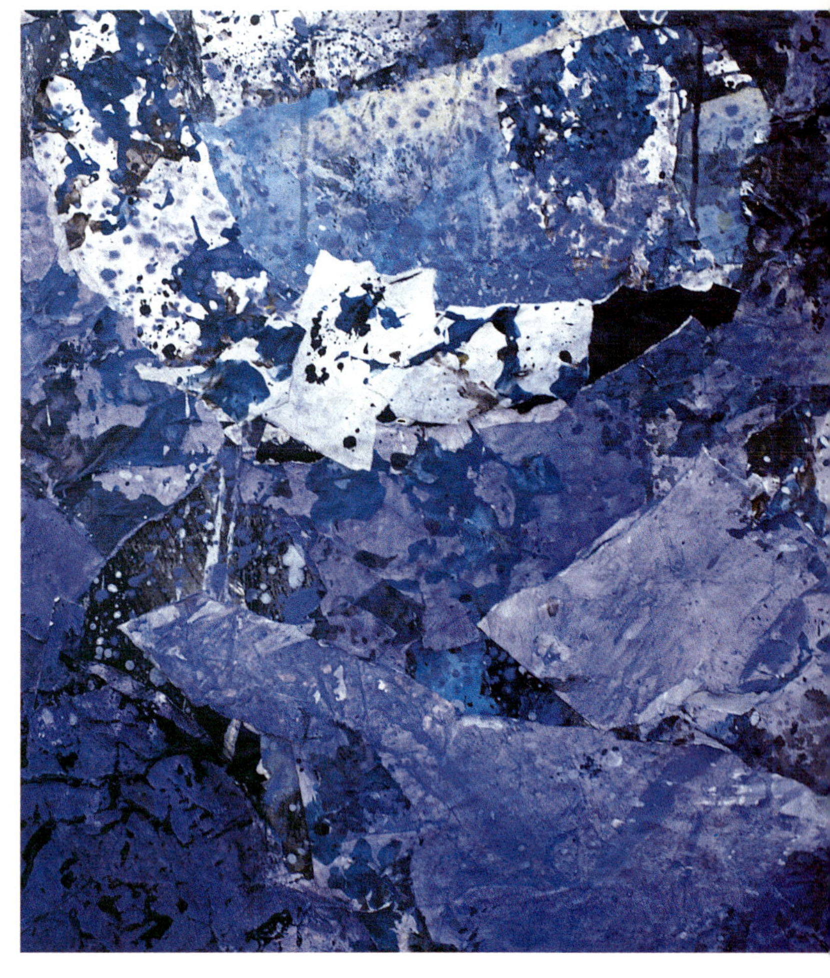

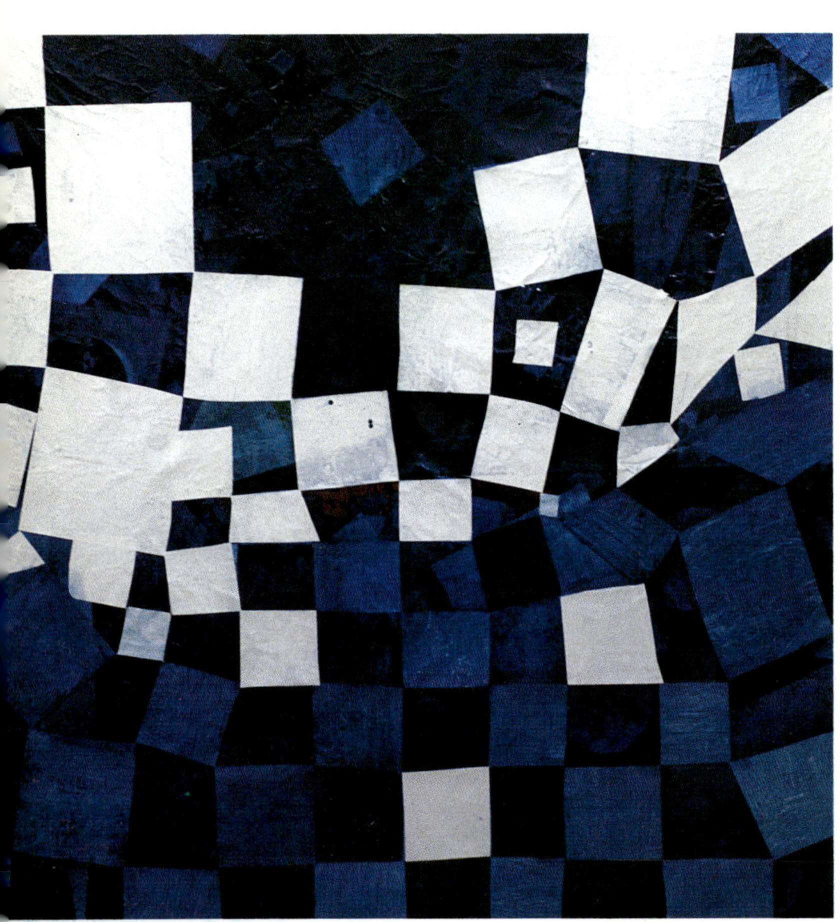

Dennis Green
Harmonica
52" x 50" (130 cm x 125 cm)
Paper on canvas

Edith Socolow
Window Series-Eve Tides
28" x 38" (71 cm x 97 cm)
Paper

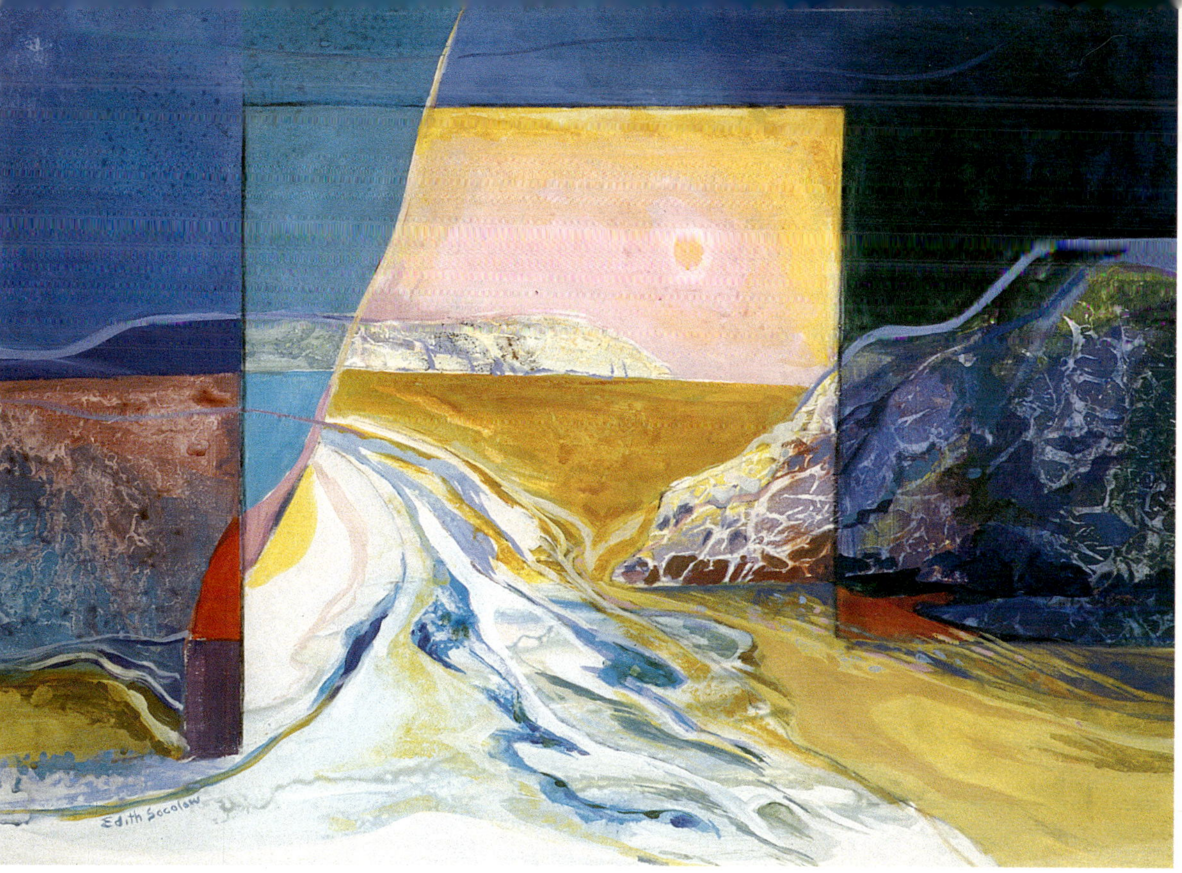

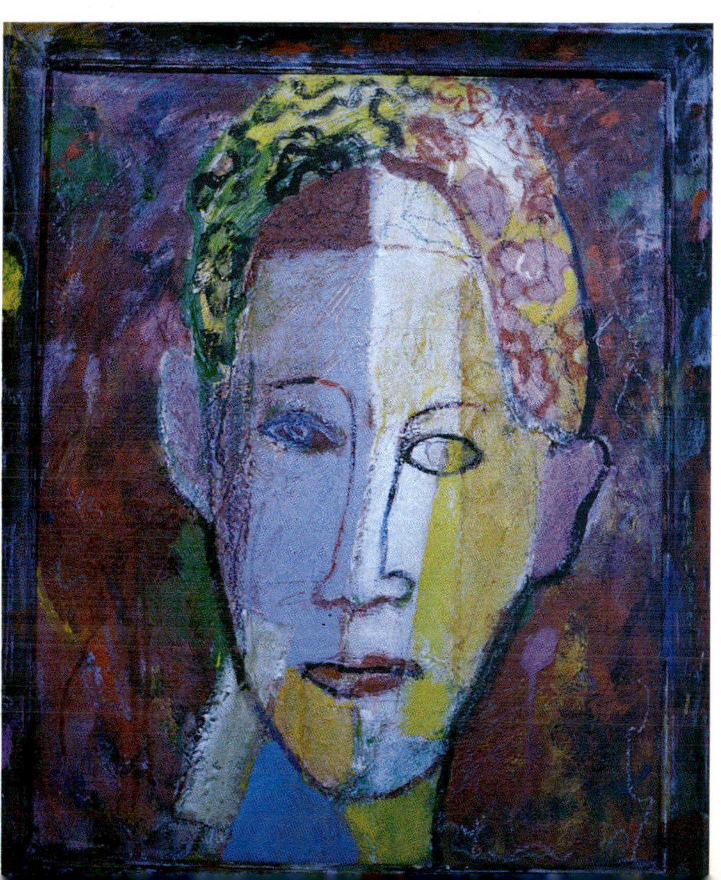

Joan Painter Jones
Woman/Hat
24" x 20" (60 cm x 50 cm)
Canvas board

Marsh Nelson
Eventide
21" x 27" (53 cm x 68 cm)
Two-ply museum board

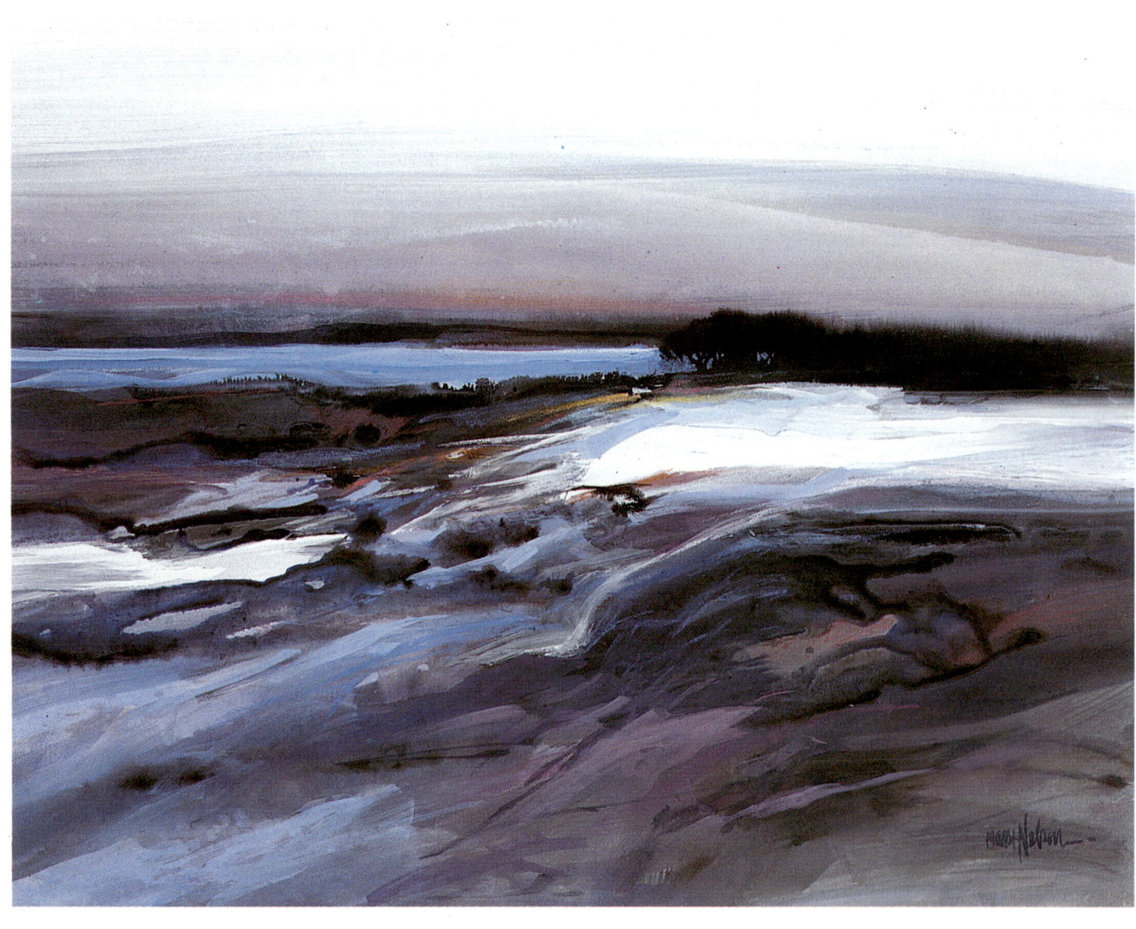

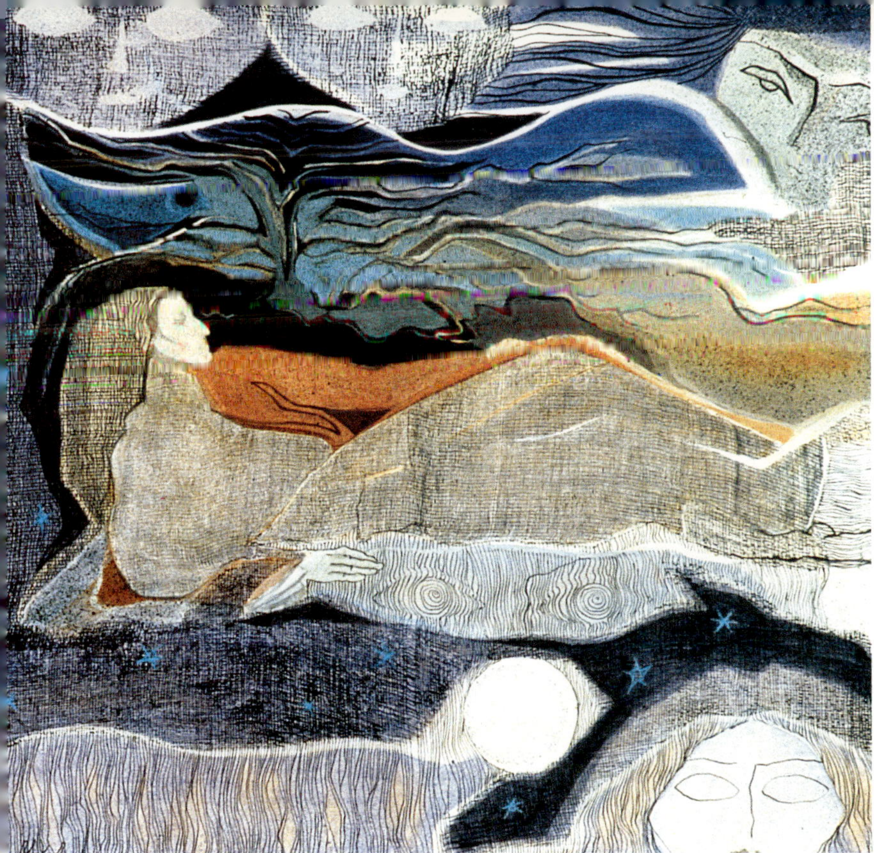

Alex Andra
Reveries I
37" x 37" (94 cm x 94 cm)
Canvas

Carla McConnell
Cora
21" x 16" (53 cm x 41 cm)
Museum board

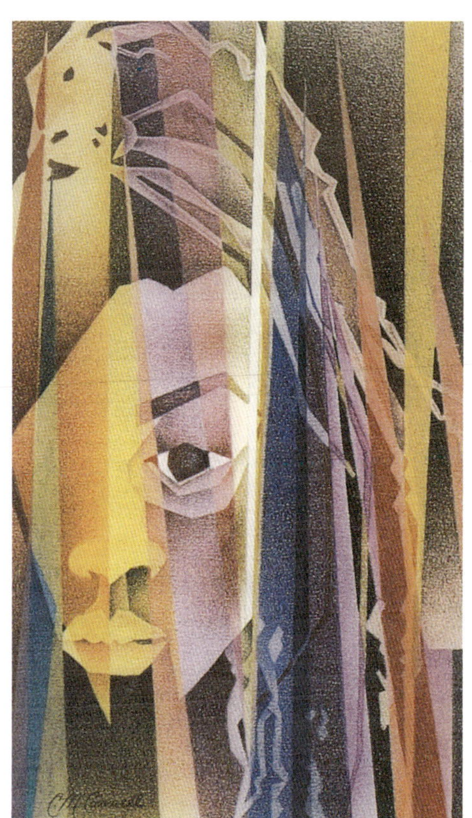

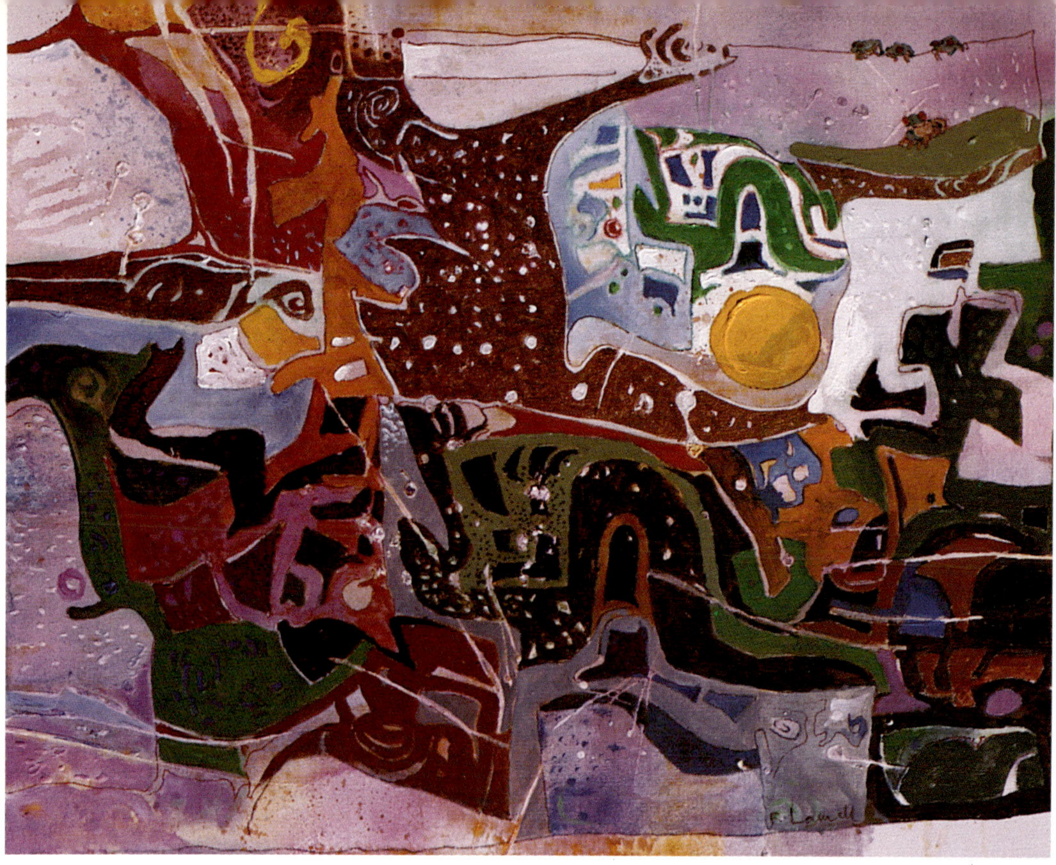

Robert Lamell
Aahscape
20" x 24" (51 cm x 61 cm)
Canvas

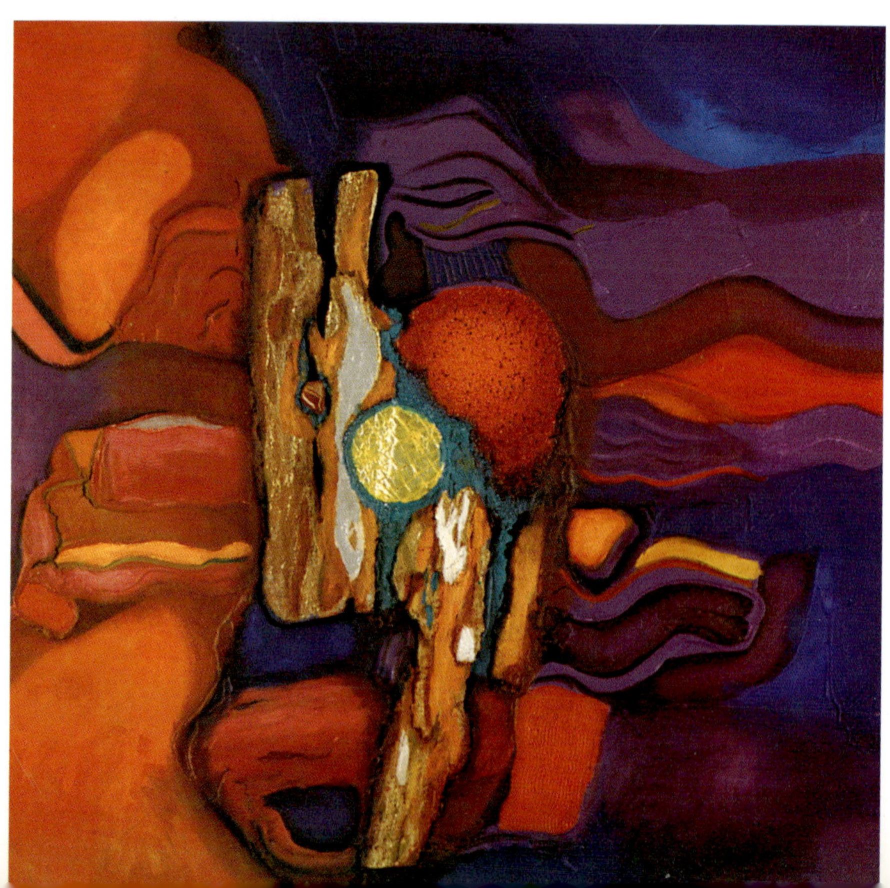

Atanas Karpeles
Yantra II
48" x 48" (122 cm x 122 cm)
Acrylic with bark, polished stone, foil, and plastic balls
Cotton canvas

Jorge Bowenforbés
Los Pescadores-Stabroek
40" x 56"
(101.6 cm x 142.2 cm)
Gesso-primed canvas

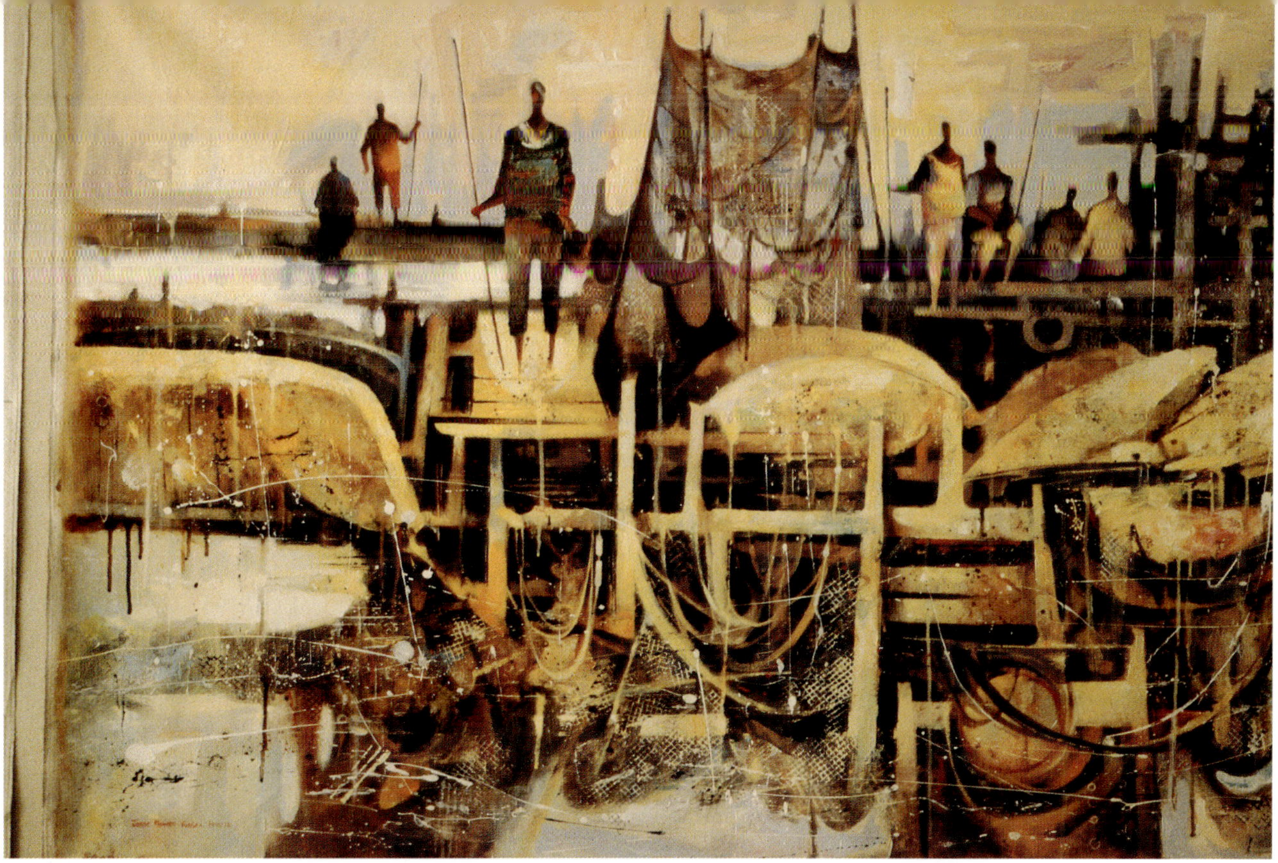

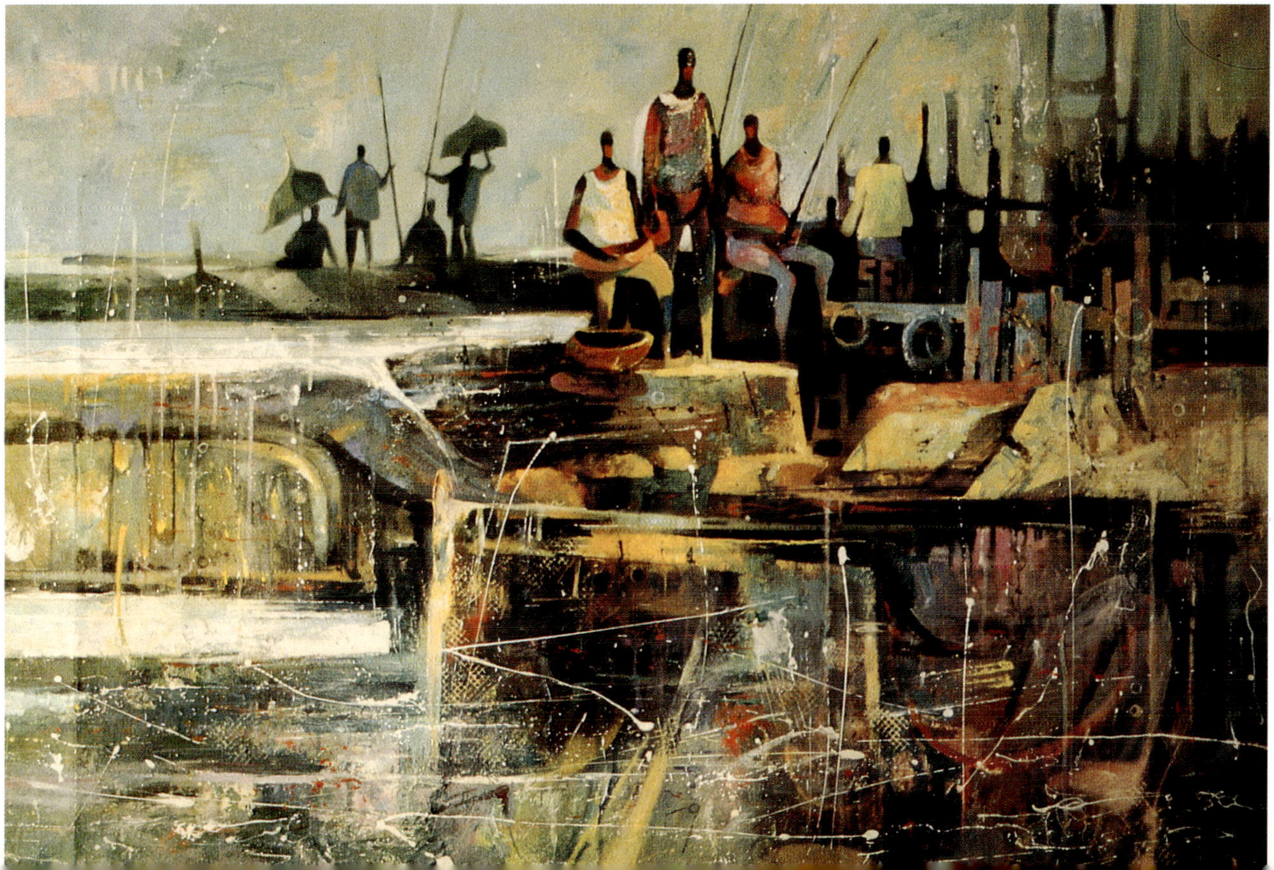

Jorge Bowenforbés
Los Pescadores-UITVLUGT
40" x 56" (101.6 cm x 142.2 cm)
Gesso-primed canvas

Lou Rizzolo
Charlevoix Breeze
25.5" x 34" (64.8 cm x 86.4 cm)
Fabriano Artistico 190 lb., rice paper

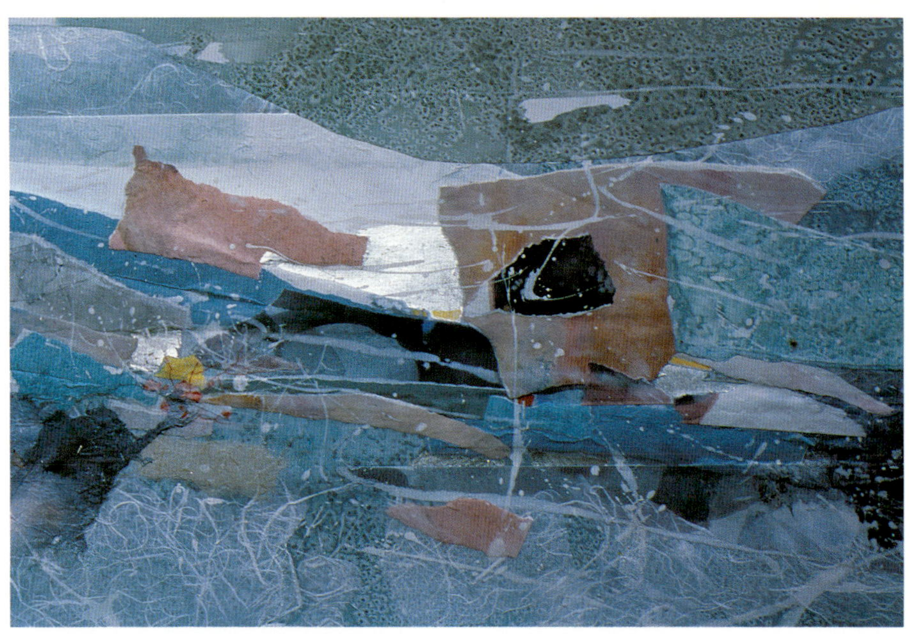

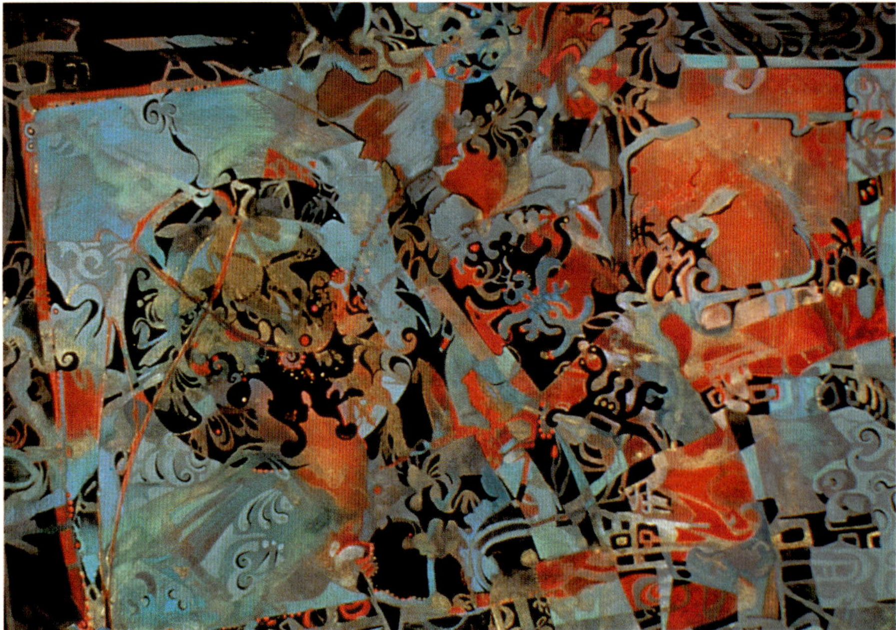

Judi Coffey, N.W.S.
Silk Scarf Series: Hidden Treasurers
22" x 30" (55.9 cm x 76.2 cm)
Arches 140 lb. hot press, rice paper
Media: Collage, acrylic

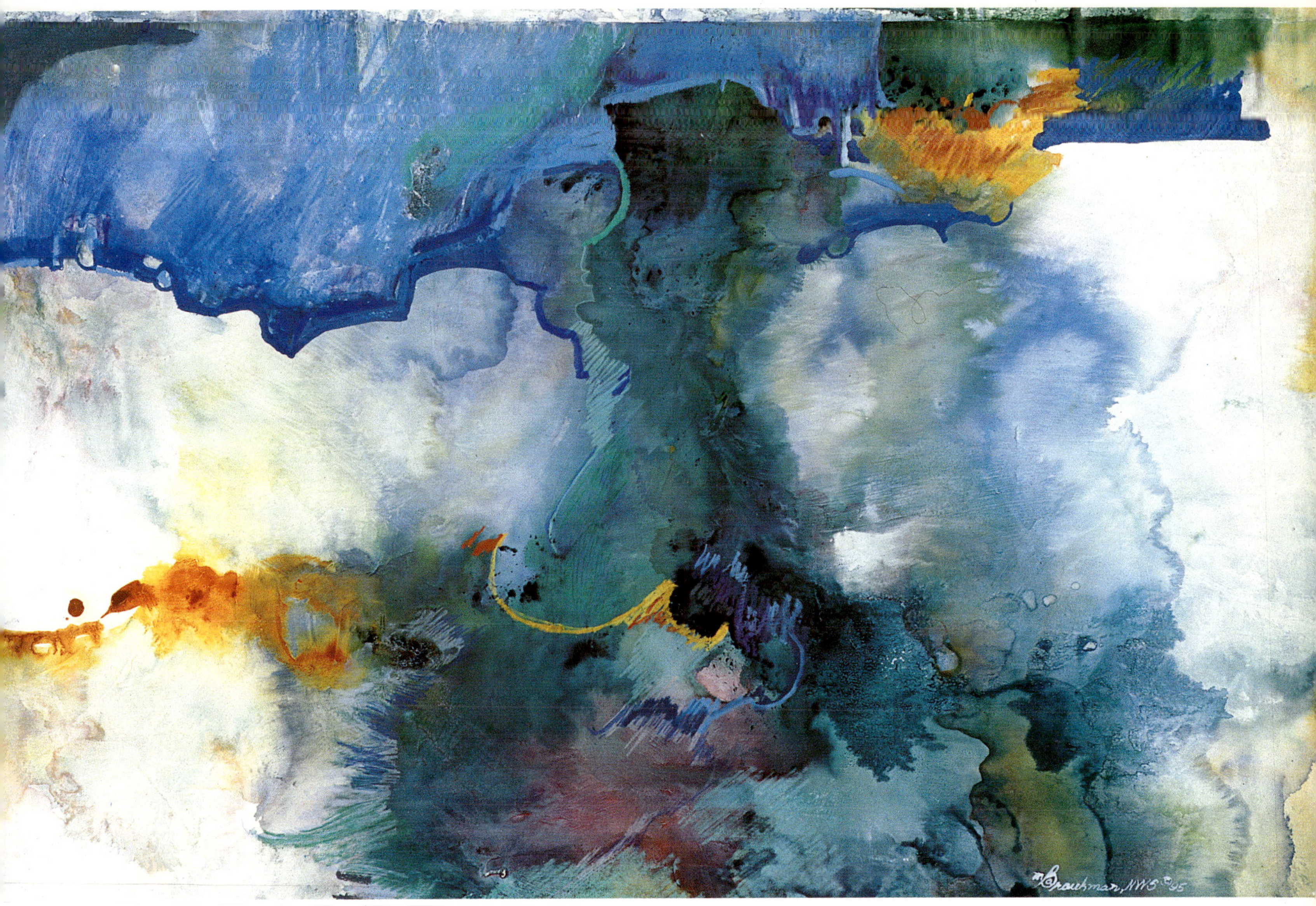

Mary Alice Braukman
Cloud Turbulence
18" x 28" (46 cm x 71 cm)
Acrylic with gesso, absorbent ground, and crayon
Strathmore #500 gesso-coated heavy weight plate surface paper

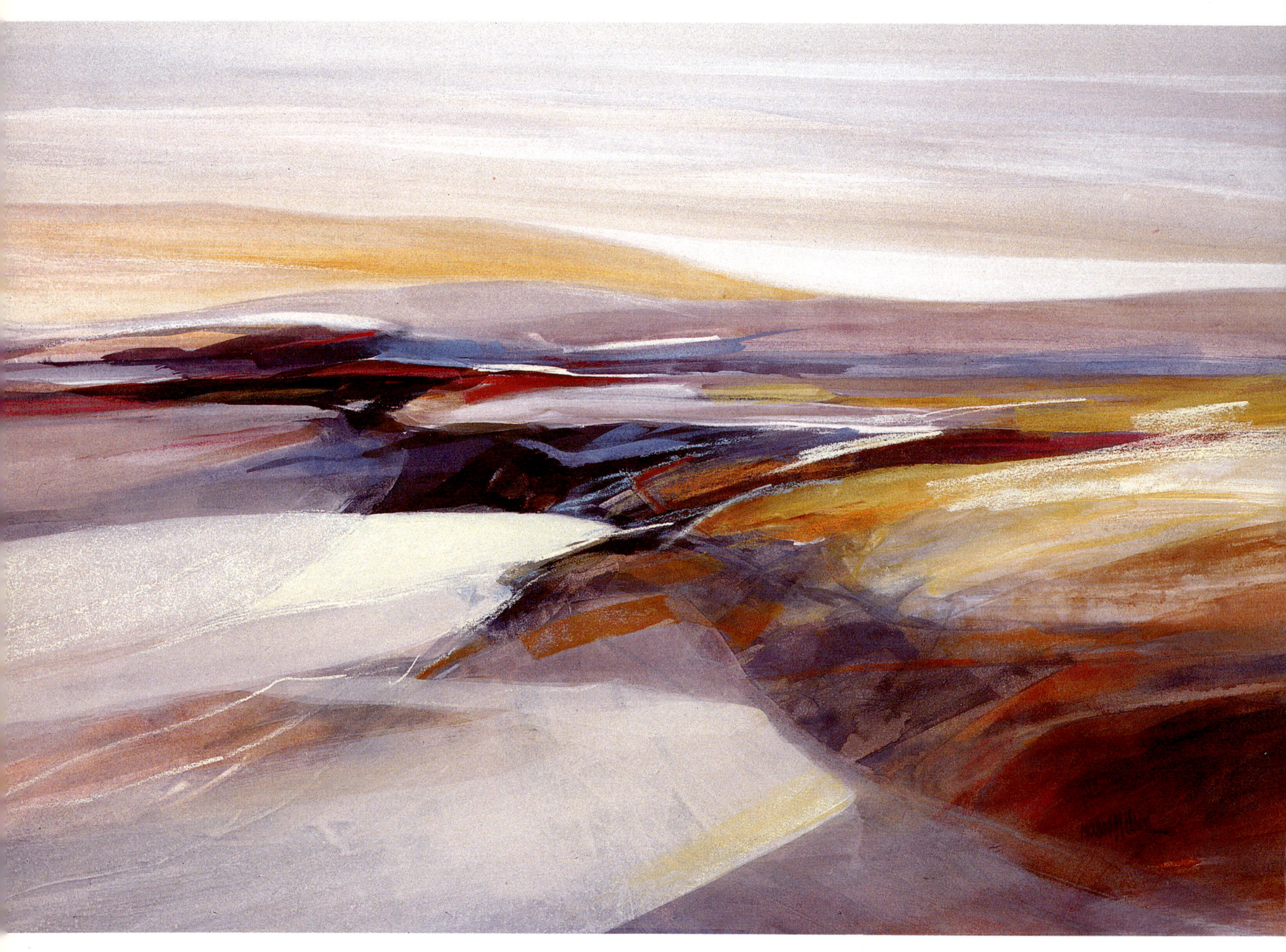

Marsh Nelson
Earth Shore
21" x 31" (53 cm x 79 cm)
Two-ply museum board

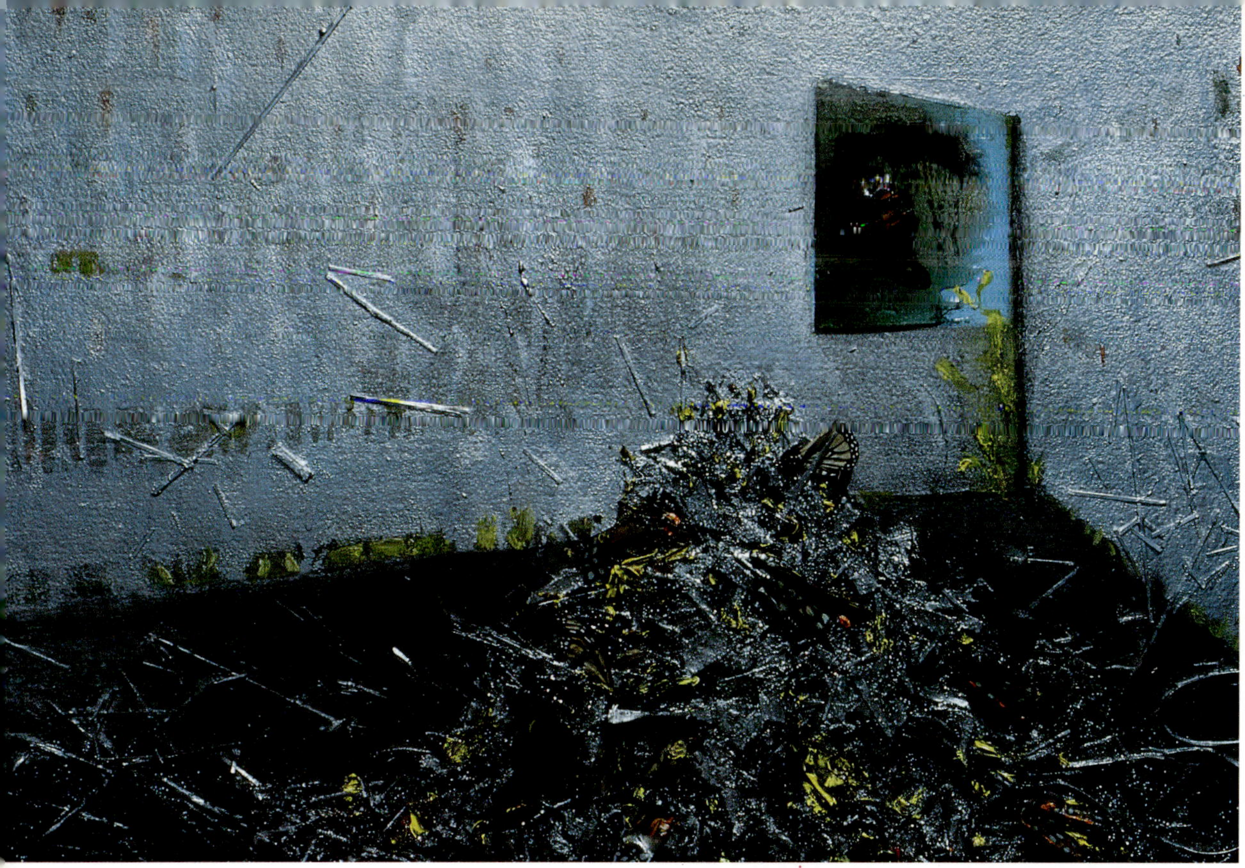

Janet L Culbertson
Butterfly Heap
22" x 30" (55.9 cm x 76.2 cm)
Oil with mixed media:
butterflies (found dead on beach),
collage, silver, and glass chips
Arches 400 lb. paper

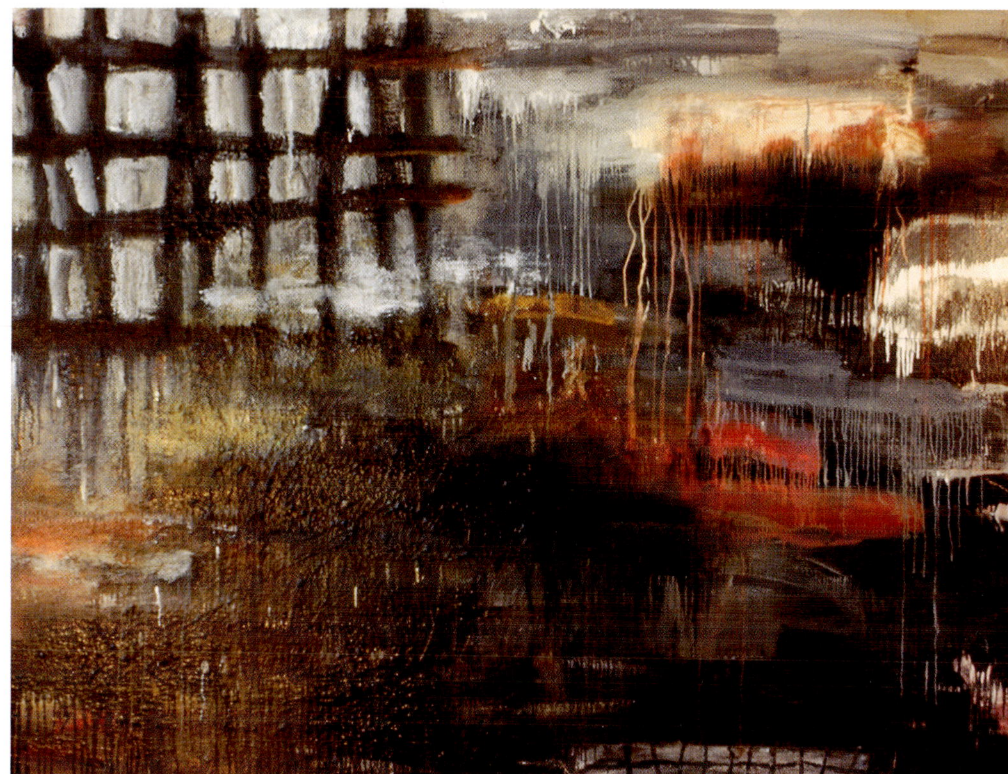

Margaret Arthur
The Raven
71" x 93" (180.3 cm x 236.2 cm)
Canvas

Directory & Index

Dennis Green 84
75 Hudson Avenue
Brooklyn, NY 11201

Marilyn Gross 34
374 MacEwen Drive
Osprey, FL 34229

Marian Hettner Grunbaum 23
1 McKnight Place, Apt 330
St. Louis, MO 63124

Phyllis Hellier 59
2465 Pinellas Drive
Punta Gorda, FL 33983-3317

Allan Hill 53
2535 Tulip Lane
Langhorne, PA 19053

E. Lorraine Hill 77
295 Gilmour Street P.H. 2
Ottawa, ON K2P 0P7
Canada

Judy A. Hoiness 49
1840 NW Vicksburg Avenue
Bend, OR 97701

Joan C. Hollingsworth 32
2824 NE 22 Avenue
Portland, OR 97212

Blair Jackson 44
6318 Waterway Drive
Falls Church, VA 22044

Astrid E. Johnson 29
14423 Ravenswood Drive
Sun City West, AZ 85375

Joan Painter Jones 51, 67, 85
7050 Talladay
Milan, MI 48160

Atanas Karpeles 14, 50, 66, 69, 88
2033 East Casa Grande Street
Pasadena, CA 91104

Joan D. Kelly 9
5611 Brandon Boulevard
Virginia Beach, VA 23464-6503

Robert Lamell 36, 88
2640 Wilshire Boulevard
Oklahoma City, OK 73116

John A. Lawn 64
200 Hulls Highway
Southport, CT 06490

Esther Levy 21, 30, 82
15 Beacon Court
Annapolis, MD 21403

Katherine Chang Liu 7, 26
1338 Heritage Place
Westlake Village, CA 91362

Margaret C. Manter 63
1328 State Street
Veazie, ME 04401

Leslie Masters 27
8197 Lake Crest Drive
Ypsilanti, MI 48197

N. L. Matus 46, 73
25802 South Cloverland Drive
Chandler, AZ 85248

Carla E. McConnell 87
729 W. Broadway
Montesano, WA 98563

John McIver 13
P. O. Box 9338
Hickory, NC 27262

Katherine McKay 25
P. O. Box 5472
Richmond, CA 94805

Elaine S. Miller 47
1003 Indian Creek Road
Jenkintown, PA 19046

Linda M. Miller 16
1642 NE 127th Avenue
Portland, OR 97230

Sybil Moschetti 70
1024 11th Street
Boulder, CO 80302

Jean Munro 29
7622 Simonds Road NE
Bothell, WA 98011-3924

Marsh Nelson 6, 80, 86, 92
185 Edgemont Avenue
Vallejo, CA 94590

Patrick O'Kiersey 21, 58, 69
3240 Telegraph Avenue
Oakland, CA 94609

Robert S. Oliver 57
4111 E. San Miguel
Phoenix, AZ 85018

Doug Pasek 57
12405 W. Pleasant Valley Road
Parma, OH 44130-5030

Alex Powers 54
401 72nd Avenue N. #1
Myrtle Beach, SC 29577

Nydia Preede 71
P. O. Box 344
Eatontown, NJ 07724

Doris Price 24
Rural Route 8, Box 511
Millsboro, DE 19966

Edward Reep 13
9021 Crowningshield Drive
Bakersfield, CA 93311

Pat Regan 59
120 W. Brainard
Pensacola, FL 32501

Jan Rimerman 32
P. O. Box 1350
Lake Oswego, OR 97035

Lou Rizzolo 90
P. O. Box 62
Glenn, MI 49416

Joan Ashley Rothermel 19
221 46th Street
Sandusky, OH 44870

Mike Russell 48
427 1st Street
Brooklyn, NY 11215

Timothy Santiorre 17, 79
311 South 4th Street
Mount Horeb, WI 53572

J. Luray Schaffner 12
14727 Chermoore Drive
Chesterfield, MO 63017-7901

Aida Schneider 42
31084 East Sunset Drive N
Redlands, CA 92373

Brenda Semanick 41
3325 North Deerspring Court
Tucson, AZ 85750

Leona Sherwood 64
615 Buttonwood Drive
Longboat Key, FL 34228

Jane Shibata 39
2024 Purdue Avenue
Los Angeles, CA 90025

Eva Sierzputowski 39
1366 W. 59th Street
Cleveland, OH 44102-2102

Lee Sims 31
735 Ridge Road
Lansing, NY 14882

Kerri McLaughlin Smith 7
13220 S. 48th Street, #1032
Phoeniz, AZ 85044

Edith Socolow 22, 62, 85
26 Salt Island Road
Gloucester, MA 01930

Kathy Stark 52, 56
35 Milbrook Road
Nantucket, MA 02539

Andy Syrbick 78
27 Clinton Street
Framingham, MA 01701-6702

Fredi Taddeucci 63
Route 1, Box 262
Houghton, MI 49931

Sharon Teabo 79
115 Virginia Avenue
Petersburg, WV 26847

S. Webb Tregay 45
470 Berryman Drive
Snyder, NY 14226

Mary Unterbrink 83
3998 NW 7th Place
Deerfield Beach, FL 33442

Susan Lucas Updyke 24
10 Brentwood
Bristol, TN 37620

David VanDenBerg 11
3325 North Deerspring Court
Tucson, AZ 85750

Ted Vaught 34
1527 NE Hancock Street
Portland, OR 97212

Maxine Warren 30, 72
Rural Route 2 Box 227
Ponca City, OK 74604

Claffy Williams 74, 75
220 Atlantic Avenue
Cohasset, MA 02025

E. Michael Yefko 20
206 Widow Sweets Road
Exeter, RI 02822